The
Struggle for Control

SUNY Series in Deviance and Social Control
Ronald A. Farrell, Editor

The
Struggle for Control

A Study of Law,
Disputes, and Deviance

Pat Lauderdale
and
Michael Cruit

STATE UNIVERSITY OF NEW YORK PRESS

Published by
State University of New York Press, Albany

For information, address State University of New York
Press, State University Plaza, Albany, N.Y. 12246

Production by E. Moore
Marketing by Theresa A. Swierzowski

Library of Congress Cataloging-in-Publication Data

Lauderdale, Pat.
The struggle for control: a study of law, disputes, and deviance
   / Pat Lauderdale and Michael Cruit.
      p. cm. — (SUNY series in deviance and social control)
   Includes bibliographical references (p.   ) and index.
   ISBN 0-7914-1311-X (CH: acid-free). — ISBN 0-7914-1312-8 (PB:
acid-free)
      1. Justice. 2. Law reform. 3. Dispute resolution (Law) 4. Deviant behavior.
   5. Social control. 6. Dispute resolution (Law)—Costa Rica.
   I. Cruit, Michael, 1947– . II. Title. III. Series.
   K240.L37 1993
   347.7286—dc20
   [347.28607]   91-47942
                                                               CIP

10 9 8 7 6 5 4 3 2 1

Dedicated to
The People of Sierpe
and
Annamarie, Rufina, T. E., Almeta, Panaman, and Daniela

Contents

Foreword

The Struggle for Control is a study of nine land disputes in the Sierpe region of Costa Rica. The region is isolated, underdeveloped, thinly populated, poor, with badly developed transport and communications. The state itself is poor and only weakly present in the region. In fact, it is so weak that the local system of justice is sometimes a fee-for-service system in which complainants must pay the transport costs of witnesses to courts, and people in need of police service must pay the transport costs of the the *guardia* if they want help. The distribution of property rights mixes small peasants and merchants with the shadow presence of absentee landlords. But because of the large amount of unused, unoccupied land, there is an influx both of poor migrants in search of land and wealthy foreigners in search of investment opportunities, giving the whole region a frontier atmosphere.

Because of the influx of migrants and the weak presence of the state, land disputes are common in the region. Land is often sold without a title search or land survey, the property rights of the region in any case separate use, ownership, and control—for example, giving rights to use and possession that do not depend on ownership—so that boundary and title disputes are endemic. Thus, the nine cases studied by *The Struggle for Control* include cases of unclear title, boundary disputes, and conflicts between rights of use, ownership, and possession, including poachers (for gold, not animals) and squatters on the land.

While the cases described in *The Struggle for Control* have the fullness of an ethnography, it is not really ethnographic in method. It is really a theoretically oriented monograph concerned with the amount and kind of social control found in disputes and the variables that determine them. Its underlying theoretical model assumes a boundary around a shared moral order, but a fragility of the moral order that requires it continually to be defined and redefined. Because the moral boundary shifts as a function of internal and external threats, the amount and kind of social control is a variable. Hence, the motivation of the inquiry is to study factors that account for variation in social control. Because it is concerned with a general social process more than a particular situation, it is unlike an ethnography in having a hypothesis to test. Not that there is an explicit null hypothesis. But there is nevertheless a fairly straightforward hypothesis at stake: How far is a theory of disputes and social control derived from the North American experience simply ethnocentric?

This calls for a certain way of reading and understanding the monograph. First, it has to be understood as a comparative study even though the comparison (to the U.S.A. but with frequent reference also to the anthropological literature on law) is mostly implicit. Second, one has to continually distinguish four very different elements of the text: metatheoretical presuppositions and directives, general theoretical principles, particular descriptions, and conclusions that depend on combining the theory and description. The metatheoretical elements of the text include its argument for integrating disputes, law, and social control, for taking a structural approach to disputes, for integrating conflict and consensus theory into one approach. The theoretical element of the text consists in abstract terms and general empirical laws. The abstract terms include words like "deviance," "social control," "access," "costs," "resources," and "multiplex" versus "simplex" relations. The general laws consist of universal conditionals that are abstract and general, but have empirical import. These include sentences like "multiplex relations tend to suppress open conflict," or "the course and outcome of disputes are determined by patterns of access to the formal and informal mechanisms of social control," or "the weak presence of the state magnifies the effects of differences in resources on the course and outcome of disputes."

The descriptive elements of the text themselves divide into two kinds of elements, though one is often implicit. The first, the more often implicit element, links the terms of the general theoretical structure to the particular instance. That is, the terms of the theory have to be instantiated if the theory is to apply to the case. Thus, "informal social control" has as instances the family and friendship networks of the region; formal social control has as instances the municipal court, the judges, the attorneys, the *guardia*. Multiplex relations have as instances overlapping of relations created by residence, employment, marriage, and the like. "Access" has as instances a somewhat complex pattern of channels connecting one either to the formal or the informal systems of social control.

A second descriptive element encompasses the initial conditions of the process in the particular instance. That is, it describes particular states the antecendent ("if") variables in the general lawlike sentences have in the particular case. Here again, one must be careful how one reads the text because this works at two distinct levels. On the one hand the Sierpe region of Costa Rica differs from the U.S.A. For example, the frontierlike region described in the monograph has an unfamiliar mix of legal systems, part rational-legal, part an almost patrimonial system described as *chorizo* (meaning "sausage"), frequently felt to be corrupt but in fact another kind of legal system.

At a more micro level, each particular dispute differs in the values of variables such as access, time, cost, distance, social relations, and social context that affect the course and outcome of conflicts over land tenure. The two levels together account for the outcomes of the process in the particular region, in general and in each particular case. The fourth element of the monograph are conclusions that derive from a combination of the theory and the descriptive particulars: conclusions about disputes in the region, though typically offered as descriptions, are derived from conditional lawlike expressions in which the descriptive particulars are substituted for the abstract terms of the theory and the particular initial conditions of a case are substituted for the abstract, general antecedents of the conditionals. Thus, one has sentences like "NorteAmericanos are outsiders with respect to both the formal and informal mechanisms of social control in the region" and "double outsiders (though the term is not used in the monograph) are the most disadvantaged actors in disputes over land in the region."

The metatheoretical approach of the monograph is a unique combination of elements that transcends the boundaries of topics within disciplines and the disciplines themselves. It integrates into a single process disputes, deviance, and social control, and the law. With respect to disputes it takes a structural approach, meaning that disputes are not really resolved; rather, they recur over and over again, though possibly in different guises. In fact the method of the book is founded on this concept of a structure underlying the apparently transient event of a dispute. Disputes are treated as if they were like an ethnomethodologist's breaching experiment; their purpose is to discover the underlying, taken-for-granted structure that is normal but normally not visible. Although the approach is structural, there is at the same time a process of negotiation on the surface that is treated as a function of this underlying structure, but at the same time is what reveals it.

These negotiations arise because disputes involve definitions of right and wrong. Hence, they involve definitions of the persons engaged in the dispute as either conforming to the rules or deviants from them. This is of course a view founded on the interactionist theory of deviance, which is central to the theory underlying the monograph. But it takes more seriously than this theory typically does the fact that it is not only deviants who are defined; the process also defines who is a conformist and who is an agent of social control. In the frontierlike region of the Sierpe, where occupation of land is in flux and complicated by legitimation of use rights, the ambiguity of ownership rights magnifies this feature of the process, bringing it more fully into view.

That disputes are determined in their course and outcome by definitions of conformity, deviance, and agents of control means that social control is an important aspect of disputing. In the first instance, this leads Lauderdale and Cruit to study the laws, courts, and police force of the region. But *The Struggle for Control* integrates the analysis of the formal system of social control with analysis of the informal system. In fact, one of its more interesting arguments is that rationalization of the law sometimes increases rather than decreases the significance of the informal system of control.

One of the useful by-products of both the integration of formal and informal social control and the ethnographic detail of each case is that the monograph continually exhibits the close interconnection of its micro and macro levels of analysis. It ranges from world system factors (which are part of the social context of each dispute) down to the social psychology of the actors involved in disputes and how it relates structure to action. While the structure is ever-present, the book is also about actors and their actions. The monograph continually displays how they are interconnected.

But perhaps the most attractive feature of the approach is that it also integrates conflict and consensus into a single theoretical structure. Like conflict models, the theory of *The Struggle for Control* sees a world that is more than one moral community. It pays close attention to the suppression of the issues in some conflicts and to the importance of control over the agenda of a dispute to its course and outcome. But it addresses both elite and collec-

tive reactions to conflict and deviance. It rejects the view that
either alone explains the course and outcome of a dispute. This
shows particularly in the monograph's analysis of the relations
between formal and informal systems of social control.

Because of its broadly general perspective, the implicitly
comparative method of the monograph deals with both similarities
and differences between civil justice in Sierpe and the U.S.A. The
similarities give one a sense of what is general about the process of
dispute management, law, and social control, such things as the
importance of access, effects of the strength of the state, and the
role of third parties, who are both activated by and determine the
course and outcome of the process. But the monograph is also concerned with differences. In comparative studies in general, differences might have either of two quite distinct interpretations: they
might indicate that what we had thought was a general process is
in fact not general; that our view of the general process was confused by ethnocentrism. Alternatively, they might in fact confirm
our understanding of the general process, showing the effect that
differences in the values given to the variables of the theory in the
particular case, acting through the same general principals, have in
producing different outcomes.

The findings of *The Struggle for Control* are of the latter
kind. They largely confirm the general theoretical structure that
guides the investigation, though they suggest a quite large number
of questions for further research and directions in which to elabo-
rate the theory further. Thus, probably fewer disputes occur that
involve people in multiplex relations in the U.S.A. than in Sierpe.
Sierpe gives us more of a sense of the effect of this aspect of social
relations than research in the U.S.A. But the differences between
Sierpe and the U.S.A. are due to the greater frequency of multiplex
relations in Sierpe rather than the way multiplexity, when it
occurs, will affect the course and outcome of a dispute.

The combination of what are usually compartmentalized
variables into one theory and the combination of a general theory
with ethnographic methods of investigation makes *The Struggle
for Control* a multifaceted work. Much of its fascination lies in the
interplay of its elements. Its complex texture makes it a book of
very general significance. The downside of this is that any one
reader, possibly not familiar with all the diverse literatures on
which the work draws, will find some of it hard reading. But the
synthesis of so many elements also means that the book should be
of interest to a large, if disparate, audience ranging from students

of disputes and their management to students of law and society more generally, from Latin Americanists to anthropologists more generally, from sociologists studying deviance and social control to sociologists more generally.

MORRIS ZELDITCH, JR.
Stanford University

Preface

Disputes provoke strong emotions and often lead to unintended consequences—loss of honor, loss of friendship, loss of liberty, loss of sustenance, and loss of life. We struggle to maintain control over these parts of our lives. However, most attempts to control disputes without understanding their origins, dimensions, and varying constructions are misguided.

We embarked on this project with the view that the story of human conflict and control has been told many times, yet most attempts to improve our understanding have served to blur rather than to sharpen our analyses. Some of the people who read previous drafts of this book were quite displeased with our approach, findings, and conclusions. Most of these readers who view themselves as dispute resolution experts included politicians, policymakers, judges, administrators, negotiators, and arbitrators. Generally, they viewed our approach unorthodox, our findings unpleasant, and our conclusions dangerous. They probably will find this final work to be, at least, as displeasing. While we agree with them that "something must be done" in the short term, we disagree with their emphasis on the paramount values of efficiency and order, especially when efficiency and order lead to more long-term inequality and rigid, hierarchical control.

Experts of dispute resolution often claim to have resolved a dispute, but later we find that they have unintentionally or, in some instances, intentionally only put band-aids of resolution on the cancerous sores of disputing. The sores may be hidden and there may be temporary resolution, but the underlying problems usually fester and grow. As anyone who has lost a dispute because of lack of resources can tell you, most resolutions do not solve underlying structural problems and often lead to long-term crises.

The other individuals who read prior drafts tried to help us explicate our nascent theoretical perspective, establish the conditions for confirmation or disconfirmation of our findings, and balance the tone of our conclusions. They are also convinced that disputes are rarely resolved, most are only in various stages of management by the disputants and others. And they are interested in studying the processes by which deviants are created and used in the disputing process. The creation of deviants and disputes appears to be a permanent fixture of social life. These readers recognize that in one dispute you may become a deviant, while in another you may create one or more. They also supported our research strategy, which suggested that we focus upon developing a theory rather than using premature models to test incomplete ideas. These scholars helped us resist the temptation to create ex post facto a theory after many years of moving back and forth among evolving ideas, dispute processes and findings. Reorganizing the book at this time by moving the clearer picture of our nascent theoretical perspective from chapters 3 and 4 to the front of the manuscript might please other scholars. However, it would not reflect accurately the research strategy, how the ideas evolved, and their relationship with our analysis of the disputing processes.

We claim to have studied such processes in detail in this work since one of us has lived in the research area since 1979. And the other has been in and out of the area since 1980. We also presented our final findings to the participants who were involved in the disputes reported in this book for their critiques. Of course, this is only one study and our results will remain tentative unless others confirm or disconfirm them, or readers find our approach inadequate.

Acknowledgments

Bob Todd helped us bring this work to fruition. His organizational skills, substantive comments, and enthusiasm were invaluable. We are particularly grateful to him for his editorial contributions.

We would also like to thank Iris Acevedo, Rebecca Bordt, Omar Castro, Victor Fernandez, Steven Katkov, and Luis Umana for their work as research assistants on this project. The research was supported in part by a Fulbright research fellowship, a grant from Stochastica Incorporated, the Office of International Programs at Arizona State University, and the Herbert Blumer Institute in Costa Rica.

The following people read previous drafts of the manuscript and offered us very useful critiques: Roberto Arias, Donald Black, David Goldberg, David Greenberg, Stuart Henry, Gary Marx, Laura Nader, Eliot Werner, and Morris Zelditch, Jr. In addition, the friendly advice and timely comments from Patricia Chang, Julia Coffman, Bo Eskay, Ron Farrell, Rebecca Fuhrer, Wolfgang Lixfeld, Connie McNeeley, Laurel Rowe, Marysue Smith, and Suli Zhu were enlightening. In the earlier stages of the work, Steven Katkov gave us important substantive, organizational, and editorial direction. Claudia von Werlhof, Andre Gunder Frank, and Michael Lauderdale were intellectual lightning rods. We also want to give special acknowledgment to Annamarie Oliverio and Victor Perez for their refreshing advice, unwavering support, and stimulating ideas throughout the course of our study.

We wish to thank Marian Buckley, Fran Mularski, Rita Higdon, and Kay Korman for their assistance in processing the various drafts of this manuscript. Kay Korman and Rita Higdon helped us through the earlier years of the project, and Marian Buckley, Fran Mularski and Janet Soper made a tireless effort in the final stages. We are grateful to them for their ability to infuse precision, humor, and compassion into the more tedious parts of the work.

The indigenous spirit of Rosalie Robertson was essential for the publication of this book. And Elizabeth Moore watched over it with thoughtful persistence. Thank You.

Finally, we deeply appreciate the help of Almeta and T.E., and the people of Sierpe, Costa Rica. We love you and your "pure" life.

P.L. & M.C.

1   The Scope

Life is full of disputes and struggles. First, we have to understand why they exist if we want to survive and live in peace.

José Gomez, Costa Rican campesino, 1980

Introduction

Conventional wisdom in North American society and most professional knowledge assume a clear and distinct line between the study of disputes and deviance. This distinction has become blurred increasingly by recent studies which reveal that law is more than simply an affair of making and enforcing rules (Henry 1983; Black 1989; Merry 1990; Nader 1990a). In this book we explore those aspects of law and their relationship to the study of deviance and disputes that typically are ignored or suffocated before they become public. We suggest some basic steps for integrating the study of disputes with research on the sociology of law and deviance by examining the conditions under which definitions and labels of deviance are created and employed in disputes, rather than studying deviants simply as violators of laws, rules, or norms.

We examine in detail nine land disputes in Costa Rica, including disputes between insiders and outsiders, and Costa Rica's place in the world system. Our analysis includes an emphasis on the power and forms of domination that can be gained from the creation and manipulation of definitions of who or what is deviant: in particular, the methods used by participants and formal agents of social control to manipulate the dispute agenda. This analysis is informed by a broader nascent theoretical framework suggesting that instead of disputes being resolved by official agents of control, they recur often in different guises over and over because they express underlying structural problems. Experts of dispute resolution, unreflective legal agents, or charismatic leaders often create the illusion of being able to resolve the disputes rather than actually resolving them or the underlying structural problems. We view law, deviance, and disputes as one integral process, a process which politically determines the negotiation of deviant identities and the control of the dispute agenda—particularly whether the underlying conflict is allowed to emerge into the open to be negotiated or is ignored or suppressed.

Having studied disputes, deviance, and law in the United States for a number of years, we turned to a comparative study in order to examine systematically those dimensions of disputing that are common across societies as well as those that are culturally different. As a first step in our comparative work, we chose a setting in Costa Rica where our type of ethnographic work was possible, since we have developed close interpersonal contact with the people in the area over the past twelve years and because the setting has some similarities to the U.S.A., yet possesses important differences. In general, the relatively small country of Costa Rica is less developed technologically, has a more socialistic political organization, and embodies a different style of law. These encompassing factors are especially relevant for a comparison of the similarities and differences in disputing and social control. The comparative setting can help us sharpen our analysis of disputes by examining the role of people who are defined either as insiders or outsiders, and the cultural versus noncultural means used to define and manage disputes. Moreover, we can examine those factors that seem to be common to most disputes, such as the importance of status hierarchies, the use of the label of deviance, access to forums of social control, and the cost of disputing. Basically, the Costa Rican community serves as a setting in which to examine fundamental ideas about deviance, disputes, and law.

Our initial chapter serves as an introduction to the way in which we approached and conducted our analysis of disputes from the broader perspective of law and deviance. We also present a brief analysis of specific geographic, cultural, and technological factors which form the background for understanding the disputes. The chapter ends with a discussion of the more specific conditions that appear crucial to the study of disputes: the nature of social and political relationships, informal and formal social control, cost, time, and access to dispute forums.

We examine, for example, one common conception of formal social control based upon the belief that law serves to improve the human condition by providing more predictability, safety, and stability in daily life. Yet, while law typically offers the illusion of fairness and equality, access to legal institutions is not equal for all. And bureaucratic control over resources such as money entails an emphasis upon regularity, predictability, efficiency, and cost effectiveness. Increases in levels of rationalization, the existence of explicit, abstract, and calculable rules and procedures that lead to an increase in predictability, do tend to make the dispute process more predictable, but typically increase formal social control as it is implemented largely through the political processes of the dominant users of law.

Next, we present a brief section on the larger context within which the disputes arise. The section includes an examination of the debate over the intentions and consequences of the Nicaraguan Contras who often operated from Costa Rican territory. It explores the sources of the simple dichotomies that persist—deviants versus patriots, or terrorists versus freedom fighters, and the impact of such dichotomous labels. In this section, we also examine overarching conflict primarily from the perspective of Costa Rica's position within the region and the world system. Costa Rica has attempted to shield itself from short-term approaches to conflict resolution by abolishing its army, developing a policy of neutrality in the disputes of other nations, and emphasizing formal, legal approaches to the management of internal disputes. Yet such measures are difficult to maintain in a world economic and political system that impinges upon its national stability and self-determination. The impact of external conflict and various attempts at external control is felt at numerous levels within any society. We pay particular attention to disputes in relation to Costa Rica's international reputation as a nonmilitarized society and recent changes resulting from the economic, political, and military instability in surrounding areas. In addition, we suggest that new nonmilitary and military aid from the United States has a significant effect on the management of disputes in that area.

In the second chapter we examine a number of specific disputes from our research period beginning in 1980. These cases, which are primarily land disputes, examine how disputes unfold, how and why they become public or nonpublic, as well as the various forms that disputes may take. In the first case, *"Resident or Squatter?"*, we examine a battle over the control of rich gold deposits in the District of Sierpe. The struggle, which takes place between a local resident and an absentee landlord, illustrates the complex dynamics inherent in most disputes. The analysis details the nature of the social relationship including whether a disputant is an insider or outsider; whether the relationship is static or dynamic; and the level of access to formal and informal social control forums.

The third chapter explores the factors that may lead to a change in social control, and offers a more comprehensive analysis of law, deviance, and dispute management. In addition, this chapter compares and contrasts the cases and reaches some preliminary theoretical conclusions about the form and content of disputes. The analysis includes an emphasis on the power and forms of domination that can be gained from the creation and manipulation of definitions of who or what is deviant: in particular, the methods used by participants to control the dispute agenda. We also offer some ideas for constructing alternative ways of studying disputes and provide a few suggestions for work on related topics.

In the fourth chapter, we conclude the study by focusing upon theoretical implications of studying disputes and their management. The discussion attempts to create a larger research agenda via the study of dispute management and law as well as commenting on the relationship among the study of social control, deviance, and justice. Our discussion also provides relevant information on part of the culture of Costa Rica. These accounts are relevant, since so little has been written about a nation that abolished its army approximately forty years ago, yet sits amid the flaming controversies in Central America. Only with a few exceptions, such as the awarding of the 1987 Noble Peace Prize to President Oscar Arias or the surrounding crises in Nicaragua and Panama, has Costa Rica received much attention. In the epilogue we also present a brief comment on the study of law and U.S. policy toward Central America. The discussion is based upon some of the central findings from our study, including the relevance of studying the structural conditions that lead to specific types of disputes and the problems associated with focusing upon popular, yet premature, ideas found in most dispute resolution and legal perspectives. Since one of the central purposes of this study is to use a Costa Rican community as a setting in which to examine several fundamental ideas about law, deviance, and the management of disputes, our study focuses upon the processes and structural factors which appear to produce and then reproduce the conditions that influence the type and amount of deviance and disputes.

Disputes, Law, and Deviance

The study of disputes has been over preoccupied with the issue of how to resolve them. Recently, we have been reminded by a number of local and global events that many of them are rarely resolved. The U.S. foreign policy disasters—for example, in Latin America—stem, in part, from a preoccupation with short-term resolutions to disputes and an unwillingness to explore more fundamental approaches to the study of conflict. The military "quick-fix" to conflicts of interest in Latin America has been touted as a fundamental approach to each "new" dispute. However, there is now little debate over the results of that approach. It has led to policy disasters in Guatemala in 1954, in Cuba at the Bay of Pigs in 1961, in Chile in 1973, in Panama and Nicaragua in the 1980s, and in El Salvador in 1991.

Much of the professional knowledge in the field of dispute resolution is increasingly challenged by the realization that important disputes among people, groups, and nations are typically in various stages of negotiation or management. A dispute that seems to have been resolved in the short run often reappears in another form via a new label, or we find that part of the original conflict reemerges in what seemed to be a unique dispute. Systematic analyses of disputes over property such as land and water as well as those regarding personal reputation typically reveal that what appeared to be settled, once and for all, is not. While an arbitrator, judge, court, or the winning side may claim that the dispute is resolved, upon closer inspection we increasingly discover that the same dispute appears again in another form usually after it has festered to the point of being intractable (cf. Elster 1989).

Our study of such disputes proceeds from the methodological perspective of sociologists and anthropologists who are interested in identifying and examining structural roots of disputes and attempts at resolving or managing them. We focus upon a number of social disputes which we began studying in 1980 in a specific area in Central America. Most of the disputes originated on the Osa peninsula along the southern Pacific coast of Costa Rica.

Our emphasis upon examining the structural foundations of the disputes and the subsequent modes of dispute management distinguish our approach from traditional approaches that have been primarily psychologistic. The peculiar development of the study of disputes has been dominated by the psychological perspective. The commitment to explaining individual motivation has excluded definitional and structural issues despite the attention that needs to be paid to such variables as subculture and access to social control forums. The psychological perspective has also focused disproportionately upon the role of arbitrators, mediators, judges, and other "professionals" in dispute resolution. While these individuals often play important roles in part of the study of disputes, the perspective has overemphasized the issue of resolution and largely ignored the broader analysis of the disputing process and institutional factors that effect the resolution of disputes (cf. Kirp et al. 1986; Elster 1989).

We view the analysis of disputes as an important part of the study of social conflict and control. From this perspective social control is the process of defining and reacting to deviance. Deviance is a definition created to refer to action that should not occur from the positions of particular disputants or agencies. This approach leads us to examine the emergence of particular rules and laws, the ways in which people dominate other people, as well as the relationship between informal and formal control. Specifically, we are interested in examining the conditions which lead to more or less social control, rather than how to implement control. We also hope to contribute to research that raises important related questions. Under what conditions, for example, does an increase in social control lead to compliance rather than subversion or rebellion (cf. Sacco, 1992)?

The resolution, management, or negotiation of disputes involves the use of different resources. A nation may turn to a third party such as the World Court, a group may enlist aid from a social movement, or an individual may ask for help from friends. Under varying conditions, people rely upon many types of informal means of social control such as collective norms, social movements, or numerous forms of political deviance. Or they attempt to use more formal means such as established rules or law. When do individuals in a community invoke norms or third parties in their attempt to settle a local dispute? When does a nation call upon law to resolve an international dispute?

In investigating the conditions under which people turn to one type of social control versus another, we seek a preliminary integration with the study of law and justice, both inside and outside the formal legal system. Our examination of law stems from the fact that many scholars view law as the key to the resolution of disputes and the advancement of justice (cf. Lieberman 1981). We have found, however, that studies which analyze law as a separate species of social control or examine informal justice apart from the formal legal system are "guilty of contributing to the ideological process whereby law is constructed as a reality" (Henry 1983:vii). We focus upon disputes, as one form of conflict and subsequent crisis situations, since they often reveal important parts of the structure of a system that are obscured during relatively normal times.

Recently, there has been a reemergence of interests in studying disputes in this context. Such interests range from studies on the jurisdiction of the World Court to those concerned with the creation of rules in intergroup conflict. In the conclusion to their research on disputes in Africa, for example, Comaroff and Roberts suggest:

> On the one hand, the logic of dispute is ultimately situated in the encompassing system and can be comprehended only as such. But, on the other, it is in the context of confrontation— when persons negotiate their social universe and enter discourse about it—that the character of that system is revealed. Because this is true, the dispute process may provide an essential key to the disclosure of the sociocultural order at large. [1981:248–49]

In an analysis of disputes employing comparative data from a number of cultures, Black suggests in a similar vein that the study of "conflict management is a prism in which larger configurations of social life are visible" (1987:46; see Black 1989).

Much has been written about the process of disputing, social control, and the evaluation of diverse behavior, usually from a conflict, control, or dispute resolution perspective. In order to employ some of this literature for our study, we explore the advantages and disadvantages of using relevant conceptual schemes (cf. Gluckman 1955; Erikson 1966; Nader and Todd 1978; Trubek 1980–81; Comaroff and Roberts 1981; Abel 1982a and b; Henry 1983; Black 1984, 1989; Munger 1988, Nader 1990a;). In comparing these perspectives, we discovered that many of them overlap in important respects, yet most current research using a particular perspective tends to ignore the others. Obviously, such a situation creates many conundrums. In this study, we redirect some of the work on disputes by focusing upon points of convergence in related areas, especially relevant research on law, deviance, and social control. Our attempt here at redirecting and integrating part of the work on disputes with this research is an extension of a similar implicit thrust in the anthropology of law forwarded by investigators such as Nader (1990a) and Comaroff and Roberts (1981). It is also a continuation of the explicit direction in the sociology of law by researchers such as Henry (1983) and Black (1989) which explicate the relevance of broader notions of social control and conflict. As Henry notes:

> The debunking of the slippery notion that law is a spontaneous and uncontrived product of the continuous flow of life, made accessible to man through reason, is as refreshing as the exposure of the processes under which law is legitimated by reference to the gods, the popular sense of right, or the general will. What sociologists and anthropologists clearly and often uncomfortably demonstrate is that law is formulated in a sociopolitical context; that it serves some interests rather than others; that different social structures or forms of societal organisation display different forms of law and legal systems, and that a combination of coercive and ideological processes are at work to ensure the continuation of existing systems of law and through these the perpetuation of existing social structures. [1983:1–2]
>
> By omitting to consider the body of informal behavioural imperatives, norms and obligations, they [functionalist and natural law theorists] contribute to, rather than analyse, the very ideological processes that render formal law the dominating social control institution. In order to unmask this kind of mystification it is necessary to reestablish the relationship between positive law and its informal counterpart... Only by considering these approaches together can we hope to comprehend what constitutes the totality of social control. [1983:4]

The study of social control has been divided into two paths. The first concentrates on social control as the independent variable, especially those factors that lead to deterrence or compliance. The second examines social control as the dependent variable, particularly those factors that lead to variations in formal and informal control (see Black 1984, for a discussion of crime as one form of social control). We follow this second path, which focuses upon factors that affect the type and amount of social control. In this context, issues concerning the control and distribution of resources, the manipulation of status, the creation of agendas as well as authority, legitimation, obedience, and related concepts become highly salient (Balbus 1977; Trubek 1977; Ashley, 1980; 1986b; Benney 1983; Walker et al. 1986).[1]

The evolution of the study of disputes has certain striking similarities to the study of social control and deviance. A brief review of these similarities can be useful in understanding why the study of disputes is so diverse and often confusing (cf. Henry 1983). Some of the pioneers in the study of deviance were interested primarily in eliminating or at least decreasing the amount of deviance. And some earlier proponents of work in the dispute resolution area claimed that they wanted, first and foremost, to decrease the amount and intensity of disputes. Despite the obvious attempts of some researchers and dispute resolution experts to control the field for instrumental, professional interests and profit individually by attempting to create and expand a new profession, a few studies on dispute resolution have been initiated with a more encompassing emphasis. These studies are used to examine the role of power and its impact on variations in dispute resolution (cf. Kidder 1980–81).[2]

Such studies are frequently ignored or seen as irrelevant, since we find an abundance of premature attempts by individuals to use power to "resolve" disputes or eliminate deviance without a serious recognition of the risk of unintentionally creating additional conflicts or more severe problems. In lieu of first identifying the social conditions that create more or less social control, some professionals have tried to define what social control should be or how to increase its effectiveness. As a partial response to the problems encountered by this approach, the Society of Professionals in Dispute Resolution made liability insurance available to their members in 1988. We have attempted to avoid the pervasive specter of ethnocentrism which has been present in many "policy" studies. Rather than impose subjective notions of "progress," "developed," or "professional care," we have attempted to avoid these contaminating factors (for a cogent analysis of these subjective concepts, see Lévi-Strauss 1955; Kirp et al. 1986).

We first review the role of power upon the type and volume of disputes. Our focus, however, is not solely upon leaders, elites, or the state, which may increase social control by reducing disputes by a variety of means (cf. Elster 1989). Despite recent elaboration of the pitfalls associated with dichotomous logic, many researchers continue to impose a conflict or consensus perspective upon their analyses. *This artificial conflict/consensus dichotomy is evidence of a prolonged preoccupation with the determinants of individual deviant behavior, a bombastic misportrayal of the dialectic between functionalist and conflict perspectives, and an unfortunate aversion to the organizational and institutional aspects of deviancy* (Lauderdale 1980). Despite a few attempts to introduce other perspectives such as pluralistic or critical ones, most thinking has continued to be framed within a conflict or consensus perspective. As Giddens aptly emphasized some time ago, the debate between the conflict and consensus proponents has proven to be based on "misleading interpretations of past theorists," and has been "a wholly inadequate way of conceiving our present tasks" (1976:717). Yet it is rare to find research that systematically examines the institutional aspects of diverse behavior or the processes that lead to the imposition of the deviant label. We explore a more fundamental examination of the basic dynamics of power attainment and the control of deviance (Lauderdale et al. 1990; Sacco, 1992).

This broader framework suggests at least that deviance raises key questions in the study of disputes (cf. Munger 1988).[3] Under what conditions do disputants gain the power to successfully define other disputants or social control agents as deviant? When are disputants able to redefine their actions as political deviance— that is, Under what conditions are their actions viewed as positive and operating from a higher moral position? What factors convince social control agents that one disputant or particular action is, in fact, deviant? In essence, this study as well as much of the current work on disputes and deviance can be usefully integrated into the study of conflict and social control (Davis and Anderson 1983; Ben-Yehuda 1985, 1990; Hagan, 1988).[4]

> There is a point at which deviations from the rule remake the rule itself. Thus, every act leads a double life: it constitutes conformity or disobedience to custom at the same time that it becomes part of the social process whereby custom is defined. [Unger 1976:49]

In this chapter, therefore, we will develop a broader approach to the study of dispute management. Initially, we will focus upon the nature of social relationships, access to forums of social control, and related resources in the Península de Osa, Costa Rica.

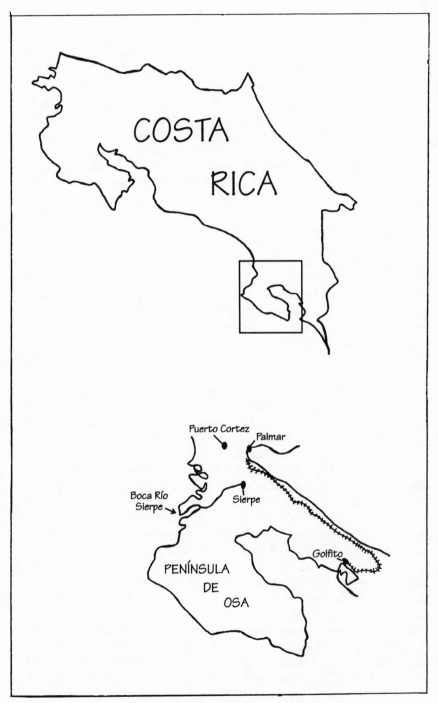

Figure 1.1
Map of Costa Rica

The Setting

We examined disputes in the Península de Osa, located some two hundred sixty kilometers south of the capital city of San José on the western coast of Costa Rica. The peninsula is on the Pacific Ocean and protrudes from the southern coastline much like a bent forefinger pointing toward South America. It is approximately sixty-two kilometers long and thirty kilometers at its widest point (see Figure 1.1).

The Península de Osa lies adjacent to the rich coastal plains that once supported the four thousand-hectare (approximately ten thousand acres) banana plantations of Standard Brands Company. Until 1985, the vast, sprawling network of banana plantations formed the economic backbone of the whole southern zone of Costa Rica. However, in December 1984, the workers began a long and bitter strike that resulted eventually in a decision by Standard Brands, which had initiated plans for such a decision as early as 1979, to cease operations in the southern zone. Such a massive displacement of economic power and human resources created economic crises, not only locally, where the effects are most acute, but nationally (Perez Vargas 1988; Lauderdale 1988b).

Transportation on the Península de Osa is difficult. Although the Pan American Highway connecting North and South America was built through the southern zone, running parallel to the coast, it bypasses the Península de Osa. There is also a railroad connecting Palmar Norte, a town situated on the northern fringes of the plantations, to the seaport city of Golfito, about eighty-five kilometers to the south. Bananas were loaded onto trains, transported to Golfito, then shipped to the various world markets. Despite this close proximity to a widely developed area, the Península de Osa remains one of the most isolated and least developed regions in Costa Rica. The Pan American Highway, power lines, and the railroad were built primarily to accommodate the economic services and needs of banana company workers and their communities and small businesses. Yet the Península de Osa has been ignored typically in the development of the economic infrastructure of the southern zone. All roads and power lines stop at least twenty kilometers from the northern perimeter of the peninsula. There are no telephones and no public electricity on the peninsula, and the only means of travel to and from it are by boat, horseback, or foot. Water travel is by far the most common means of transportation, usually with long dugout canoes pushed by paddles or propelled by small outboard motors. The majority of the people living on the peninsula are concentrated in small communities around the one hundred fifty kilometers of coastline.

Most of the Península de Osa is covered with thick, tropical hardwood forests on rolling hills generally unsuitable for large-scale farming and the banana plantations found in other parts of the southern zone. A major national park, Corcovado, with a nascent reforestation program, covers a large portion of the peninsula. The major economic activity on the peninsula consists of small, independently owned farms and cattle ranches. Fanning out from the small coastal communities, small parts of the jungle have been cut back to provide pasture for the grazing of cattle and clearing for the planting of various tropical fruits and vegetables, the most common of which are cacao, platanos, rice, beans, and corn.

The cattle and produce are usually sold or traded in those towns that have transportation connections to other parts of Costa Rica; principally in Sierpe, Palmar Norte, or Puerto Cortez, all situated close to the northern regions of the peninsula, and in Golfito, the southern port city which is located twenty kilometers across the water from the southern tip of the peninsula. Thus, time and cost in transporting commodities and people to the major markets and transportation centers has left small independent producers and cooperatives relatively isolated. The Península de Osa has not been an important part of the Costa Rican national economy and, in general, has not benefited from government or private-sector economic development programs.

Gold mining is another major economic activity in this area. Along the northern and southern coastal area of the peninsula, gold mining continues to contribute to the local economy. The gold mining ranges from a few large operations employing many workers and using heavy equipment to local people working in the small mountain streams with shovels, wooden sluice boxes, and gold pans. However, for the most part, this is a seasonal activity, primarily because the only time sufficient water is available to work the streams and rivers is during the rainy season—from August through December.

The disputes we observed and recorded took place in an area along the northeastern coast of the peninsula, on a point between the knuckle and first joint in the forefinger of the peninsula. At this point, the Sierpe river, the major waterway for the northern region of the Península de Osa, meets the Pacific Ocean. The area is known as the Boca Río Sierpe, the Boca ("the mouth"). All the disputes we examined, except one, took place in and around the Boca Río Sierpe.

The Boca is within the legal district of Sierpe, which, along with the districts of Palmar and Puerto Cortez, form what is called the Cantón de Osa (cantón roughly translated means "county"). Puerto Cortez is where the Municipalidad de Osa, the "county seat," is located. In the county seat of Puerto Cortez is the alcaldía (typically, a mayor who has limited legal authority), along with the criminal and civil courts and judges. Palmar and Sierpe have only their own police forces, usually made up of members of the Rural Guardia. The guardia maintain social order partially by making arrests and carrying out small-scale investigations, but have no authority or facilities for the hearing or judging of cases. All cases, whether criminal or civil, must be processed and adjudicated in the Municipalidad de Osa in Puerto Cortez.

The districts of Puerto Cortez, Palmar, and Sierpe form three points of a triangle arranged around the northern boundaries of the banana plantations. The easternmost point is Palmar, which is located on the Pan American Highway. This district of Palmar includes the town of Palmar Norte and 447 square kilometers of the surrounding countryside. The total population of the district of Palmar is 14,729, with approximately seven thousand inhabitants residing in the town (Costa Rican Census 1984).

The district of Puerto Cortez is situated slightly to the north and to the west of Palmar. This district includes the town of Puerto Cortez, which has a population of about nine thousand and includes 384 square kilometers of the surrounding countryside. The total population of the district of Puerto Cortez is 14,592 (Costa Rican Census 1984). The southernmost point in the triangle is the district and town of Sierpe, also connected to Palmar by a rough dirt road which winds through fifteen kilometers of a banana plantation. Sierpe is a tiny river port community of about three hundred fifty inhabitants and is the departure point for transportation for all small farming communities up and down the river to the Península and the northern regions of the Península de Osa.

The size of the district of Sierpe is 1,252 square kilometers, almost three times the area of either the districts of Palmar or Puerto Cortez. Yet the total population of the district is only 4,211 (Costa Rican Census 1984). The reason for the relatively small number of people is that this vast area, including the northern third of the Península de Osa, consists largely of jungle wilderness. This area is the focal point of our study.

Sierpe has a different economic base than either Palmar Norte or Puerto Cortez, which depended heavily on the patronage of hundreds of banana company workers and their families. Sierpe is located on the other side of the plantations from both the Pan American Highway and the railroad. In addition, all roads and power lines stopped short of Sierpe prior to 1982. The town is surrounded on three sides by water: to the south by the Estero Azul, a wide spring-fed stream, and to the east and north by the Sierpe River ("Snake River"), which bends and twists some sixteen kilometers southwest from Sierpe to the Pacific Ocean. This water highway provides the fastest and most practical means of travel for most of the district's inhabitants. Commodities and people destined for other points in Costa Rica pass through Sierpe. Sierpe has not suffered as much as Palmar Norte and Puerto Cortez from the pullout of the Standard Brands Company.

Sierpe is relatively isolated. The organization of social relationships is characterized by homogeneity. Residents typically engage in "dependent" relationships and retain many other forms of mechanical social solidarity. Also, this isolation is not simply related to physical circumstances, but also because of the lack of television and print media. Prior to November 1982, Sierpe had no electricity and no regular delivery of the various national newspapers (newspapers that were read in the area were usually brought in by travelers).

Furthermore, isolation has contributed to the development of a certain autonomous identity in the Sierpe District. Along with the attendant cultural anomalies specific to this area such as legends and "folktales," there is insider knowledge about the natural environment and a specialized language that has created a unique identity for the Península de Osa. Two other factors that have also encouraged and sustained this autonomous cultural development include transportation limitations and the effect of the ocean tidal cycle.

The ocean tide has had a significant influence on the local sociocultural development and transportation in the area. Although Sierpe is approximately sixteen kilometers upriver from the Pacific, the water level in Sierpe goes up and down at least two meters every six hours. These conditions, which residents view as "inevitable and unchangeable," continue to have an impact upon local social life. Individuals, for example, plan arrivals and departures according to the continuous ebb and flow of the tide. People generally travel upriver as the tide is rising, because it aids upstream travel. People have adjusted to "waiting time" in and around Sierpe. That is, people traveling on the river usually make arrangements to stay with friends or family, either for their meals or to spend the night, while waiting for the tides to change. Thus, during certain times of the day and days of the week, there is much socializing in Sierpe among people from many different parts of the district. People come together in the churches, in the cantinas, and on street corners, where they exchange news and messages, and also arrange for messages to be sent to other parts of the district. Thus the changing of the tides have created an opportunity for frequent reinforcement of social solidarity and community identity (see Nader 1990b for a similar analysis of other means of maintaining or achieving solidarity).

Along with mechanical solidarity and a relatively clear sense of community, there are few apparent status differentials in Sierpe. Some people, of course, are known to be rich or well-off, while others are said to be poor or *corrompido* ("corrupt") but, nevertheless, there is no conspicuous division of status. This factor, combined with the tendency of the residents to live their entire lives at home or close to home, has created a cohesive social atmosphere—everyone knows virtually everyone else, including most of their problems and personal history. Strangers are noticed quickly and are subject to the open, and usually friendly, curiosity of the locals. This sense of community is important for at least two significant reasons. First, under such circumstances, there is likely to be a high degree of consensus among local residents concerning attitudes and beliefs toward the "resolution" of disputes including the role and effectiveness of the law and the kind of information available about where and how to conduct a dispute. For example, if a Sierpe resident becomes involved in conflict she or he will most likely turn for assistance or advice to a family member or friend who is also a resident of Sierpe. Second, many of the cases we describe involve "outsiders"—that is, those who own land or have business investments within the Sierpe district but live outside the area. These individuals, such as North Americans, with very little or no experience of the Costa Rican culture, and Costa Rican absentee landlords are not fully integrated into the Sierpe or Boca communities.

The residents of the Boca Río Sierpe, which is about sixteen kilometers down river from the town of Sierpe, seem particularly conscious of outsiders. The area is sparsely populated and most of the residents have lived the majority of their lives there. New resi-

dents or workers are immediately the subject of conversation—
who are they, where do they come from, what are they doing
here? Also, since the Boca is a wilderness area, with no electricity
and no telephones, the local residents have come to depend on
each other in times of emergency or trouble. In addition, they help
each other by sending messages for friends or by going upriver and
bringing back needed supplies. Thus, locals ask what are the new-
comer's resources, can they be depended on for assistance, or do
they need help?

For example, shortly after one North American outsider
moved to the Boca Río Sierpe in June 1980, he was visited by an
unfamiliar local resident. The man had paddled to the house by
dugout canoe, bringing his son who had been badly injured in an
accident with a machete. He said he wanted the North American
to take his son to Sierpe where he could get public transportation
to Palmar Norte for medical attention. The man explained later
that he had brought his son to the North American because he had
heard that the gringo was a good person and had the fastest boat on
the Boca. (Because of this incident, and many related ones, over a
period of years this outsider eventually became an "insider" in
most interactions.)

In the case of absentee landlords, however, there is a much
more subtle relationship between "insiders" and "outsiders" on
the Boca Río Sierpe. Most absentee landlords are either Costa
Ricans or foreigners who live outside the Sierpe district and have
limited contact with the local residents. They may be well known
to the local residents, perhaps because of having owned their land
for a long time or because of frequent visits, or they may be complete strangers. However, in either case, they are not considered as
being *of* the local community—that is, there is no sense that they
truly belong. In interviews with local residents, absentee landlords
usually were spoken of in terms that clearly indicated that the
landlords were considered beyond control of the informal social
network of the Boca. It was one of the rare instances where residents exhibited a sense of "class consciousness." The landlords
were usually described in reference to their wealth, status, or occupational position somewhere "out there," either someplace else in
Costa Rica or in a foreign country.

There may be several consequences of such an arrangement
of relationships. First, in the case of absentee landlords involved in
a land dispute with a local resident, it might be expected that the
landlord would be closer to the formal social control agencies,

enjoy better access to more accurate information, and have greater resources available to successfully manage or resolve a dispute. On the other hand, if the outsiders are foreign and know little or nothing about Costa Rican land, laws, and customs, they may not have the most basic information about where to go or whom to see in the event of a land dispute. In fact, they may even have difficulty soliciting assistance or advice from people within their own informal social network.

There are other ways in which the differences between insiders and outsiders on the Boca Río Sierpe have become evident. Since such differences may bear directly on our study, we want to further clarify what it means to be an insider or an outsider in this particular area. For example, there are "secrets" about life on the Boca which only long-term residents or their families could know about, secrets which are consciously withheld because of pride or profit or because the knowledge is regarded as commonplace. These secrets are related, for example, to the location of Indian burial grounds, the best places to pan for gold, local folklore and legend, and special knowledge about the environment that helps residents to survive and prosper.

One of these secrets, for example, is significant not only because it provides a better sense of the Boca Río Sierpe but also because it is important environmentally and ecologically. In this instance, information about the physical environment among the local residents is regarded as common knowledge and could not be shared with an outsider unless the outsider had become redefined as at least a marginal insider. After about a year and a half of living on the Boca, a North American was invited by the daughter of a local resident to go fishing. This was possible only because the father and the North American had recently come to the understanding that the North American was courting the daughter, and it was expected that they would eventually be married. As they paddled into a vast maze of mangrove swamps that cover several square kilometers along the eastern part of the Boca, the daughter stopped occasionally to catch small black crabs crawling on the lower limbs of the mangrove trees. "These crabs are the bait," she explained. "They live in the holes in the mud, but since it's now high tide they're up in the trees." Finally, she pointed to a particular stand of mangrove trees and as they came close she quickly jumped from the small dugout to the lower branches of a tree. Carrying only a hand line, she baited her hook with one of the small crabs, looked around for a few seconds, then began howling and yelping and shaking the leaves and branches of the tree at the same time. Her high, loud shouts echoed off the water and into the swamp. The North American was startled and said something about scaring the fish away. The young woman replied that, on the contrary, she was actually "calling" the fish.

She then began whistling and squawking like a bird and breaking off pieces of crab and throwing them in the water while still shaking the leaves and branches. Suddenly, as a piece of crab hit the water, the surface rippled and there was a flash of silver and red; a large beautiful red snapper. She leaned over and carefully threw her line in the water. The fish had the crab and the hook in its mouth almost before it hit the water. The woman explained later that the monkeys and birds in the area love to eat the small black crabs, as do the fish. The fish have learned to follow the monkeys and birds as they feed, relying on sound and vibration, hoping to catch the crab crumbs or the crabs trying to escape by jumping into the water. "You actually *hunt* the fish," she said. "Either you follow the monkeys and birds yourself, or you act like one. Yet, the technique only works during certain times of the day and during certain periods of the month." She then went into a long explanation about the correlation between the phases of the moon and the *ritmo*, or rhythm, of life on the Boca.

To put this example into context, there are several absentee landlords, both Costa Rican and North American, who are well-known among the residents of the Boca Río Sierpe, and who have had a long association with the area. One North American, for example, has been coming to the area for six months a year for the past fifteen years and is an avid fisherman, yet has never heard of this relationship between crabs, monkeys, birds, and fish. The differences between insiders and outsiders on the Boca Río Sierpe is both profound and subtle. Such differences are the result of the unique organization of social relationships on the Boca. They are based, in part, on sharing special knowledge about the physical environment; the preservation of ancient traditions, stories, and legends; and the interdependence of the area's residents faced with the inconvenience and potential dangers of living in an isolated wilderness.

We make special note of these circumstances because the situation is changing quickly as the outside world gradually penetrates the relatively "closed" social universe of the Sierpe district. This is due primarily to a combination of at least three factors: (1) the world recession in the 1980s rocked the Costa Rican econo-

my—the national debt soared, inflation accelerated to unprece-
dented levels, unemployment increased dramatically, and the
colón (the Costa Rican currency) was devalued significantly; (2)
the influx of refugees from El Salvador and particularly Nicaragua
increased substantially, especially as the so-called Contras—led by
former Somoza guards who waged war against the Sandinista government—began receiving money and military assistance from the
United States; and (3) the withdrawal of Standard Brands Company
from the southern zone of Costa Rica resulted in a massive displacement of economic and human resources in which hundreds of
people lost not only their jobs but their homes as well.

The workers had been living in company houses on company
property and, thus, could be "legally" evicted. These events have
had a direct effect on the Sierpe district, considered one of the last
frontier areas in Costa Rica; that is, still relatively undeveloped
with vast wilderness regions available for settlement and a wealth
of natural resources open to exploitation. In 1986 and 1987,
a Costa Rican government agency, the Institute of Agrarian
Development (IDA), sent homeless families to the northern part of
the Península de Osa for resettlement. These families quickly
experienced some of the dependency relationships of the Sierpe
community upon the rest of Costa Rica, as Costa Rica experiences
various levels of dependency in the world system.

The world is beginning to penetrate in other ways as well. In
November 1982, electricity was turned on in Sierpe and the town
had a fiesta. The introduction of electricity has since influenced
everything from fashion to language to eating habits. People are
buying, for example, electrical appliances such as food and juice
blenders, refrigerators, and freezers. Now Sierpe residents can purchase fresh meat and vegetables, and store them safely at home
until they are eaten. This was not possible in the past due to lack
of cold storage facilities in homes and in the pulperías, or general
stores—which consequently could not sell highly perishable items
in any large quantities. Now, however, the local pulperías often
stock frozen chickens, meat, many kinds of fresh vegetables, milk,
and ice cream. However, since not everyone can afford a refrigera-
tor, some families share their cold storage space in exchange for
partial payment of their electrical bill. Thus, there has been a
change in both buying and selling patterns, as well as in dietary
and eating habits.

The purchase of other electrical appliances, such as irons,
sound equipment, sewing machines and, of course, televisions, has

had an influence on local fashions, political opinions, and perspectives about world reality. Before November 1982, for example, there were perhaps five or six televisions in all of Sierpe. Those with televisions and the generators necessary to power them watched regularly, while those who saw one at a neighbor's house regarded television as a curiosity and a novelty. With the introduction of electricity into Sierpe, however, televisions were among the very first electric appliances purchased and television antennas began appearing on the rusty tin roofs of Sierpe.

With changing times, the local *pulperías*, which up to that time had primarily stocked basic foodstuffs, tools, and a few clothes items, began featuring consumer-oriented goods and even a few luxury products. The sudden exposure to television may have contributed to this observed shift in buying and selling patterns. Costa Rican television, like the television programing in the United States, is saturated with slick, mass-oriented "commercial breaks" designed to sell the latest in fashions, kitchen soaps, disinfectants, electronic appliances, household goods, and related commodities.

The effects of television viewing in Sierpe was evident in various comments by the residents concerning the product commercials. The general feeling is summed up in these words by one local resident:

> What I don't like about television is the commercials. They usually show half-naked men and women, all very handsome and beautiful, sitting around on a yacht and drinking a particular brand of scotch. Everybody is laughing and having a great time. What do my sons and daughters think about this? Will my boy believe that if he drinks this kind of scotch he can expect to be surrounded by five beautiful girls? The good life, as they say? This is *Sierpe*! All we have here is beer and hard whiskey. No yachts, no naked people. But what if he picks up that part of the message about drinking? I'm afraid he might see drinking as glamorous, a part of being a man. That's not right, not a good thing to teach the children.

The more pervasive effects of television on the residents of Sierpe is still not entirely known. Suddenly a bombardment of outside news and political propaganda from around the world began entering the small houses and bamboo huts of Sierpe de Osa on a daily basis. The electronic news media provided the residents of

Sierpe with a rapid "education" in war, murder, terrorism, drug abuse, economic crises, and political revolution. One resident reflected that, "When I see what's going on in the world—all those countries fighting each other, *terrorismo,* people going into space, the dangerous fight between Russia and the United States (they have atom bombs, you know)—I realize how tiny Costa Rica actually is! We don't have anything to do with what's going on out there. It's as if we don't even exist. But if there should be a big fight with atom bombs, we're fried!" A news documentary aired on Costa Rican television about the U.S. space program, and as one local resident watched footage of one of the Apollo moon-landing flights, he burst into laughter, pointed at the television screen, and said, "That's crazy! They can't do that! How can anybody walk on the moon? It's a fake!" Even after hearing a short history of space flight and an explanation of space vehicles and spacesuits, the resident still shook his head and refused to believe it had ever happened. "There's nothing up there. How could they spend so much money? You know what I think? I think they lost a few billion dollars somehow, so they told people they used it to go to the moon. I don't believe it."

Such comments seem to reflect a mixture of attitudes ranging from detachment, to resentment, to a sense of "otherworldliness" about events and programing residents see on television. Also, there is something about the element of "world context" which causes confusion and cognitive dissonance among some of the residents, primarily because the information they see and hear on television sometimes contrasts sharply with their preconceived views of world reality. Most people in this area, for example, regard the United States of America as a kind of glorious land of milk and honey, where everyone has a lot of money, beautiful clothes, fancy houses, and big automobiles. There is also the image of the United States as a kind of cross between Elmer Gantry and John Wayne; that is, the U.S.A. is seen as the supreme example of democracy and moral righteousness in the world that has the power—"the iron fist," as one resident put it—to stamp out any country causing trouble or practicing evil (cf. Vargas 1989).

Another report, on the Costa Rican national news program, mentioned a study done in the United States which revealed that there were approximately eight million people in the U.S.A. suffering from hunger or malnutrition. This news also created quite a sensation among those who saw the program. They immediately asked a barrage of questions about the U.S. economy and wanted to know how it could be possible to have so many hungry people in the United States. One young girl made this comment: "Why that's terrible! All those hungry people! My god, the entire population of Costa Rica is only two million! Imagine if we were all hungry. I never thought there could be (any) hungry people in the United States, but *eight million!*"

The introduction of electricity into Sierpe appears to be having an effect on more than buying and selling patterns and eating habits. The effects of watching television is also influencing opinions and perspectives regarding the world reality and Costa Rica's place in the world context. It is unclear in what ways these observed changes and reactions may eventually effect the social reality in the district of Sierpe, and such events will require further study. The introduction of electricity in Sierpe is, however, clearly one example of how influences from the outside world are having an effect on the cultural qualities of a community of people living in relative isolation.

Another element of the "outside world" which has entered into this isolated area is the addition of regular and reliable bus service, introduced between Sierpe and Palmar by a local entrepreneur in 1983. Before this time, the bus service was almost nonexistent. Old buses were often out of service for days at a time or, more often than not, broken down along the road while carrying a load of passengers. With the introduction of reliable and affordable bus service, travel has increased and the daily newspapers and mail are now delivered fairly regularly.

Also during the 1980s, construction began on a road that will eventually connect the town of Sierpe with Drake Bay, which lies along the northern coast of the Península de Osa. This road has been planned for a long time, in part because of the many drownings reported from this area, particularly in the mouth of the river Sierpe, where the river meets the Pacific Ocean. People living on the northern third of the peninsula must pass from the ocean through the Boca to get to the town of Sierpe. This trip can be dangerous because of the unpredictable nature of the combination of storms at sea, wave patterns, and the force of the tide. During the past fifty years according to estimates by the local *guardia,* 46 people have drowned in the Sierpe district, most of them in an attempt to pass into or out of the Boca Río Sierpe.

It is not clear how the pace of such changes and innovations have influenced the social structure and economic activity in the Sierpe district. However, one particular influence is the large number of people moving into the area. These are not simply homeless people looking for a place to settle, but also entrepreneurial outsiders who are interested in the development of a tourist industry and in taking advantage of the many kilometers of deserted white-sand beaches in the area and the excellent deep sea fishing just outside the Boca in the Pacific Ocean. For example, a group of North Americans built a tourist business on Drake Bay in early 1984 and began expanding it in 1989, and a Costa Rican absentee landlord recently initiated construction on what he calls a "luxury tourist resort" just inside the Boca on the river. Also, the gold in the area continues to attract outsiders, not only individual gold prospectors, but also large operators with heavy equipment.

Nevertheless, the Sierpe district still retains the distinctive features of a frontier area exhibiting a high degree of social solidarity among the local residents, combined with only a weak presence of state power and authority. In fact, formal social control in the district of Sierpe is not one of enforcement; enforcement of the letter of the law is viewed as impractical in a wilderness area of over one thousand square kilometers without telephones or graded roads. Rather, the guardia plays a reactive role; it typically responds only if called upon. The consequences of such circumstances in the process of social control in the area is fairly obvious; a very low, weak presence of formal social control with a correspondingly strong presence of informal social control. Thus, the control of crime is usually a responsibility of the residents, and the data we have been able to gather regarding theft of personal property confirm this statement. More often than not, such theft is handled in an informal manner by alerting family members, friends, or local acquaintances, and enlisting their help in recovering stolen items. Furthermore, when and if the guardia are called to investigate such theft, they too use the informal social network in the course of their investigation. There have been few incidents of violent crimes such as homicide, rape, or armed robbery reported in the Sierpe district since 1980.

In cases of a civil nature, however, such as conflict over property ownership, boundary lines, or rights of possession, the process of social control becomes more problematic. Because water travel is so important throughout the district of Sierpe, land which is easily accessible by water is usually valued highly. Disputes involving such property are likely to be considered as serious and worthy of intervention by the formal social control agencies. Since the Rural Guardia, however, is typically incapable of providing technical reactions in such cases, and since the town of Puerto Cortez is the site of all legal services and the administration of law for the Cantón de Osa, cases involving civil law suits must be held there. If two landowners are feuding over disputed boundary lines on the Boca Río Sierpe, an offended party must travel to Puerto Cortez to file a complaint or *denuncia* against the other person. This trip is fifteen kilometers up the Sierpe river to the town of Sierpe and can take from one to six hours, depending on the type of boat used. Once in Sierpe, they must take a bus to Puerto Cortez. After conducting their business at the Municipalidad de Osa in Puerto Cortez, they must return home by the same route. In all, such a trip can take at least one day and most likely two. Moreover, if they have witnesses for the claims, they must arrange to transport the witnesses to Puerto Cortez to testify. In addition, the disputants typically are obligated to pay for their witnesses' travel expenses, meals, or hotel rooms, and to compensate them for lost salary from their regular jobs.

This procedure simply *initiates* a civil lawsuit, after which the person against whom the *denuncia* is made will be required to make the same trip to Puerto Cortez with any witnesses. Depending on the circumstances of the case and where the disputed territory is located, there may be other required trips to Puerto Cortez. At least once during the course of the lawsuit, the *alcaldía* ("mayor") usually makes an inspection trip to the area to see the disputed territory or boundaries in question. The offended party is usually expected, but not required, to pay any expenses incurred by the *alcaldía* in making this inspection trip, such as meals or transportation costs. If a person cannot pay or refuses to pay, she or he can ask the court to cover all expenses of the inspection trip. However, if there are insufficient funds in the court or county treasury, she or he must wait until funds become available.

Most of the land disputes we examined took place in the area of the Boca Río Sierpe. Since all jurisdictional power and authority in the Municipalidad de Osa is in Puerta Cortez, *access* has a significant influence on the management and outcome of civil disputes. Indeed, access will affect the form of the dispute—that is, whether a dispute is actually referred to the formal court system or managed informally by the disputants. After each dispute became public, we noted who was involved and the nature of their relationship, the conduct and management of the dispute, and the outcome. Those individuals involved in the disputes were interviewed, as were other observers and interested parties, such as lawyers, judges, and the police.

We were able to examine systematically nine cases beginning in June 1980. The disputes involved the ownership or control of scarce resources in the district of Sierpe, especially property easily accessible by water. Earlier investigations had discovered that when control of a scarce resource forms the basis of a dispute, interpersonal relationships between the disputants are often sacrificed in an attempt to force the issue to resolution (Starr and Yngvesson 1975; Lauderdale 1988a). In addition, our preliminary field research, theoretic framework, and the dispute literature suggest that we focus upon specific factors, such as the nature of the social relationship among disputants, access to forums, as well as related time, cost, and cultural factors. These factors form a "variable continuum" that defines the language and limits of the dispute. Thus, these variables are not to be regarded as definitive categories in which to rank the data, but rather as a language strategy to identify and differentiate the various elements that might influence the dispute process (Kidder 1980–81).

As we mentioned in the preface of this book, the following work is neither an attempt to test a particular theory nor a narrative of specific disputes. In the twelve years of research we discovered new information from a variety of sources on the study of disputes and deviance, which helped us move further in the gradual development of our arguments. In essence, we thought the best strategy would be for the reader to witness our attempt to develop a theoretical framework for future studies of law, disputes, and deviance by moving back and forth among initial theoretical ideas, what those ideas suggest for appropriate methodology to study the dispute processes, and the impact of the evolving theory and methodology on specific findings.

Social Relationships and Disputing

The nature of the social relationships among disputants will have a significant effect on the methods chosen to manage the dispute, and consequently the outcome of the dispute (Gluckman 1955; Nader and Todd 1978; Black 1984, 1989). Yngvesson (1984) delineates a series of assumptions that underlie the attendant analysis: (1) disputes vary in meaning relative to particular circumstances; (2) defining the meaning of a dispute is a political process; (3) the meaning of a dispute is negotiable—however, the balance of power among the actors influences the nature of this negotiation; and (4) the negotiated meaning, which influences the definition of the dispute, ultimately shapes the outcome of that dispute. Relationships defined as continuing involve many mutual interests and demand certain kinds of dispute strategies that will allow the relationship to continue—for example, through negotiation or mediation. On the other hand, single-issue relationships will not be valued highly and will typically lead to adjudication or arbitration in the settlement of the dispute (Gluckman 1955; cf. Van Velson's situational analysis 1967). In essence, the more highly valued the relationship between disputants, the more likely the management of the dispute will be conducted to minimize the chances that the relationship will be destroyed or damaged seriously.[5]

In addition, our focus upon the nature of the social relationships includes a plethora of sometimes subtle, sometimes obvious factors such as the status, power, and prestige of disputants as well as their level of integration into a social situation or community. Level of integration, for example, can be characterized by the degree to which disputants are perceived as being inside or outside the community. And, while it is clear that this integration is a matter of degree, we initially simplify the analysis by dichotomizing the integration by referring to people as insiders or outsiders. We will also examine some of the more analytic concepts related to social relationships by discussing the usefulness of cross-linkages, symmetry, and social hierarchy.[6]

In analyzing the status and power of disputants, we examine the relative resources that are available for managing a dispute. In cases where disputants have a significant advantage in resources, we might expect that they would have a number of advantages in the dispute process. Advantages come, for example, not only in the power to access the formal control system but also, more fundamentally, in the ability to control the definitions of the situation. Who is defined initially as a deviant, as a complainer, or as a victim, and how are such definitions created and maintained?

The nature of the social relationship is just one variable among many others that may influence the course and outcome of the dispute process (cf. Welton et al. 1988). These variables are interrelated and in some cases they cannot be easily differentiated. Thus, throughout our discussion we frequently explain actions or events in terms of a particular variable that under certain conditions may be inextricably linked to another variable—for example, cost and time. Nonetheless, human actions and larger events cannot and should not always be placed neatly into categories, and we try to avoid arbitrary classifications that might lead to forcing information into our framework (see Augelli and Murphy, 1988).

Rationalization and Access to Dispute Forums

A dispute is created and bound within a particular social context. Sheldon Ekland-Olson (1984) refers to a dispute as a disruptive event that results in "relational disturbance." Grievances and disputes are socially defined, and as such, result in some disturbance or discord in social relations. If expectations are breached, what alternatives are available to the disputants and under what conditions will a particular alternative emerge? The answer also depends on factors such as the perceived "seriousness" of the event, expectations about successful pursuit of the dispute, access and control of information, and a variety of other resources. Regardless of which alternative emerges, alternatives typically have been encompassed by two broad forums: informal and formal social control.

We view formal social control as the system of institutionalized legal structures that form the backbone of state authority and power. This form of control includes, for example, police, judges, lawyers, and other components of the court system and penal institutions. In most cases, the formal legal system is considered the preeminent form of social control within national boundaries—that is, the state has the authority and power to define and administer the law as well as to prosecute and punish deviance. Increased rationalization of law is viewed typically as progressive, since explicit, abstract, and calculable rules lead to more predictability (Weber 1954). Merry (1987) points out that related conceptions of formal social control are based upon the belief that the formal rational law serves to improve:

> The lot of the average person, who is increasingly guaranteed a level of predictability and stability in his or her social life and whose protection is based on principles other than sheer might or the number of strong and powerful allies she can muster. [1987:2]

However, in any analysis of formal social control, it is important to consider how law becomes legitimized within a society. Law is one form of domination and control that often is accepted as a legitimate means of managing a dispute. Law typically offers the illusion of "fairness and equality" because access to legal institutions can appear equal for all (cf. O'Barr and Conley 1988). While law is justified often as representing the views of each member of society, it is structured and controlled to legitimate various forms of domination (Weber 1978; Merry 1987; Inverarity et al. 1992). Legitimacy is grounded in assumptions about authority; people often follow orders of an authority because they believe that formal social control will produce decisions irrespective of pressures from personal goals or group norms (see Bauman 1989). Because law, which represents only one type of formal control, typically is accepted as legitimate in most societies, it continues to exert a dominant force in the management of disputes (cf. Turk, 1976; Weber 1978; Merry 1987 Marx, 1988).

There are varying theories relating to how law, for example, is created in a society. Many perspectives focus upon the role of judges and courts in making law (Shapiro 1981). User theory, however, offers a broader perspective by showing how law can be primarily a function of the cumulative impact of the dominant users, rather than simply that of judges, court, or defendants (Nader 1984b). A major determinant of the characteristics of users of the formal legal system is whether the predominant system is viewed as a viable means of managing a dispute or as unresponsive and indifferent to peoples' needs. Those who use the formal system and who manage to achieve access are referred to as "voicers"; those who are more cynical or disillusioned and do not access the formal law are "nonvoicers." These nonvoicers are likely to utilize extralegal or informal approaches to law, such as self-help (Black 1976; Nader 1984a).

Informal social control includes symbolic systems of shared meanings and expectations about what constitutes normative behavior. These meanings and expectations are constantly both redefined and created as a product of social interaction, and can be applied to societies or small interpersonal groups. One recurring view relating to the perception of normative behavior focuses upon solidarity; the sense of collective sentiment, the dependence or interdependence of social relations, and the maintenance or adjustment of the identities of individuals or collectivities (cf. Durkheim 1964; Erikson 1966).

While important prior work has focused on disruptions in solidarity and the ostensibly attendant increases in deviance, it is also important to note that the identity and solidarity of a collective revolves largely around predictability and control. That is, the interest in "belonging" and achieving a sense of security are directly related to these concerns with increasing rationalization. Rationalization in the context of this study refers to the existence of explicit, abstract, and calculable rules and procedures that lead to an increase in predictability within a social system. Agreements over the relative value of money, for example, have led to relatively fixed standards. Bureaucratic control over resources such as money entail an emphasis upon "regularity, predictability, efficiency and cost effectiveness" (Henry 1983:15). Increases in degrees of rationalization tend to make the dispute process more predictable at the formal level, yet typically increase informal as well as formal social control as they are implemented partially through political processes.[7]

Access to dispute settlement forums in "traditional" societies has often been characterized as unproblematic. These societies are usually described as composed of homogeneous groups of people organized around informal principles with relatively clear procedures for the handling of a grievance or dispute. This does not suggest, however, that the distribution of power is equal or that all members of the society have equal access to decision makers. The variety of reactions to and definitions of deviance and disputes within traditional societies has received considerable attention. Access to forums in traditional societies has been characterized as being part of *informal social control.*

Although informal social control is rarely encouraged, except on the margins in some mediation or negotiation settings or self-help clinics, it nevertheless exerts considerable control over human behavior. This can be explained in part by the social psychological principle of the "generalized other;" each person is a part of a larger social group organized around a common system of values, beliefs, and moral boundaries that provide identity and meaning to members of that particular group. As George Mead (1934:155) notes, "it is in the form of the generalized other that the social process influences the behavior of the individuals involved in it and . . . the community exercises control over the conduct of its individual members." This "control" can be *informal* if it refers to the socially derived meanings and definitions about normative behavior, or *formal* if it concerns the effect of state-administered sanctions against particular kinds of behavior.[8]

Since there are numerous systems of informal social control, access to informal forums of dispute settlement may be as varied as the many different kinds of social groupings possible in a society—for example, religious, occupational, racial, ethnic, and familial groups. Moreover, among these many different groups, considerable conflict and disagreement exists; for example, those who urge gun control versus those who demand the "right to bear arms," abortion advocates versus antiabortion advocates, or local merchants against "gangs."

In complex heterogeneous societies, access to forums has been described as problematic, to say the least. In these societies, the formal system of law is often perceived as the only forum "legally" available. In fact, the state expressly forbids its citizens to "take the law into their own hands." To settle their dispute "outside the law" is, in most instances, itself a crime (Black 1984).

The formal legal institutions of the state are ostensibly impartial agencies that regulate and "police" these various relationships, acting as an intermediary force in resolving conflict and dispute. However, as has been demonstrated by other research [notably by Lynn Mather (1979) on criminal law, and Merry (1990) on civil law], the state's legal institutions are influenced and manipulated by particular informal groups. Black and Baumgartner (1983) present a typology of "third parties" that they suggest are endemic to the management of human conflict (see Figure 1.2). Their typology categorizes third-parties along two dimensions: the nature and degree of intervention. Black and Baumgartner designate twelve third-party roles, including five "support" roles— "informer, adviser, advocate, ally, and surrogate"—and five "settlement" roles—"friendly peacemaker, mediator, arbitrator, judge, and repressive peacemaker." Each role is ranked according to the degree of intervention involved, with the extent of "partisan" involvement central to the various support roles and the extent of "authoritative" involvement central to the settlement roles. Finally, the authors assign one role that entails features of both partisan and nonpartisan involvement—"negotiator"—and one role that is removed entirely from these categories—"healer."

Access to formal forums of social control in a complex society often begins among one's own informal contacts. However, in large cities, for example, informal networks of friends, family, and associates are not always in close proximity. It is quite common for neighbors in these cities to be strangers. People do not general ly call upon a stranger for help in the settlement of a dispute unless immediate physical threat is involved. Thus, in the case of a breach of contract, for example, a person might call a trusted friend or close relative who will be expected to sympathize with the grievance and perhaps suggest alternative courses of action.

This "complaining" stage of the dispute process is the point where most conflicts become public and the designation of deviance often emerges. The complaining typically includes claims about the broader violation of moral boundaries. Perhaps the friend knows a lawyer who can help. The person contacts the

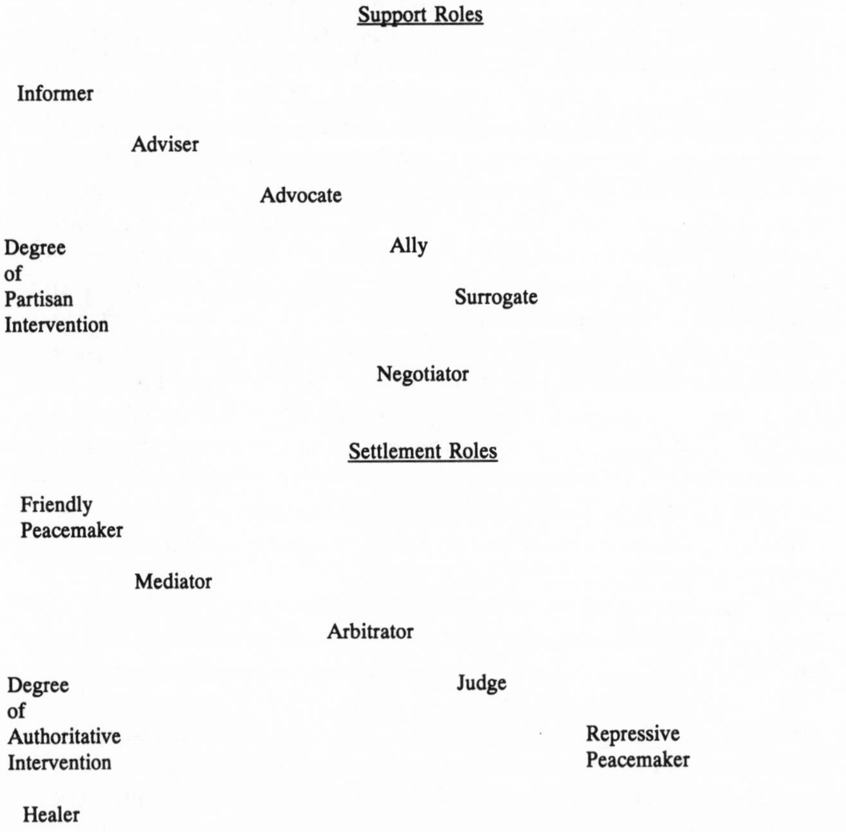

<u>Support Roles</u>

Informer

    Adviser

        Advocate

Degree   Ally
of
Partisan   Surrogate
Intervention

       Negotiator

<u>Settlement Roles</u>

Friendly
Peacemaker

    Mediator

        Arbitrator

Degree   Judge
of
Authoritative   Repressive
Intervention   Peacemaker

Healer

Figure 1.2

Adapted from Donald Black and M. P. Baumgartner, 1983, "Toward a theory of the third party" in *Empirical theories about courts*, Keith O. Boyum and Lynn Mather, eds. New York: Longman, p. 87.

lawyer by means of identification with the mutual acquaintance before discussing the case, which often includes reiterating claims of who or what was deviant. Up to this point, the dispute process is handled primarily on an informal basis. The lawyer makes predictions and observations, and determines if the person requires "formal" representation. If so, the lawyer often takes the dispute into the formal legal arena of the state. As this scenario demonstrates, access to the formal agencies of social control often is preceded by contacts within one's own informal social network, which may include not only technical claims, but deliberations over the moral order. Then there may be other assistance offered to access the formal system, such as, for example, a loan to help retain a lawyer, as well as information about the lawyer's office or the court.

In other societies, however, particularly in the rural, isolated regions of the "Third World" or "developing" countries, the power and authority of particular representatives of the state is often weak and their presence is minimal. (In fact, there may be vast areas of the countryside under the control of those who directly or indirectly oppose the national government). The Osa Península in Costa Rica, the area studied, is one such region. In the legal district of Sierpe which contains the peninsula, there are only three members of the Rural Guardia in an area of thirteen hundred square kilometers with a population of approximately four thousand people. Also, the seat of government power is located in the town of Puerto Cortez, at least one day of travel from the closest parts of the Sierpe district. Given such circumstances, most conflicts will probably be responded to initially in some informal manner.

Access to forums refers to the social control agencies or agents available for the resolution of disputes, such as the formal legal system of the state or third party mediators including associates, friends, and family members. The term "forum" incorporates a broad range of alternatives in the reaction to deviance. Disputants, for example, must know what courses of action are open to them in managing a dispute. If access to the formal court system is difficult to achieve or if the formal system is viewed as unnecessary, imposing, or corrupt, other forms of settling the dispute will often be utilized (cf. Kozolchyk and Greenberg, 1988). In "developing" societies, especially in those communities where the influence of the state is weak, access to the formal legal system appears to be quite problematic (Greenberg 1989).

Reactions to disputes may find expression in several ways. In general, these reactions may be implemented in either of the two forms of social control—informal or formal. Whether social control is implemented through formal or informal means depends upon factors such as access to social control agencies, the nature of the social relationship among the disputants, the object or basis of the dispute, and when and where the dispute occurs. As Nader (1980:29) notes in reflecting upon two elements of social control, "we have to get into deterrence and prevention by working back from the case studies down the chain to the source of the problem." This emphasis upon dissecting the dispute is particularly relevant (Miller and Sarat 1980–81). The recent return to decoding discourse, and a more general focus on reassessing simple classifications, is important particularly in the study of disputes (see Taylor 1986).[9]

We view the distinction between informal and formal control as largely heuristic. Obviously, the distinction is basically theoretical, since we often find a great degree of overlap between them. In addition, formal control usually has been conceptualized as highly organized and rigid, while informal control has been regarded typically as disorganized or loosely structured. We think that work following such a perspective is misleading. Formal control *may* be easier to identify and place on an organizational chart, but it does not follow necessarily that informal control is unstructured. The structure exists, although it may be difficult to identify and document. In fact, in many situations formal social control is subordinate to informal control, especially when considering its impact on the social system (see Balbus, 1973). That is, the formal system of control is used often as a tool by certain groups of people who are organized around informal principles and perspectives. One of our goals is to explore the degree of structure in the informal social control infrastructure in the Península de Osa, Costa Rica.

Time

Time can influence the process of social control in several different ways—for example, the time and distance needed to travel to social control agencies; time as a strategy in the management of a dispute (e.g., using a "cooling off" period or delay tactics); or time as a function of court proceedings (e.g., the rate at which cases can be heard and decisions made). Time as it relates to formal social control is closely associated with cost factors. In cases such as those occurring in the Osa Península, time affects access to the forums of social control. Time can also be used as a strategy in the dispute process, such as when a "recess" period is declared to allow tempers to subside and allow disputants the opportunity to reassess their relative strengths and weaknesses. This "cooling off" period can also act as a delay mechanism in an effort to increase legal costs and force an opponent with fewer resources to withdraw from the dispute. As Kidder notes:

> ...many of the cases one finds in the "dispute processing" institutions, whether formal or not, may be simple strategic confrontations over limited resources, with both sides claiming prior "rights" or the violation of some principle of "justice" only because that is the appropriate language for those fora, not because it is what the partisans feel. They initiate dispute processing action when they feel the time is right to "go after" whatever resource they seek to control and think that legal (or dispute processing) action can help them secure control. In such cases, the language of *justice*, far from being a support for equality, may be seen as an ideological basis for unequal distribution. Its primary function is to legitimize the authority of the distributing agent. [1980–81:723–24]

Time as a factor in informal social control is less obvious. Baumgartner (1984) suggests the importance of time on the process of informal social control in a study of the dispute process in suburbia. One factor, for example, accounting for the predominance of nonconfrontation among the middle-class residents of suburbia is "their high rate of mobility [which] means that bonds between persons are frequently ruptured and replaced with new and equally temporary ones, so that relationships often have short pasts and futures" (1984:95). The consequences are twofold: first, people tend to tolerate deviant behavior because they can look forward to an eventual separation from the deviant; and second, "it makes bitter enemies and resentments difficult to sustain and limits the ability of people to accumulate damaging information about one another" (ibid.).

Where residency is more permanent, the opposite is true. Here confrontation is more likely because grievances are cumulative and there is greater opportunity to accumulate damaging information (cf. Marquez 1983). Time is especially relevant in the present study because of the nature of the social structure on the

Osa Península. People tend to live in close familial networks near their birthplace. Because there is limited, if any, social mobility, their pasts and futures are inextricably linked with each other. Moreover, the possibility of collecting damaging information—the building of "grievance portfolios"—is substantially increased and often involves the use of family histories from several generations.

Time may also be a main cause or focus of a land dispute. It is common in the definition and interpretation of Costa Rican land laws that a person who occupies a particular piece of land for a given length of time, usually more than three months, and who makes general improvements on the land has a legal "claim" to the land (see Locke 1960, especially pages 328–29). These claims are described as the "rights of possession." General improvements, which may bring about these claims, include building a house, clearing trees and underbrush, and planting crops. A claim may be applied under two general conditions: in situations where settlers move onto "free" or untitled land; and in situations where settlers move onto land that has already been claimed or is "owned" by somebody else. It is the latter situation that leads to most disputes of this nature.

It is most common for *precaristas,* or squatters, for example, to move onto land owned by an absentee landowner. In fact, some people continually live as *precaristas,* and become, in effect, professional squatters. They move onto desirable pieces of land, hold onto the land as long as possible, make improvements to the land, and then negotiate with the landowner over control of the land. In cases where the landowner has already been granted a clear and formal title to the land, they can have a *precarista* removed, but only after agreeing to pay the *precarista* for improvements made on the land. In cases where no clear title exists, the issue of determining ownership becomes especially problematic and complex. Frequently, a *precarista* is able to establish such a firm presence that the landowner must pay more for land improvements than the land is worth. There has been a dramatic increase recently in disputes of this kind, partially as a result of the withdrawal of Standard Brands Company from the southern zone of Costa Rica.

Cost

Cost may also influence the amount and type of social control, and it may be particularly important in determining whether a dispute is referred to a formal social control agency. Court costs, lawyer's fees, and the cost of transporting witnesses, for example, may be inhibiting factors that will affect whether an individual will appeal to the formal court system for the management of a dispute. Cost can also be expressed in social psychological terms, such as the loss of status, or "face," in one's community, or the loss of pride and self-respect.

Some disputes may not be pursued in the formal court system, because of the costs involved. In deciding to respond to some perceived deviance or problem by initiating a formal lawsuit, for example, disputants must have the resources to access the formal legal arena, as well as reasonable assurance that there is a fairly good chance of success, and that the outcome will be worth the cost of the fight. The costs in this sense can be figured both in actual money spent on lawyer's fees and court costs, plus the time and effort one is expected to invest. On the other hand, there are those disputes that are considered "not worth the bother" in pursuing by formal complaint; for example, those disputes that are managed more easily and economically in an informal manner such as toleration or avoidance (Baumgartner 1984). Of course, these concerns may depend on how disputants or social control agents assess the degree of seriousness of the offense.

Cost has also been referred to in a social psychological sense, such as loss of pride or social standing among one's peers or the loss of "honor." An in-depth analysis of such social psychological costs may help explain why "self-help" is one viable alternative in societies where law is highly developed and readily available—particularly in those cases where "crimes of passion" are involved.[10] In fact, a main clue in helping us to understand this problem is contained in the very phrase we use to describe it: *self*-help. If someone commits an offense against *my* parent, or *my* property or *my* honor, it evokes a powerful emotional reaction.[11] This type of response is related to the very essence of who I am or who I think I am; that is, to my *self* (and is attenuated in cultures that stress individual possessions and desires). Cooley refers to the "self-feeling" or the "my feeling" as the substantiation of the self as a social fact:

> A formal definition of self-feeling, or indeed of any sort of feeling, must be as hollow as a formal definition of the taste of salt, or the color red; we can expect to know what it is

only by experiencing it. There can be no final test of the self except the way we feel; it is that toward which we have the "my" attitude. [1902:172]

It is the sentiment of appropriation or the intentions, opinions, beliefs, values, feelings, and material objects (including other persons) to which I impart the possessive pronoun "mine" or "my."

Thus, it would appear that the social psychological costs of dispute and conflict deserve further consideration and investigation (see Gurevitch 1988). For our purposes in the present research, a study of disputes in Costa Rica, we want to emphasize that threats of violations made against "my land" are an important aspect in the determination of how a dispute will be responded to and defined (for a discussion of the importance of how events are defined, see Mather and Yngvesson 1980–81:820–21).

In the Osa Península, cost can be assumed to have a considerable influence on the conduct of the dispute process, because of the formal requirements and distances involved in initiating a lawsuit, or any civil complaint. Simply making contact with the formal social control agencies may involve considerable expense—for example, when traveling from forty to one hundred twenty kilometers through country where the only means of travel is by foot, horseback, or boat. Furthermore, a person is required to present witnesses who can substantiate her or his claims, and is expected to pay for witnesses' meals, hotel rooms, and any loss of salary from time off the job.

In addition to the factors of cost, time, access to forums, and the nature of social relationships, cultural factors—including definitions of beauty, friendship, family, knowledge, progress, peace, and justice—are also part of our analysis (cf. Felstiner et al. 1980–81; Ben–Yehuda 1990; Cohen 1991). These cultural factors are discussed explicitly in the following cases and analyzed from our nascent theoretical perspective.[12]

The Politics of Dispute Management in Costa Rica: An Introduction to the Cases

Costa Rica has been a fairly stable, democratic country existing within a regional context of political, economic, and military instability. It has a continuing international reputation as a peaceful nation, and has not had an army since 1949. The government has promoted parliamentary and civilian control of its security forces and has a tradition of encouraging international research and teaching regarding peace (cf. Biesanz et al. 1982). Yet nascent militarization of the country plays a vital role in the development of the Central American region, and dispute management in Costa Rica has evolved within the context of an area embroiled in intense, dynamic conflict (Vargas 1989).

A number of national and international factors contribute to the volatile environment in which disputes are difficult to resolve. The factors include social protests by groups in Costa Rica responding to severe austerity measures imposed by international lending organizations, unpredictable changes in work location and policy by transnational corporations operating in the country, and an increasing number of attempts by other nations to impose their strategies of international security. Our analysis of dispute negotiation focuses upon the southern part of Costa Rica—an area obviously affected by changes endemic to the surrounding area. While we focus upon particular disputes in a limited geographical area, the impact of more widespread disputes—including refugee problems and military conflict on the border between Nicaragua and Costa Rica, and disputes between Nicaragua and the United States—provide a context for examining outside pressures which influence the character and style of the dispute process in the southern zone of Costa Rica.

The disputes we explore include issues of the rights to possession and use of land in Costa Rica. Appendix A examines agrarian reform in Central America and provides an overview of the legal policies on possession of land and land use in Costa Rica and their development. It contains a broader theoretical perspective on the impact of the world system on the rationalization of law and economy in Central America. The analysis suggests that the management of disputes in this book is often influenced by more encompassing factors. Disputes involving land reform, for example, can be examined in light of the external pressures on Costa Rica to rationalize via agrarian reform (see Torrealba Navas 1991).

Historically, Costa Rica has been viewed as an area bound by the rich cultural heritage of Indian cultures; it exhibits strong Mayan, Aztec, and Chibchan influences. The arrival of the Spanish during the colonial period, and later arrivals of European immigrants, African, Jamaican, and Chinese minorities and others shape the culture. Costa Rica shares a three hundred kilometer boundary with Nicaragua on the north, and to the south it has a three hundred and sixty three kilometer border with Panama. Costa Rica emerged as an independent nation in 1821, after a liberating process took place in Guatemala. Its first political constitution, the Pacto de Concordia, was issued on December 1, 1821. As the name of the act indicates, its main purpose was to avoid tensions and to regulate a productive and harmonious society (Perez Vargas 1981):

> Costa Ricans call themselves Ticos. This name is said to stem from the colonial saying "We are all hermaniticos" (little brothers). It also reflects their custom of referring to many things in the diminutive. . . . In some respects the land itself suggests diminutives. With roughly 51,000 square kilometers or 19,965 square miles, about the same area as West Virginia, it is the second smallest country in mainland American; only El Salvador is smaller. [Biesanz et al. 1982:1]

Another vital aspect of this small country and culture is its emphasis upon improving the educational system. In 1823 public instruction was defined as the principal foundation for human happiness and common prosperity. The constitution of 1869 led to compulsory primary education paid for by the state; presently, 30 percent of the annual budget is devoted to education and there is a 90 percent literacy rate. In striking contrast to the U.S.A., the budget dedicated to education and health in Costa Rica is over twenty times larger than that of the Ministry of Public Security.

Costa Rica is divided politically and administratively into seven provinces (San José, Alajuela, Cartago, Heredia, Guanacaste, Puntarenas, and Limón) that are in turn divided into 80 *cantones* or counties, and 409 districts. The population of Costa Rica is approximately two and one-half million people. The center of power is located increasingly in the city of San José where the final forum for the settlement of disputes, the Supreme Court of Costa Rica, is located.

Costa Rica has appealed frequently through its courts to international organizations in order to solve conflicts within the framework outlined by international treaties and agreements. These conflicts are often couched in the rhetoric of geopolitical considerations, considerations that often appear central to political stability in Central America. The creation of an effective democratic system and the constitutional abolition of the army in 1949 are important elements contributing to Costa Rica's uniqueness in the region (see Schlesinger and Kinzer's *Bitter Fruit*, 1982, for a comparison with Guatemala). The court system is independent and operates on a fixed percentage of the annual national budget. There is also an independent Supreme Electoral Tribunal that has full authority over the electoral process, including campaign ethics, and commands the security forces for six months prior to elections.

We try to provide an understanding of the dynamics of the specific disputes and to allow readers to view the gradual development of a theoretical approach to dispute management. A focus on particular factual and procedural details in each dispute is necessary. However, it is also important to offer an analysis of the broader contextual factors involving the increasing rationalization of law in Costa Rica and possible effects on the management of disputes. Appendix B offers a more detailed analysis of the process of rationalization and an attempt by a progressive advocate of the Costa Rican legal system and the Supreme Court to bring increased predictability and fairness to disputants, including formal rational procedures designed to meet national concerns such as social change and welfare (see Perez Vargas 1988, and Torrealba Navas 1991).

Interference from the outside has been a longstanding issue for Costa Ricans. In the mid-1850s, a U.S. adventurer, William Walker, imposed himself as the ruler of Nicaragua with the formal recognition of the U.S. government. The "Napoleonic" Walker believed that it was his "manifest destiny" to turn some of the weak nations of Central America over to his U.S. supporters in the "Confederacy of Southern American States." In 1856 Walker invaded northern Costa Rica. Some nine thousand Costa Ricans were prepared to respond to such an invasion under the authorization of their legislative assembly and the direction of President Juan Mora. Although approximately half of the Costa Ricans died in the struggle, they drove Walker's troops back into Nicaragua. Walker and his forces were defeated. (A few years later Walker was executed by a Honduran firing squad.) The imperialism of Walker and the Costa Rican response has been touted as one of the most important ingredients in Central American history, "more important than independence" (Biesanz et al. 1982:19).

Importantly, one of the most fundamental and potentially catastrophic contexts for disputes is related to the history of Costa Rica's response to militarization and war. While Costa Rica generally has attempted to maintain a nonmilitarization stance, the country is surrounded by intense conflicts, as well as numerous pressures to create models that imitate more economically powerful countries (cf. Paige, 1987). These models typically include the notion that "modern, progressive societies" must have expansive military capabilities, sophisticated technological abilities, and interdependent economic relations (see Frank, 1972; Lauden, 1977).

The recent history of Costa Rica reveals an acceptance of increased nonmilitary aid from the United States, as well as new forms of military aid. This latter aid is referred to usually as foreign contributions to "police professionalization" (Lincoln and Lauderdale 1985). The United States' "security assistance" to Costa Rica has increased dramatically since aid was resumed in 1981. The aid is distributed through two programs; the International Military and Education Program (IMET) and the Military Assistance Program (MAP). In 1981 the total assistance was $34,000 (U.S.) via IMET with no expenditures to MAP. In 1986 IMET's budget exceeded $250,000 and MAP's budget greatly surpassed the $9 million allocated in 1985. In addition to this enormous increase in U.S. military aid, nonmilitary aid of various types also increased until the early part of 1987 (see Block 1988 for a more general discussion of the privatization of covert military aid).

The different definitions of nonmilitary aid have created heated disputes. The boundary between military and nonmilitary aid is ambiguous, since nonmilitary aid has often included assistance from the U.S. Army Corps of Engineers and components of the U.S. National Guard. *Debates rage over the activities of these outsiders, with disclaimers from groups inside and outside Costa Rica that point to new bridges, roads, and communication systems, while their opponents point to these developments as part of the construction of a growing infrastructure for war.* These conflicts and forms of aid have led to perplexing levels of dependency for Costa Rica, especially in light of attempts by former Costa Rican President Oscar Arias to increase political self-determination in the midst of ongoing economic austerity programs.

In addition, the conflict surrounding Costa Rica has led to other problems, such as the cost of supporting recent refugees who comprise approximately 10 percent of the total population:

> By the end of 1986, the country had absorbed at least 30,000 documented refugees, of whom over half were Nicaraguans. But the more serious problem is that there are also 200,000

undocumented refugees, mostly Nicaraguans who arrived before 1979. Caring for the refugees has further strained the Costa Rican economy. The Nicaraguan community has also been fertile ground for contra recruiting, which Costa Rican authorities have had difficulty controlling. [Fagen 1987:115]

Different types of aid to the Contras who operated in Costa Rica and the increasing tensions emerging from Panama contribute further to the volatile environment in which disputes are difficult to resolve.

In 1987 President Arias was awarded the Nobel Peace Prize for his role in developing and implementing a peace plan for Costa Ricans and their war-torn Central American neighbors. The peace plan, which was a culmination of years of dispute negotiation by more than a dozen Latin American countries, responded in part to outside pressure from the U.S.A. Only a few days before the presidents of the five Central American nations signed the accord, the Reagan administration had presented its own plan. However, the ostensible bipartisan peace plan was interpreted as a thinly veiled attempt by the Reagan administration to garner U.S. congressional support for another upcoming Contra aid proposal. The interpretation was constructed amid a larger historical analysis of relations between the U.S.A. and the Central American nations. The Central American analysis included a reexamination and discussion of events such as the World Court decision of 1984, which ordered the U.S.A. to cease all military and paramilitary activities against Nicaragua, the exposure of the CIA psychological warfare manual, the 160-year-old policies of the U.S.A. in Central America and, in particular, key policies behind the Iran/Contra scandal (cf. Marshall et al. 1987).

The Iran/Contra scandal was viewed in the light of evidence that suggested that the illegal U.S. network could be traced back to its clandestine war in Laos, its longstanding involvement in drug smuggling and arms sales, and the CIA's plot against Fidel Castro. In general, the acceptance of the Arias plan sent a message both to the U.S.A. and the larger international community. The Central American nations want to manage disputes without undue interference from the outside, and choose peaceful and diplomatic negotiations, even in the face of potential loss of financial and strategic support from other nations and international lending agencies.

This stance on outside interference, nonetheless, was particularly unsteady for the primary architect, former President Arias, since Costa Rica has recently been the second largest recipient of U.S. aid per capita. The U.S. aid has helped Costa Rica pay its enormous debt-service demands, and continue to enjoy the highest standard of living in Central America. Many Costa Ricans are also well aware of their economic dependency on transnational corporations. Throughout most of the history of the United Fruit Company, for example, which is known as the "Octopus" in many of the rural regions, there have been heated debates over the advantages and disadvantages of dependency relationships. These debates entail discussions of the advantages of modernization via the transportation systems built by the transnational corporations and the disadvantages of such "progress" resulting in the related deterioration of the ecosystem (cf. von Werlhof 1989). More general discussions focus upon the short-term versus long-term effects of economic dependency on workers, natural resources, and political development (Bornschier and Chase-Dunn 1985; Greenberg 1989; von Werlhof 1991). In recent years, Costa Ricans have also become concerned with the precarious position of being heavily dependent on the export of only a few items such as beef, coffee, bananas, some fabrics, and the ensuing problems with terms of trade with other countries.

And, more specific to the rural area of Costa Rica where our study began, we observe the related impact of larger economic and social forces:

> Eight small farmers began a hunger strike in the Costa Rican capital, demanding that the government reopen negotiations on agricultural policies with them. The strike followed a peasant march held on 15 September [1987], Independence Day, when over 1,000 peasants and supporting community organizations protested government cutbacks in subsidies on corn, rice, and beans. The subsidy reduction, demanded by the International Monetary Fund, was also the cause of a similar march one year ago, which ended after rioting forced marchers to seek sanctuary in the capital's cathedral. [Morris 1987:12]

Other austerity measures were imposed in 1989 and 1991. The people who are involved in the following disputes are directly and indirectly affected by such encompassing forces as these austerity programs, the subsequent subsidy reductions, natural disasters such as the major earthquake in 1991, the numerous conflicts in the bordering countries of Panama and Nicaragua, and the seemingly endless war in the region. Although the nature of their dependency relationships is not always readily apparent, the disputes are impacted by numerous economic and political forces at both the local and national level (Frank 1984; Edelman 1988; Perez Vargas 1988). In addition, the following disputes reveal there is a pervasive yet subtle relationship between economic dependency and other forms, such as those engendered by interpersonal conflict or cohesion. Emotional dependency, for example, is one of the more obvious forms that penetrates each case, regardless of the nature of the dispute.

Our descriptions and analyses of the disputes are guided largely by the methodology of field research provided by Muzafer and Carolyn Sherif (1964). One of us has lived in the research area since 1979 and the other has been a frequent visitor, including most of 1985. In 1991, after we completed the following chapter, we discussed the general findings with most of the disputants and other participants. They provided us with useful critiques which we integrated primarily into the last two chapters of the book. Their comments also reminded us, once again, that many people in the United States of America are unaware of the relatively unique culture of Costa Rica (cf. Deloria, 1973, on North American Indian culture). The following cases also reflect part of that culture.

2 The Disputing Process

Case 1:
Resident or Squatter?

The history of the first dispute has important roots in the geographical setting of southern Costa Rica as well as human relationships. Violínes Island forms the northern part of the mouth of the Sierpe River and is within the legal jurisdiction of the district of Sierpe. It is called Violínes because it resembles a violín—the thin neck pointing west into the sea, and the broad, blunt end facing east, upriver.

Violínes Island has been the source of many legends and is featured prominently in the local folklore. Most maps of Violínes, for example, show the general location of a tunnel, which bores deep into the sheer rock face of the island's northeastern seacoast and is visible only during low tides. The existence of this tunnel has intrigued people for generations. It is generally regarded to be the hiding place of gold and other treasure stolen from Spanish settlements in South America by the crews of Sir Francis Drake. Drake visited the Península de Osa on the Golden Hind in 1549 and his memoirs say he spent about three weeks roaming from Drake Bay to the Boca Río Sierpe, obtaining provisions for his ships for the voyage across the Pacific Ocean. Stories range from speculation about what the treasure might include—for instance, a three-foot high solid gold statue of the madonna and the "spirits" who are said to guard the treasure. These spirits ostensibly have created many mysterious problems for treasure hunters and, on at least one occasion, actually "caused the death" of a local campesino (farmer) who had supposedly found the treasure.

These stories are legend and none have been substantiated; however, Violínes does have generous natural deposits of gold. The gold has attracted individual prospectors who work the small streams each rainy season. In fact, before Francis Drake arrived in the area, the Boruka Indians lived around the Boca. The Indians mined the gold, melted it, and fashioned ornamental and ceremonial artifacts. Some of the burial rites of the Boruka included burying personal possessions along with the body. Because of this, the Indian cemeteries that remain have attracted a different kind of gold prospector, the *huecero*, who is a professional grave robber.

By law, all minerals (including Indian artifacts) are owned by the government. Costa Rican citizens have the legal right to search for gold, provided that they use only a shovel and a pan. However, gold miners using heavy equipment must first be granted a mineral concession by the government, and all gold found must be sold to the Central Bank of Costa Rica. Once the concession has been granted, the prospectors have the right to mine the gold within specific boundaries. The creation of claim boundaries creates potential conflicts, since it is possible, for example, and very often the case, that one person owns the land and someone else has been granted the concession to mine the land for the minerals. If the landowner has questions concerning how and where to look for gold, or the amount of compensation to be paid for damaged property or the percentage of the gold profits she or he is entitled to, conflict often arises.

There were no major gold mining operations using heavy equipment on Violínes until 1967. In that year, a North American named Hammer was granted a concession to mine gold on the eastern side of the island—the blunt end of the violin. The only person living on the island at that time was Pablo, an elderly man of Boruka ancestry. Pablo came to Violínes Island in 1936 and staked a claim to thirty acres of the island. In those days, there were very few people in the area. In fact, it was not until the early 1940s that the government sent professional cartographers and land surveyors to the peninsula to make an accurate map of the area. Pablo was their guide.

Hammer was granted a mineral concession to mine gold on the east side of Violínes, close to Pablo's farm. Although Hammer built two buildings outside the boundaries of Pablo's property, he began mining part of the area inside those boundaries. Pablo reports that his first action was to confront Hammer, telling him he did not want machinery on his farm. Hammer showed Pablo the papers granting him the concession and the map of the concession. Mineral concessions also have boundaries, but they are nothing more than arbitrary limits within which someone has the right to mine for gold, and they may or may not correspond with farm or property boundaries. In this case, the limits of Hammer's concession included all of Pablo's farm. And although a gold miner must reach an agreement with the landowner over property damage and a percentage of the gold revenue, Pablo did not have legal title to the land he claimed.

Pablo traveled upriver to Sierpe to ask several of his friends for advice. They suggested that he go to the Municipalidad de Osa in Puerto Cortez. There Pablo was told he needed a survey map of his property before the process of gaining formal title to the land could begin. Since Pablo had to pay for the services of a professional land surveyor, he had no choice but to wait until he secured the money. During the next two years, Hammer mined gold on Violínes but did not reimburse Pablo for damaged property or give him a percentage of gold revenue. Pablo reports that although Hammer's mining operation produced a considerable amount of gold, most of it was stolen by Hammer's workers. In 1969 Hammer died and the mining operation ended. By this time, Pablo had paid for a survey on his farm and had begun the process of acquiring formal title to his property.

In 1970 this same concession was granted to another North American, Peterson, who bought Hammer's machinery in addition to bringing his own. By this time Pablo had established a legal claim to his farm, which consisted of a formal "recognition" of his rights of possession by the government authorities in Puerto Cortez. This formal recognition meant only that, while Pablo's application for legal title was still pending, Pablo was regarded as the owner of the farm and was entitled to all landowner's rights. Peterson, however, located his operation outside the boundaries of Pablo's farm thereby avoiding having to interact with Pablo.

During the two years Peterson operated his gold mine, Pablo also applied for the "rights of possession" to the "milla maritima," a two hundred meter stretch of riverbank property that is owned by the Costa Rican government. A portion of the milla maritima can be leased from the government by making proper application and agreeing to pay the yearly taxes. Since this land had not yet been claimed by anyone, Pablo secured the right to lease it from the government and agreed to pay the taxes. By the time Peterson left Violínes for the United States, after having taken out approximately three hundred pounds of gold, Pablo had been granted the rights of possession to the milla maritima on Violínes. This land included the buildings built by the gold miners, but since they had left the area and the buildings were vacant, Pablo did not challenge their existence on what was now his land.

In 1977 Peterson sold his heavy equipment to a Costa Rican, Fernando. Fernando owned several businesses in San José and a cattle ranch near Puerto Cortez, from which he sent his cattle to graze on the flatlands that cover the southern half of Violines Island. Shortly after Fernando bought the machinery, he sent two of his workers to occupy the houses built by the gold miners. Pablo called Fernando by telephone from Sierpe and told him that the houses were on his land and that he did not want Fernando or his workers occupying them. Fernando refused to remove his workers from the houses.

Pablo says he again sought the advise of several friends in Sierpe and Palmar. His friends warned him not to bring his dispute to the Municipalidad in Puerto Cortez because Fernando had considerable influence in the area and Pablo could not expect a fair hearing. Pablo, nonetheless, went to San José and brought his case to the government agency, ITCO (the Institution of Land and Colonization). Pablo made a denuncia (formal complaint) against Fernando for living in the houses within the milla maritima which was now under Pablo's control. At this time, Pablo was told to wait until ITCO could send one of its investigators to the site for an inspection trip. He was told this would occur within three weeks. Pablo returned to Violínes Island and waited for the inspection.

However, after more than a month had passed and no ITCO investigators arrived for the inspection, Pablo made another trip to San José to determine what progress had been made on his *denuncia*. This time he hired a lawyer and asked him to review the denuncia he had made earlier. The lawyer discovered that ITCO was still waiting to send an investigator to Violínes. The lawyer then persuaded ITCO that it would not need to send investigators to Violínes because the land involved in the dispute was the milla maritima, the riverbank property already leased to Pablo. ITCO then issued an order to the authorities in Puerto Cortez to remove anyone who was living within the milla maritima. Pablo went back to Violínes and waited for the order to be enforced. Again, nothing happened. He waited for two months and then made a trip to Puerto Cortez where he was told that the order had been received from San José but was "still under study." Pablo was told by the *alcaldía* that he had requested a confirmation of the order from the authorities in San José and was waiting for their answer. Pablo then called his lawyer in San José to ask him about the order issued by ITCO. The lawyer said that no request for confirmation had been received by ITCO and that the order was still in force—it was the responsibility of the alcaldía in Puerto Cortez to enforce the order.

Pablo said that at this time he became completely discouraged with the formal legal system and decided to take matters into his own hands. He began by studying Costa Rican land law. He remarked:

> The law in Costa Rica has become a monopoly, a bureaucracy. People sit in the bureaucracy for years with their hands at the controls; moving up, moving down, manipulating the law like a machine. And the grease is money. The law favors the rich over the poor. This is not democracy, it is bureaucracy. The problem with the law in Costa Rica is not the constitution or the legal codes but with the people who enforce it.

Pablo then made another trip to San José to make his own denuncia against Fernando, this time at the Department of Agriculture. Pablo included documentation in the denuncia from an earlier inspection trip he had paid for by the Sierpe *guardia*. Pablo followed the progress of the denuncia through the various legal procedures until another order had been issued to remove Fernando's workers from land on which Pablo had the rights of possession. Pablo then returned to Violínes and waited for the order to be carried out. Once again, nothing happened. Pablo subsequently decided to carry out his own investigation regarding the orders sent to Puerto Cortez. He went to Sierpe, Palmar, and Puerto Cortez asking his friends and acquaintances with "connections to local government representatives" about the two orders issued by officials in San José and why they had not been carried out.

His investigation revealed that Fernando had been paying bribes to the guardia in Sierpe and Palmar and to the alcaldía in Puerto Cortez assuring that they would *not* comply with the ITCO orders to remove the workers from Violines Island. Pablo never received irrefutable proof that such bribes had occurred, but he learned enough to convince him to drop his formal complaints against Fernando. Pablo reasoned that if the formal law depends on one's resources and who pays whom, then he would have no chance against Fernando. Pablo made the decision to allow Fernando to occupy the houses of the abandoned gold mine, because he had done all he could do legally without receiving the expected response from the formal legal system. Instead, Pablo concentrated his efforts on consolidating his control over the remaining portion of the milla maritima on Violínes Island. In 1983 the Costa Rican Institute of Tourism granted Pablo the sole right to build cabins and any other structures within the milla maritima. Pablo says he did this mainly to keep Fernando from building any other houses on land Pablo controls.

Pablo has continued to manage this dispute on the informal level by complaining to friends and allies as well as supporting other insiders in their disputes with Fernando. In this respect, Pablo and the residents of the Boca Río Sierpe have had a general "dispute relationship" with Fernando since he took over the property in 1977. The problems result from land-use conflicts on Violines Island, which is rich in natural resources—particularly gold and coconuts. The residents use the coconuts to make cooking oil, or as chicken and pig feed. During the rainy season, many residents search for gold in the numerous mountain streams on the island. However, Fernando has discouraged any trespassing on his farm and claims the coconuts as feed for his pigs and cattle. He has made threats to "call the guardia" on several residents in response to the "stealing" of his coconuts. In addition, his workers on the ranch have a standing order to prevent trespassing or coconut gathering. The residents have responded with "self-help" tactics, including supporting each other in making secret trips to Violínes by passing on information about Fernando's whereabouts or the movement of his workers. In addition, Pablo allows gold miners to enter Violínes from his farm, out of sight of Fernando's workers.

While at one point it appeared that the dispute had been abandoned on the formal level, in early 1985 it resurfaced. At this time, the alcaldía in Puerto Cortez was replaced and key posts in the municipalidad also changed hands, including the person in charge of administering the milla maritima in the Cantón de Osa. Primarily due to these changes, Pablo decided that he might receive a more unbiased hearing in Puerto Cortez than he had in the past. In his first meeting with Juan Carlos, the new person in charge of the milla maritima, Pablo learned that Fernando had applied for and been granted the rights to the milla maritima on Violines Island in 1977, the same year Fernando bought the houses and machinery. Juan Carlos explained that the law governing the milla maritima had been changed on March 2, 1977, when jurisdiction of the zone was transferred from the central government to the local municipalities. Under the new law, the municipality could not grant rights of possession on this land without first marking the limits of the "public zone," a fifty-meter area contained within the milla maritima. Furthermore those people with leasing agreements based on previous laws were required to inform the National Geographic Institute and hire an engineer at their own expense to conduct the necessary survey.

Pablo protested that he was unaware of the new laws and that he had been granted the rights to the milla maritima from ITCO in San José in 1974 and had been paying taxes ever since. However, Fernando had also applied directly to the Municipalidad in Puerto Cortez for the rights to the same land in 1977, complying with the requirements of the new law. Thus, Pablo learned that both he and Fernando had been granted rights to the same portion of milla maritima.

Upon further investigation, Pablo discovered that various documents sent from ITCO to inform the *municipalidad* of his right of possession were "missing" from the legal files. We have seen Pablo's copies of these documents, which include a signed contract between him and ITCO as well as receipts from the Central Bank for his tax payments. These papers do not appear in the records at the *municipalidad*. Juan Carlos said he knows nothing about the missing files or how Fernando could have been granted rights to the milla maritima, but he pledged to help Pablo track down these documents and "resolve the dispute." During the past year Pablo has been writing letters to various government offices in San José requesting copies of the missing documents.

In a recent interview, we asked Pablo to confirm the accuracy of reports of the missing documents and he agreed that the sequence of events are correct. "But," he said, "the dispute is not over! I have most of the papers I need right now and when I'm ready I'll go to court again." He went on to explain that the matter of the missing documents had spawned a new dispute between the *municipalidad* and the central government in San José. "That's why I'll win," he said, "The new government is coming down hard on corruptions and Puerto Cortez is full of it. We're going to jump on those guys and Fernando will lose." Pablo appeared confident and said he is eager to continue the dispute. As part of our inquiry, Fernando was asked to comment on the case but refused to answer questions.

In review, this case involves a dispute between a local resident, Pablo, and an absentee landlord, Fernando. The nature of their relationship is simplex; they are neighbors who know one another but do not have a continuing personal relationship. Their particular informal social circles do not overlap and they do not have a desire to foster a close or continuing relationship.

The insider/outsider status of the two men is also important. Even though both men are well-known in the Sierpe district, Pablo is *of* Sierpe, his close friends and relatives are also Sierpe residents. Fernando, on the other hand, is known only because of his business associations in the area and, because he lives and works in San José, visiting Sierpe only a few days each month, he is considered an outsider. Pablo's insider status allows him considerable advantage in gaining access to the informal social network in Sierpe and the Boca.

Moreover, Fernando is known to be a wealthy man with extensive business interests in San José, and a large cattle and pig operation on Violínes Island. He owns several cars, trucks, boats, and outboard motors that, because of the relative poverty and isolation of Sierpe, are highly visible. In casual conversations with several Sierpe residents it became evident that Fernando is not particularly well liked, even among those individuals who depend on him for their livelihood; he is considered aloof, arrogant, tough, powerful, and far outside the social status hierarchy of anyone in the local Sierpe community. Sierpe residents comment that he is a "rich and powerful man," a "rich son-of-a-bitch," or a "big man *sin vergüenza.*" The phrase *sin vergüenza* translated means literally "without shame," and carries with it a definite negative connotation. A more general translation is "without conscience" or "without principles."

Pablo, on the other hand, seems to be popular and is considered a near permanent feature of the Sierpe district. He first settled in Sierpe more than fifty years ago and has been living there continuously since that time. He is a private and unassuming man who goes about his personal business without pretense. Also, among local residents, Pablo has attained a legendary status, particularly concerning the amount of gold he is said to possess. Because he has lived for so long on Violínes Island—itself a source of many legends and well-known for its generous gold deposits—it is believed generally that Pablo has found a fortune in gold over the years and is hoarding it somewhere on his farm, probably beneath his home. (This rumor gained some credence when, several years ago, a North American was mining gold on Pablo's property. Pablo refused to allow the miner to tear down his house to gain easy access for his large machinery, even though the North American offered to build him a larger house at no expense.) Despite the general belief that Pablo is a rich man, he is respected in the community because he lives a frugal, almost humble, existence.

The consequences of the arrangement of these social relationships for the dispute process are very subtle and difficult to ascertain precisely. On the one hand, the process of formal social control seemed unaffected by how popular Pablo may be among the residents of the Sierpe district. On the other hand, Fernando was apparently more "popular" among those who can most significantly affect the dispute—that is, by the formal authorities in Puerto Cortez who represent the formal social control network. Indeed, as far as Pablo and his friends and relatives are concerned, the formal authorities in this case were manipulated by Fernando.

Thus, Pablo "lost" the initial stage of this dispute, because he lacked the money and power necessary to influence the formal authorities in Puerto Cortez. The nature of the dispute process here served to reinforce the general attitude among the people of Sierpe that, in most instances, they believe that the application of the formal law in Costa Rica depends more on one's personal resources and on who one knows than on any objective criteria based upon notions of fairness, justice, or the strict interpretation of written law. Despite Pablo's claim that two different government agencies in San José decided the case in his favor, Fernando was able to maintain control of the disputed property and continues to do so.

Additionally, the fact that access to forums of social control can depend on where one is in the social system, what one's resources are, and who one knows, is illustrated clearly in this case. When the dispute with Fernando arose, Pablo sought out the advice of those closest to him—his friends and relatives in Sierpe. He was told that Fernando was likely to have considerable influence with the formal authorities in Puerto Cortez and that he should instead take his case to the authorities in San José. Whether or not this was sound advice is unimportant in this situation—the fact is that Pablo did place trust in his friends' and relatives' advice; he bypassed the formal authorities in Puerto Cortez and brought his case to the government agencies located in San José. Apparently, Pablo had the resources to travel to San José, but complained that it was a long trip and cost a lot of money. Access to the formal social control agencies in this case was preceded by contacts among Pablo's informal social relations. In addition, because Pablo chose to take his case to the authorities in San José, he was committed to deal with them and thus was required to make repeated trips to San José to manage the progress of his dispute. Pablo estimates that these trips took on the average of about four days.

Fernando, on the other hand, did not experience the same inconveniences in transportation or communication; he had his own vehicle and telephone. Furthermore, he had the kind of informal access to the formal authorities in Puerto Cortez that Pablo's friends and relatives had forewarned. Fernando's relationship with the formal authorities demonstrates another important aspect to the question of access; even though Pablo managed successfully to contact the formal authorities in San José, he apparently contacted either the wrong authorities or authorities who could not or would not enforce their decisions. In addition, Pablo entered into a formal relationship with these authorities—that is, as a citizen making a formal denuncia before the representatives of the law. Fernando, on the other hand, had apparently established an informal relationship with the representatives of the law in Puerto Cortez, those who are responsible for carrying out the orders of their superiors in San José and enforcing the law in the Cantón de Osa.

However, this arrangement directly counteracts Costa Rica's attempts to increase the formal rationality of the law, particularly in the establishment of strict rules and procedures governing the management of civil complaints, including formal regulations controlling how citizens should approach the law and how *enforcers* of the law should manage disputes among citizens. And it would appear that most residents recognize these procedures and act accordingly. There was, for example, a general agreement that Pablo should take his complaint to the formal authorities. When asked why, most people referred to the predictability and power of the formal law: "The law is the *law*," as one resident put it. This illustrates how the process of rationalization has also become a part of the social construction of reality among the people of Sierpe.

Nevertheless, most residents believe that the formal law is not always formal and rational in its application. In fact, they are convinced that personal sentiments and special interests sometimes shape particular elements of the formal-legal landscape. It was this consideration that led Pablo's friends to advise him to take his case to San José rather than Puerto Cortez. This action was not a rejection of the state's formal legal system, only specific parts of it—those believed to be corrupted.

Thus, while access to the formal social control network may not be particularly problematic, this fact alone does not ensure a fair and impartial management of one's dispute. Relationships and communications *within* and *among* the institutions of social control may be interfered with or incomplete, introducing additional elements into the dispute process that may be completely beyond the control of one or more of the parties to the dispute.

When control of the formal management of a dispute is lost, the formal law is no longer being applied in a formal, rational manner and an element of unpredictability occurs. We suggest that this unpredictability is, in part, the result of use of *informal* law. Fernando, for example, was said to have reached informal agreements with the formal authorities. Because of this, Pablo's informal social network cautioned him to bypass this weak link in the formal chain of authority, even though this meant more costs and hardships for him. However, Pablo could *expect* to be treated fairly in San Jose—which meant an impartial forum, control, and predictability—while in Puerto Cortez he could *never be sure*. In Pablo's words, "I can respect the law in Costa Rica if it operates fairly. But if I think there's any bribery or greed going on, I won't trust it and I won't go near it. I'll look someplace else."

The elements of cost and time have important implications in this case, as well. Fernando allegedly paid bribes to the formal authorities in Puerto Cortez, which is for Pablo the main focal point of this dispute. At one time, Pablo chose to drop all formal attempts to resolve the dispute, based on the belief that the authorities in Puerto Cortez had been paid to ignore the orders of their superiors in San José.

Even though Fernando held the initial advantage in the formal management of this dispute, Pablo began achieving his objectives on the *informal* level of social control. Among his peers in Sierpe, Pablo was considered to be "in the right" and Fernando was believed to be "in the wrong." That is, with the passage of time the management of this dispute shifted from the formal to informal level of social control. And though Pablo was not able to impress his definition of the dispute on the formal authorities, his view of the dispute has been accepted and validated by those who count most to him—his friends and neighbors in Sierpe.

In addition, there is the element of sociopsychological cost to be considered in this dispute. Pablo is a proud man and takes himself and his behavior very seriously. Also, he is extremely careful with his possessions and how he presents himself in public. He has his *reputation* at stake and he knows what that reputation is; "I believe the people of Sierpe like me and respect me," he once said. Thus, whenever he talks about his dispute with Fernando it is apparent by his manner that he is upset and angry. Further, as his language refers increasingly to "honor," "dignity," and "self-respect," it is evident that he is not simply debating who owns what land, but rather defending and protecting his *personal identity*. And since identity is often socially defined, the management and maintenance of that identity will naturally involve both the formal and informal levels of social control.

Thus, although Pablo may have "lost" the initial, formal stage of this dispute, it is apparent he has a deep emotional commitment to continue the dispute on the informal level in the form of complaining and continuously keeping a watchful eye on Fernando's activities. In fact, Pablo vows never to forget or forgive Fernando for "stealing my property." Pablo now considers Fernando his "enemy" and says that he is constantly on the alert for any opportunity to strike back at Fernando, short of any violent actions, including supporting anyone who later becomes involved in a dispute with Fernando. This element of social psychological cost may one day prove to be a decisive factor in this ongoing dispute between Pablo and Fernando.

Time as a phenomenon affecting the dispute process is also important in this case. Pablo admits that had he continued to push his formal denuncia against Fernando, he might have exposed the alleged bribery and general corruption of the formal authorities in Puerto Cortez. However, Pablo said that he did not have the energy to invest any more time in pursuing the dispute on a formal level. He points out that he spent nearly a year and a half trying to resolve the dispute in the formal social control agencies and "it all came to nothing." Although Pablo still regards this particular dispute as "not over," he no longer has much interest in managing the dispute. "I have other things to do now," he says. "I have other problems."

Finally, one of our goals in this study is to explore the degree of structure in the informal social control infrastructure in the district of Sierpe. The above discussion suggests that the informal social control process in Sierpe is a highly organized part of daily living in this area. In fact, we get a brief glimpse in this case of how the informal process can offer a kind of "compensation" for local residents in the management of their disputes, allowing for what they perceive as more control and predictability than they might expect from the formal legal process (cf. Greenberg 1981, 1989). And Pablo's redefining of Fernando as a deviant, a thief, has been accepted by Pablo's reference group.

Moreover, this case illustrates how the informal social control network can become increasingly important to disputants who are unable to achieve their objectives within the boundaries of the formal legal system (cf. Merry 1990). In addition, because one disputant expected to have a multiplex relationship with the other disputant, he avoided initiating a formal legal battle that could create animosity or hostility. While this factor was important, the case also suggests that inconsistencies and disparities in formal rationality can contribute to a shift in the way a dispute is managed. Another aspect of this case, that has proven to be important in many disputes, is the element of social psychological costs as a reason for the maintenance of a dispute. In this case, for example, one disputant, the insider, is vitally interested in maintaining his reputation in and around the Boca as well as in achieving his formal objectives in the dispute. Thus, this desire to maintain a person's social identity within their informal social control network may often have a significant affect on the management of a dispute.

Case 2:
The Colorado Camp

This case begins with the arrival of Wilson, a North American, in the Sierpe district in 1974 and his purchase in that same year of eighteen acres of land from the Simo family. The Simo's have owned several hundred acres of land in this area for about thirty years. The land, called *Campamento Colorado*, the Colorado Camp, is located approximately five kilometers upriver from the Boca Río Sierpe (the mouth of the Sierpe River) and includes about one hundred thirty meters of river frontage on the Sierpe River. Wilson and the Simos had papers drawn up and a survey made of the property to be sold. Wilson paid the agreed price and took control of the property. At the time they were negotiating the sale, Wilson told the Simos that he was buying the property for a Baptist church in San José which had connections to a Baptist church in the United States. He described himself as a missionary and said he wanted to build a church on the property, as well as a small summer camp for visiting members of the congregation. The sale actually included two parcels of land; the first consisting of sixteen acres that was recorded in the Public Registry, and the second containing two hundred meters by fifty meters of river frontage that was not recorded in the Registry, because it is considered part of the milla maritima, which is state land. The Simo family did not have the right to sell this land, because it was not legally defined as private property; however, under certain circumstances, the milla maritima can be leased from the government for a specified period of time. In 1975 Wilson signed a lease agreement with the Costa Rican government agency that at that time enforced state land laws and regulations, ITCO (Institute of Land and Colonization). This lease agreement was for a two-acre strip of land in the restricted zone that ITCO named "Río Sierpe Lodge" and listed as a place of interest for tourists. These events are important because changes in the formal law eventually played a crucial role in the development of this dispute.

From 1974 to 1976 Wilson was engaged in a number of business activities including taking tourists from the United States on fishing excursions and a clandestine cocaine trafficking business. Ostensibly, the cocaine was manufactured in Columbia and secretly sent to Wilson's property on the river to be distributed in San José or smuggled to the United States. Jorge Simo noted that Wilson received the cocaine by airplane. Occasionally—once or twice a month—a small plane would make a low pass over the river in front of Wilson's property and drop a small plastic package into the water. Simo witnessed the drop several times. On one occasion he paddled his boat toward the drop sight in an attempt to view the contents of the package, but one of Wilson's workers arrived ahead of him. Simo did not contact the guardia (rural police) about these activities because he never thought they involved drugs or were illegal. In his own words, "I was curious but not suspicious." However, in 1976, Wilson was arrested in Columbia for cocaine trafficking.

A short time later, Wilson's wife returned to Sierpe and proposed to sell the property back to the Simos. She had a signed authorization from her husband giving her the right to sell the land. The Simos, who were told by Wilson's wife that she needed the money to get her husband out of jail in Columbia, agreed to the sale and paid her for the land. The Simos retook possession of the land and held it for the next three years.

Then in 1979 Wilson appeared at the property with members

of the guardia and a signed order by the judge in Puerto Cortez. The order commanded the guardia to evict the Simos from what Wilson claimed was his land, thereby giving Wilson the rights of possession to the land his wife had sold to the Simos three years earlier. Jorge Simo has no idea what papers Wilson could have presented to convince the judge to make such an order. He speculated that Wilson and his lawyer arranged something with the judge in Puerto Cortez—that is, the judge was paid a bribe. Also, Simo guesses that Wilson made up a new set of papers based on the original 1974 bill of sale, or that he simply presented the original papers and completely disregarded the sales transaction made by his wife in 1976. In any event, Wilson returned in 1979, took over the land, and the Simos were evicted.

The Simos then put a denuncia against Wilson in Puerto Cortez. The evidence produced included the 1976 bill of sale made with Wilson's wife, a copy of the signed authorization she presented giving her the right to sell the land, and a survey of the property. However, the denuncia was never officially recognized and Simo does not know what happened to it. But Simo emphasizes that he had dealt with the same judge who issued the order to have his family removed from the land.

The Simos's claimed that Wilson must have made false representations to the formal authorities in Puerto Cortez and thus had no right to reclaim the land bought from Wilson's wife. Jorge Simo claims that "nothing ever happened to this denuncia—there was no action." However, official court records indicate that the Puerto Cortez court absolved Wilson of any guilt and responsibility. This decision was appealed to the appropriate Superior Court and was subsequently upheld. In this same action, the same court named Wilson as the provisional caretaker of the land until a determination could be made regarding who actually owned or legitimately controlled the property. In his defense, Wilson submitted a copy of the lease contract he had made with ITCO in 1975. The Simo family refused to accept the decision of the Superior Court and vowed to appeal the case.

Meanwhile, Wilson continued to maintain control over the property, expanding his tourist business by organizing "treasure hunting tours" to several Borukan Indian burial grounds located around the Boca Río Sierpe. Early in 1981 Wilson signed a lease agreement with ITCO for an additional five-year term. Then, in June 1982, Wilson was granted a mineral rights concession by the Costa Rican government to mine gold in an area on the Boca called

Playa Blanca. At this time Wilson claimed to have rich partners in the United States who were helping him to finance his operation. He brought several pieces of heavy equipment to the Boca; a drag line, a bulldozer, a front-end loader, a gold-washing machine, and several powerful water pumps.

Toward the end of September of the same year, while Wilson was still mining in Playa Blanca, a member of the Simo family filed a denuncia against Wilson at the Bureau of Mines in San José claiming that Wilson was smuggling fourteen kilograms of gold a day out of Costa Rica instead of selling it to the Central Bank. This would have been a major violation of the agreement for the granting of gold concessions; all gold miners operating a government concession are required to sell their gold to the Central Bank. The bank pays world market prices for the gold, but does so in the deflated Costa Rican currency, the *colón*. The government then sells the gold for U.S. dollars, which it uses, in part, to make payments on its foreign debt.

The Simo family supported their claims of gold smuggling with sworn statements from two local residents; one of them was a distant cousin of the Simo family and the other who was the caretaker of their lawyer's summer cottage on the Boca. Yachts allegedly stopped in front of Wilson's fishing camp—or were met by Wilson on other parts of the Boca—and gold was transferred onto them for transport to either Panama or the United States.

The Ministry of Mines could not ignore the significance of such a report; the amount of gold obtained per day by Wilson was rumored to be worth over $100,000—a significant amount to the Central Bank. Also, the national news media reported the story on several radio and television news programs, and newspapers carried reports of the gold smuggling activity on the front page. One day after these reports, members of the guardia from Puerto Cortez and Palmar were dispatched to the Boca with orders to close down Wilson's mining operation and supervise the removal of all machinery from the site.

According to most local residents, the essential facts of the story were considered to be false or at least quite exaggerated. No one except the Simos and their supporters had seen the yachts, and the report of fourteen kilos of gold per day would undoubtedly have been considered a spectacular mineral discovery. Very few people in Sierpe believed these stories; in the words of one local resident, "this whole story is pure shit, pure fantasy, right out of the head of [Jorge] Simo."

Jorge Simo admits that the land dispute between his family and Wilson prompted him to make the denuncia against Wilson; it was seen as a chance to strike back at Wilson for stealing their land. However, Simo still maintains that Wilson was smuggling large amounts of gold out of Costa Rica and that members of his family were witnesses. Wilson thinks that this denuncia made at the Bureau of Mines was probably a result of his land dispute with the Simo family. However, the description of the land dispute Wilson offers is inconsistent with the facts of the case as they appear in Supreme Court records in San José. When Wilson was asked what motives Jorge Simo might have had for making the denuncia, Wilson replied:

> Look; we've been hassling over his property for years. He hasn't been able to keep up with loan payments to the bank. The bank has title to his land because he had defaulted so many times. Now I want to buy his place from the bank and there's nothing he can do about it.

Officials from the Central Bank in San José are reported to have said that although Wilson had been mining in Playa Blanca for almost three months, he had sold no gold to the Central Bank. Wilson, on the other hand, denied all allegations of gold smuggling and maintained that he had not sold gold to the bank, because he was not finding enough even to pay his daily operating expenses.

The land dispute between the Simo family and Wilson continued while Wilson acted as absentee landlord of the property. Wilson hired a caretaker for his businesses and moved into a house in San José. The Simo family continued to complain, not only about Wilson's stealing their land, but also about what they see as the inability or unwillingness of government authorities to act decisively. As Jorge put it:

> The law in Costa Rica doesn't work; it's like a piece of rubber—if you're rich and powerful you can bend it any way you like. We couldn't get the government to take us seriously. Too much time and money for lawyers to argue back and forth. Finally, we decided to take matters into our own hands.

On November 14, 1984, the Simo family entered Wilson's fishing camp and took over the property. They moved into each of

Wilson's three buildings and removed his caretaker. The caretaker immediately went upriver to Sierpe and telephoned Wilson to tell him what had happened. The next day Wilson drove to the Municipalidad de Osa in Puerto Cortez and requested the assistance of the chief of police. The chief went to Sierpe and asked that the rural guardia accompany him downriver to remove the Simo family from Wilson's fishing camp. When the guardia arrived at the camp, Jorge Simo argued that his family had a right to live there, presenting as proof the documents pertaining to the sale of the land by Wilson's wife. Nevertheless, the Simo family was evicted and escorted back upriver by the guardia. Since Wilson insisted on pressing charges, the guardia were obliged to take the Simos to the police station in Puerto Cortez. When they arrived in Sierpe, Jorge Simo requested that he and his family be allowed to go to a relative's house to change clothes and eat: the guardia agreed to his request. However, the Simos's had a boat waiting in the river behind their relative's house, and they walked through the house, got into the boat, and escaped, disappearing for the next three days.

This incident caused considerable reaction throughout the Sierpe district. People talked about it for days, especially the Simo family's "mass escape" from Wilson and the guardia. This appealed directly to the Costa Rican blend of courage and humor, and local sympathies were decidedly in favor of the Simo family. Nevertheless, Wilson made a denuncia against the Simos and again regained control of the land. However, the act of civil disobedience and subsequent appeals by the Simos led to further legal action. In January 1985 this case was referred for final disposition to the Supreme Court of Costa Rica in a formal legal action called Petition for the Causation Recourse. This case was referred by the judge in the Municipalidad de Osa because of the "counterposition of the titles and documents," referring to the fact that while the Simo family had legal documents proving they had sold and bought back the property, Wilson also had legal documents proving that he had leased the fifty-meter stretch of state land from the Costa Rican government. A critical entry appearing in court records entered on June 1, 1985, states the following: "the attorney who is defending the Simo family proves that they are the real owners of the property and the Causation Hall states that the Causation Recourse was admitted erroneously." Despite the fact that this latest entry implies that the Simo family may have won the lawsuit, there is still no final determination regarding the case.

Wilson continues to occupy the camp and is planning to bring more tourists to the area, and the dispute remains unresolved.

———

In review, the disputants in this case have a simplex relationship; they are neighbors and have bought and sold land from each other, but they do not have a continuing relationship. When Wilson first came to the area he was an unknown North American outsider, while members of the Simo family have been insiders in the district of Sierpe for many years. Also, their initial contact with each other was through the formal-legal process of a land transaction. Thus when conflict arose, neither side had any incentive to protect whatever relationship had been established.

However, one of the most interesting aspects of this case concerns the fairly large number of people who eventually became involved—both insiders and outsiders. Indeed, at one time the attention of Costa Rica turned briefly toward the Boca Río Sierpe; many people were drawn by the drama and intrigue of gold smuggling. Also, the community of Sierpe was witness to the takeover of Wilson's fishing camp and thus became directly involved by discussing the event and passing the story on to others in the Cantón de Osa—including those who occupied official positions in the Municipalidad in Puerto Cortez. In this sense, the dispute involved the nature of the relationship between the informal and formal social control networks. In this case, the strategy of civil disobedience was used to transform a private dispute into a public concern. In fact, the takeover was specifically designed to capture the interest and attention of as many people as possible, the idea being, according to Jorge Simo, "to shake up the *municipalidad*, to get them to take some action."

A type of "self-help" described by Black (1984) that is especially relevant here is one in which private citizens commit criminal acts as a form of informal social control—"to take the law into their own hands." The takeover by the Simo family, however, also involved an attempt to generate a reaction from the formal agencies of social control. The takeover was not simply a rejection or usurpation of the state's authority to administer the law, but rather an attempt to speed up the process of administration. Of course, it is very difficult to document how much this event actually influenced the formal court system. But it is perhaps more important that the Simo family and their supporters, including many other local residents, are convinced that this act of civil disobedience resulted in faster action by the formal authorities. When the Simos returned to Sierpe from hiding, one resident said, "You see! The people have power too."

This comment suggests some interesting aspects regarding access and the insider/outsider relationship of the disputants; specifically, how the social construction of reality can influence the way a particular definition of a dispute is to be judged or evaluated. Most people in Sierpe, for example, were acquainted with the details of this dispute, because of the frequent complaining by the Simos and their relatives. Since Wilson was an outsider and had little or no access to the informal social control network, local residents were exposed primarily to the facts of the case as they were presented by the Simos. Considering that Wilson was portrayed as the "bad guy" in these accounts, it is not surprising that community loyalties favored the Simo family. Wilson had generally been regarded as an outsider, since he was arrested in Columbia on drug trafficking charges. We have heard Wilson described typically in terms such as "he [Wilson] is bad for Costa Rica" or that Wilson "is a dangerous element" or—"full of the devil". Although we do not know of any outward displays of resentment or hostility directed toward Wilson, he was nonetheless regarded with a general attitude of disapproval—an attitude that normally may not surface or seem significant until some crisis brings it to the surface.

Furthermore, most people who commented on this dispute also mentioned Wilson's arrest and the gold smuggling charges, implying that if he is capable of such actions, then he could also steal land. Naturally, this made it all the easier for the community to believe he had stolen the Simo property. This aptly illustrates how the building of a "grievance portfolio"—the accumulation of damaging information—can have a significant effect on the dispute process and can be especially relevant in a small, close-knit community such as the district of Sierpe. This development can prevent a disputant from gaining access to the informal social control network.

Having considered the question of access to *informal* social control in the Sierpe district, it is clear that most people thought that Wilson enjoyed more access to the *formal* legal system. Wilson was seen as a rich outsider who had close access to the formal authorities. The vast majority of the people in the community perceive Wilson to have both favorable proximity and close relational distance to the agents of formal social control. Thus, while he was an outsider with respect to the informal network in and around Sierpe, Wilson ostensibly enjoyed much greater access to the formal legal system and was considered an insider at the Municipalidad in Puerto Cortez. This may be primarily because he lived outside Sierpe and had faster and more convenient access to the formal authorities.

In addition, Wilson has commented that he "is not afraid to spread a little money around to get things moving." Wilson managed, for example, to make what was apparently an informal agreement with the formal authorities when he pressured the guardia to evict the Simo family without securing the necessary court order. It is also significant that Jorge Simo planned the takeover on a Saturday morning, knowing that the *municipalidad* would be closed and no official action could be taken until Monday. It seems apparent that the formal authorities acted on the basis of informal, personal motives and private arrangements.

Furthermore, the Simos frequently complained about the slowness of the formal court system and the high costs of continuing the legal dispute. The time and cost factors combined to create a situation the Simo family eventually considered intolerable; they found themselves in a "catch-22" situation. As Jorge Simo stated, "if we drop the suit, we lose. If we continue the suit, we lose. Seven years of fighting in the courts and paying lawyers is too much. It's crazy!"

Once again, we see that merely gaining access to the formal authorities does not assure that a case will be pursued effectively or that the "facts" will be judged on a formal rational basis. The Simo family felt frustrated and stifled in their attempts to resolve the issue as quickly as possible. But we have seen how the time element plays an important role in land disputes in Costa Rica; generally the longer land is controlled, the more legitimacy or rights of possession are accumulated. In Wilson's case, he took the time to continue building and improving on the property, further solidifying his claims on the land. The Simo family watched this development with a growing sense of resentment and futility; even if they should eventually win the case, they may still be liable to pay Wilson back for the buildings and improvements he made on "their" land. As time passed, Wilson's hold on the property tightened and the Simo family felt their control slipping as the case was stalled in the formal legal bureaucracy.

The Simos turned to the informal social structure of the community where they had the assurance of faster and easier access as well as confidence of immediate action and control. These familiar communication channels offered the opportunity to make informal inroads to positions of power in the formal legal system since, for example, some *municipalidad* officials were also members of the Sierpe community and thus a part of the informal social structure. By moving the dispute to the informal level, the Simos had an opportunity to "win" their dispute through the informal social control mechanisms by having their definition of the dispute accepted and approved by significant members of the community. The Simos are convinced of the rightness and fairness of their definition of the dispute and the "deviant" behavior of Wilson; this view has been validated and supported by their friends and neighbors.

The Simos also increasingly avoided the formal social control agents, because of their belief that Wilson had "perverted" specific parts of the Costa Rican formal legal process. However, they still have hope of winning the dispute on the formal level if they can convince certain formal authorities to agree to their view of the dispute. In fact, Jorge Simo made a comment that indicates he and his family are no longer disputing so much with Wilson as they are with the formal legal system. "The judges and the guardia in Puerto Cortez and San José are "chorisero" [meaning that they are "on the take"] and we have to fight with them to fight with Wilson," he said. Thus, while the Simo family continues to pursue this dispute on both the formal and informal levels of social control, they are fighting more vigorously on the informal level. In fact, Jorge explained that during the past two years, the family has been devoting most of its attention and resources on constructing and operating a tourist business. They are beginning to take groups of tourists on day-trips to the area's national parks and also deep-sea fishing. And when Jorge says, "we'll run a better fishing camp than Wilson ever did!"—it is evident by his tone and manner that they mean to continue the original dispute by other means—in this case by competing directly with Wilson for tourists.

The dispute process that is revealed in this case and other cases allows us to comment further on the degree of structure in the informal social control infrastructure. In Sierpe, for example, the informal channels of communication are often the fastest and most reliable means of communicating. Also, the social structure is relatively static with the boundaries of community identity well-delineated, while the social fabric of the community is made up of tightly woven networks of informal social relationships that are internally quite dynamic. There are, of course, general rules and regulations that are used as guidelines, but the variations in interpretation and application are infinite. The informal law is in a constant state of change, emerging from the process of human interaction. Superimposed on this process—indeed, a *product* of this process—is the formal law, law that is relatively fixed into bureaucratic form by written codes, articles and constitutions, and is supported by the power of the state, which, in most cases, is considered final and absolute.

Within the clash of these two systems of social control, we note some additional insights about the nature of the relationship between informal social control and formal social control. For instance, at the point where these two systems merge, apparently there is a paradox between the simultaneous process of integration and conflict. *Integration* occurs because informal social control affects everyone and penetrates into most areas of human affairs, including formal legal institutions. Thus, there is *conflict* because these formal institutions are vulnerable to the dictates and manipulations of certain groups of people organized around informal agreements and relationships. There are informal inroads of access into the formal law that obviously become more available to some than to others.

Our study of the understandings and social contracts among private individuals in this case are suggestive of the various informal social control factors that influence and sometimes overwhelm the effects of the formal law. Thus, an act of civil disobedience, which resulted in a bypassing of the formal law, was used as a tactic to generate a reaction by agents of formal social control (cf. McAdam 1989).

Our analysis also suggests that inconsistencies in the formal law can also affect the management or outcome of a dispute. In this case, for example, while there is evidence to suggest that via the formal law the case has been decided in favor of one disputant, the other disputant has ostensibly gained rights of possession by occupying and improving the disputed property. Moreover, in part because of these inconsistencies, management of the case shifted increasingly to the informal level—an arena where access and a "sympathetic ear" were assured for the insiders, and their portrayal of Wilson as a deviant (Ben-Yehuda 1990).

Case 3:
The House Without a Home

In March 1979 George, a North American university professor, traveled to Costa Rica with the intention of buying land near the Pacific Ocean. He had visited Costa Rica once before several years earlier, could not speak Spanish, and was relatively naive with regard to the local culture. While reviewing the real-estate advertisements in the local English language newspaper, *The Tico Times*, he found a listing which interested him and contacted Tom, the realtor handling the property. Tom was also a North American, but had lived in Costa Rica for several years and operated his own real estate company. George and Tom then entered into a single issue or "simplex" relationship—that of buyer/seller.

Tom took George to the Boca Río Sierpe, in the southern zone of Costa Rica, to show him the land that was for sale. The land was located on the mouth of the Sierpe River next to the Pacific Ocean and included about two hundred meters of river frontage. Tom told George, "This will all be yours, from the banks of the Sierpe River up and over the mountain; one hundred acres." George liked the site, agreed to the purchase price of $50,000, and promised to return in June of that same year with a cashier's check for the full amount.

George initially did not have the $50,000 and upon his return to the United States he immediately began soliciting "investments" from several of his friends and associates. Most of the people George approached were other professors or graduate students. George told them this was an "excellent opportunity" to create an alternative academic organization by buying land on the Pacific Ocean for the "very cheap" price of only $50,000. In three months, George persuaded more than fifteen friends and colleagues to contribute money in amounts ranging from $500 to $10,000—and he eventually raised the necessary $50,000. He told his associates that they would be collective members of an academic organization, owning part of the land together, as well as receiving title to the land they had bought at $500 an acre.

In June 1979 George returned to Costa Rica with his associate Mark and contacted a lawyer in San José who had been recommended to him on his earlier visit. George, Mark, and the lawyer delineated the terms of the bill of sale; terms which had been discussed and agreed to in earlier meetings between George and the realtor, Tom. These agreements included promises by Tom to arrange and pay for a survey of the property, plus the building of a road from the property. The road was to be built from the property to the town of Sierpe to Drake Beach, along the northern coast of the Osa Península about fifteen kilometers south of the Boca Río Sierpe (mouth of the Sierpe River).

A few days later George, Mark, and Tom met in the lawyer's office. Also present was Tom's lawyer and a Costa Rican national who was never introduced and whose presence was not explained. Although George and Mark could not read or speak Spanish, it was agreed that the bill of sale would be read in Spanish to save time. George and Mark had confidence that their Costa Rican lawyer would see to it that the terms agreed to would be stated fairly and clearly. After the bill of sale was read and the lawyer had announced his approval, George and Tom signed the document and the $50,000 was given to Tom.

Approximately a year and a half later, in November 1980, a dispute involving this property became public. A local Costa Rican living on the Boca Río Sierpe told Mark, who had been living on the property since that June, that the house George and his associates had built on the banks of the Sierpe river was not built on land they purchased. The Costa Rican explained that the house actually was located in the milla maritima. The Costa Rican also said that another Costa Rican national named Sanchez had already been granted the "rights of possession" along that particular piece of land, and that the land purchased by George and his associates actually began two hundred meters inland from the river on the side of the mountain.

George and his associates had never heard of the milla maritima. Tom had never mentioned it and neither had the lawyer in San José. Mark later said that he did nothing regarding this information because he did not want to believe it and because he was not in a position to do anything about it. The only papers the North Americans had establishing a claim to the land was the bill of sale that was in George's name. Mark was not the legal representative of George in Costa Rica, however, and could not consult with any lawyers or initiate any legal action involving land in another person's name. Furthermore, he did not know what he could do about the situation even if he was George's representative; he could barely understand or speak Spanish and had no knowledge of Costa Rican formal legal procedures or customs. He decided to consider the information a mistake, and continued to live and work on the site.

A few days later, Sanchez, the Costa Rican who had supposedly been granted the "rights of possession," began making threats to come to the Boca and tear down the house built by the North Americans. These threats were relayed through a local Costa Rican, Pancho, who lived adjacent to George's property. After two threats in one week, Mark decided he could no longer ignore what was happening and on his next trip to Sierpe he telephoned George to tell him what was going on. The information caused a minor panic for George and his associates, and they immediately contacted another lawyer in San José. They instructed the lawyer to determine if the milla maritima existed on their property and, if it did, who had been granted the "rights of possession."

Also, at this time, George made several attempts to contact Tom. George and his associates were very upset and concerned over the news about Sanchez and were anxious to determine the exact location of the boundaries. According to the terms of agreement in the bill of sale, Tom was obligated to arrange and pay for a survey. By the time the dispute with Sanchez became public, however, Tom had not made any efforts toward having the survey completed. It was at this time that a second dispute began to develop. George and his associates tried to contact Tom by letter, phone, and visits to his office in San José, but Tom never answered the letters or returned the calls, and was usually "out of the office" whenever George or one of his associates went to see him.

George eventually talked to his lawyer in San José about the possibility of applying some kind of legal pressure against Tom without actually bringing a formal complaint through the courts. The lawyer then made several attempts to contact Tom, but was also unsuccessful.

Meanwhile, Mark continued to build and develop the property, particularly within the contested area, primarily because it was the only suitable building site on the whole property. In December 1980 Sanchez arrived at the property on the Boca Río Sierpe, and Mark immediately recognized him as the Costa Rican national who was present during the reading and signing of the bill of sale in June 1979. Mark had a guest staying with him at the time, who was fluent in both Spanish and English, who acted as an interpreter. Sanchez was very agitated and yelled at Mark in rapid-fire Spanish such comments as "I've had this land for over twenty years and now you rich Americans think you can come in here and just take over! I'm a big man in these parts and I have powerful connections and you'll never get away with it!" After hearing several statements of this nature, Mark asked Sanchez what he wanted him to do. Sanchez replied, "Tear down the house and get the hell out of here!" Mark refused, terminating the meeting by telling Sanchez that if he had any problems he should contact George's lawyer in San José. Mark returned to the house and Sanchez left upriver.

During this time, George and his associates made further attempts to contact Tom to ask him about the relevance of the milla maritima and attempt to determine what claims Sanchez might have on their property. However, Tom remained out of reach. George then made the decision to arrange for the surveys and decided to pay for them himself, if necessary. He said later that there were two main reasons why he made this decision; one, he felt that time was running out due to Sanchez's increasing threats to tear down the association's houses; and two, he did not want to get involved in what might prove to be a costly or protracted legal battle against Tom. Also, George had no previous experience in Costa Rica, knew nothing of the legal customs and procedures, and was therefore reluctant to get involved with something beyond his understanding or control.

In January 1981 George had two "surveys" completed on the property on the Boca Río Sierpe. The first survey established the western and eastern boundaries along the riverfront, and was also expected to determine if the property actually began two hundred meters up the mountain as Sanchez claimed it did. The chief engineer on this particular survey asked for and received $1,500 for his services, which consisted of three hours of work. Included in the sum was a formal declaration from the engineer that George's land actually began fifty meters in from the river bank and not one hundred fifty meters as Sanchez claimed (as described in the bill of sale). The second survey was conducted three weeks later and also cost $1,500 but, this time, the chief engineer and three assistants cut a path two meters wide up and over the mountain outlining the boundaries of the entire hundred acres.

Meanwhile, George's lawyer in San José told George he could not determine if a milla maritima actually existed on the Sierpe River, because he claimed that the laws pertaining to river property were "vague and ill-defined." He counseled George and his associates to continue to live and work on the property, and adopt a "wait and see" attitude about Sanchez and his threats to tear down the house. Later in 1981, George returned to Costa Rica. He became gravely ill while on the Boca Río Sierpe and died.

During the next five years, approximately every six months, Sanchez continued to make threats of coming to the Boca and tearing down the houses built by George and his associates. Sanchez, however, had not attempted to carry through with his warnings. The last time he made any such threat was over a year ago, and the North Americans continue to live and work on the property. In January 1986 the dispute resurfaced. In that month, another group of North Americans from Miami, Florida, represented by an agent, Lester, bought five hundred acres of land on the Boca next to the property purchased by George. They bought this land from the same real estate agent, Tom, and paid approximately $200,000. A few weeks later, Lester talked to Mark while on a trip to the town of Sierpe and complained he was having problems with a man named Sanchez. It seemed that Sanchez was claiming the rights of possession along the entire beach front property adjacent to the land they had bought.

Mark told Lester about his troubles with Sanchez. Lester noted that Tom had never mentioned the existence of the milla maritima and his lawyers in San José knew nothing about it. Lester said that his partners in the United States had extensive plans to develop the property for tourism and that they certainly could not do this without free access to the beaches. He said that they had already paid a substantial down payment to Tom and could not afford to simply back out of their investment.

Lester then told Mark that he was going to make a formal complaint against Sanchez and agreed to include the complaints of Mark as part of the same legal actions. Lester said he and his partners had the financial resources and "high-powered lawyers" to take the dispute as far as necessary within the formal legal system.

Lester then went to Puerto Cortez and made a formal complaint against Sanchez. During the next few months Lester and Mark worked together in an attempt to resolve their common dispute with Sanchez. They testified before a formal hearing of the Consejo—the council—of the municipalidad. Sanchez was also required to appear before the council. Both sides argued their position and appealed for a resolution of the dispute. Although the council does not perform the same function as a criminal or civil court, it does have the formal authority to resolve all land disputes falling within its jurisdiction in the Cantón de Osa.

Based on private conversations with various members of the council, it appeared as though the formal authorities would grant the rights of possession to Lester and Mark. Most council members, however, emphasized the necessity of proceeding cautiously, because Sanchez had paid taxes on the milla maritima for more than thirty years and was a well-known and powerful member of the Puerto Cortez community. They said they could not treat the issue lightly nor appear to exhibit any favoritism. One member of the council put it this way:

> We would rather go with Lester in this dispute because he has the money and desire to develop the area. This is good for the local economy. On the other hand, Sanchez has never done anything in thirty years to improve that property. But if we go with Lester, we have to at least appear to do it legally. We have to cover ourselves in case of any future legal action against us by Sanchez.

The issue remains unresolved. Lester has already built one house within the milla maritima and has plans to build several more. Mark and Lester are continuing to lobby the council for their support in granting them the rights of possession to the milla maritima.

Despite the fact that the actors in this dispute have had a "simplex" relationship and despite the fact that the issue involves control of scarce resources, no attempt by either side had ever been made to force a formal resolution of the issue in a court of law for approximately five years after the dispute became public. (It was not until third parties became involved that this dispute was referred to the formal legal system.) In fact, *no* attempt at resolution had been made, not only within the formal court system, but other forms of settlement as well, such as negotiation or mediation. This is primarily because Sanchez and his informal network of associates, and George and his informal network of associates, interrelate in only one respect. The point where both groups overlap is related to Mark, who was living on the property on the Boca and could be considered to be included in both networks. However, George did not ask Mark to attempt conciliation with Sanchez, and Sanchez's seemingly intractable attitude toward the North Americans does not indicate a willingness to negotiate. Almost all communication occurring in this dispute was conducted through the separate informal networks of communication— between George and his associates and lawyers in San José, and between Sanchez and his associates. The only communication between these two unrelated groups consisted of Sanchez's threats.

Moreover, George and his associates control the contested land. The North Americans cleared the land, built several houses, planted fruit and other trees, and have been living on the land. Although Sanchez's motives for not making a formal complaint against the North Americans remain obscure, subsequent conversations with his "messenger" on the Boca, Pancho, offers some clues. It appears that Sanchez's claim to the property in question is not secure; he has merely claimed the land by making a verbal announcement to those who live in the area. In addition, although he had owned the land sold to George, it appears he was never formally granted the "rights of possession" on the milla maritima. Pancho thinks that because the North Americans had built a house, improved the land, and had been living there for over three months, Sanchez was reluctant to contact the formal authorities. It is believed that, for this reason, Sanchez kept the dispute on an informal basis and tried to get rid of the Americans by making threats—something which Sanchez apparently had tried successfully before under different circumstances.

According to land records in the *municipalidad*, Sanchez has had the rights of possession and has been paying taxes on the milla maritima since 1974. In response to questions concerning this case, a land office official suggested that Sanchez probably did not make any formal complaints because he had allowed the North Americans to live and work in the milla maritima for too long. The official said, "After one year of living on the property, building a big, expensive house, and making land improvements, the Americans could claim the `rights of occupation'." When asked what these rights might be, the official replied, "I don't know. The legal code is very vague on this issue. The interpretation or definition of the law is usually made on an individual case-by-case basis." He explained further that if Sanchez won any court battle for possession of the milla maritima he would probably be liable to pay back the North Americans for the building they had built and the improvements they made. "Maybe that's why Sanchez hasn't made any formal complaints," said the official.

Pablo, on the other hand, offers a different view. He says that Sanchez could regain possession of the property whenever he wishes; he is waiting for the North Americans to build more houses and make more improvements. He suggests that Sanchez will then take over the property and gain substantial profit for himself. In fact, a slight variation on this view was revealed later in a public session of the council in the *municipalidad*; Lester stated that after he had bought the five hundred acres, he was approached privately by Sanchez, who offered to sell him the rights of possession to the milla maritima for $100,000. At this time, according to Lester, Sanchez mentioned he was prepared to offer the "same kind of deal" to the other North Americans, meaning Mark and his associates. Several members of the council became very upset over this offer, because no one can buy or sell state property; only the Municipalidad de Osa has the right to grant the rights of possession to the milla maritima—actual ownership remains permanently in the hands of the state.

As far as the dispute with Tom, the real estate agent, is concerned, George chose not to attempt to force a formal resolution of the dispute. He had planned on suing Tom to recover the cost of the two surveys, but he eventually decided against this, due to fear of incurring even more cost, in lawyer's fees, as well as in transportation and communication costs. George did not force a resolution of the dispute, through formal court procedures or negotiation or mediation, because he thought he had neither the time nor the money. Instead, he chose a course of action which has been referred to by Hirschman (1970) as "avoidance"—that is, termination of the relationship. George made a decision never again to have social or business dealings with Tom. George decided to take his losses, deciding not to press his claims.

This dispute initially arose, in part, due to the disparate status of the actors within the local community. Sanchez, who has lived on the Boca for many years, contested the North Americans' claim to land that he said was located in the milla maritima. Sanchez's long-time insider status gave him an "inside" knowledge of local land laws, and this status may also have resulted in more sympathy from the local community. In addition, while Sanchez may not have had strong legal control over the disputed land, he hoped that the North Americans would be sufficiently unaware of their formal rights to the land that they would respond to his repeated threats by leaving the land. However, Sanchez apparently avoided bringing the dispute to the formal level, because his chances of winning the dispute were limited.

In review, the North Americans, including Mark, George, and their associates in the United States, were considered outsiders throughout the course of the dispute (Mark, however, gradually has gained an insider status, for he continues to live and work in the Boca area). As outsiders, the North Americans had limited access to the informal social control network and limited knowledge of local language and customs. This lack of knowledge made it difficult for the Americans to respond to Sanchez's allegations. However, as the Americans continued to work and improve the disputed land, their outsider status has become less important to the management of the dispute and their rights of possession under Costa Rican law have increased.

Cost, as a variable affecting the nature of the dispute process, is also central to this case. In January 1981 George spent $3,000 of his own money for two different surveys of the property in an attempt to establish boundaries and to find out the truth of Sanchez's claim. The results were mixed—one survey suggests that Sanchez has no claim and the other suggests that he might. Nonetheless, George decided not to pursue the issue in a formal court, primarily because he faced growing reluctance on the part of his North American associates to contribute any more funds to the project.

Here we see how secondary or related disputes can influence the management of an original dispute, even though the actors in these secondary disputes may be far removed from the action and unknown to one or more of the disputants. For instance, by the time the dispute with Sanchez became public, George was already facing dissension and doubt on the part of his associates in the United States. This is important to note, because after several conversations with most of these people, it became apparent that George now generally was regarded as a "deviant."

This attitude toward George, added to the fact that almost all the associates knew nothing about the Boca Río Sierpe, led to the social construction of a reality far removed in both definition and distance from the original dispute. They were unhappy and nervous about not receiving titles promised for the land for which they had already paid (for a more thorough discussion of this issue, see the case, "The Fruit of the Land"). When the dispute with Sanchez became known among George's associates, it only increased doubts about the soundness of their investments.

Complaining by a group of the associates led eventually to a dispute between several members of the association and George. Apparently, these associates had entered into an agreement with George based on particular expectations about the responsibilities and obligations of each party—that is, the associates were supposed to pay the money and George was expected to "deliver the goods." But, since George had not yet delivered on his promises and because he now had a "tainted identity," the associates were ready to believe they had lost everything when the dispute with Sanchez became known.

Since most associates had no idea of the social circumstances of Pancho and Sanchez, not to mention the existence of the milla maritima or the exact location of their land, their reaction to this particular dispute was to hold George responsible. They found it extremely difficult to control or predict the management of a dispute which had its roots so far away from their own immediate social reality. Instead, they managed their disputes with George and Sanchez within a social context they understood and could control—usually through the informal social control network at George's university. (So far, only one out of the eighteen original members of the association has taken the secondary dispute to the formal level by suing to recover a "lost" investment.) The comment made by one associate about his interaction with George was typical of the general attitude; "It's beginning to smell more and more like a Florida land-swamp swindle."

Therefore, George assumed that he stood alone in this dispute with Sanchez, and this possibly accounted for his reluctance to force the issue on the formal level; he knew he could not count on any more financial or social support from his associates. This development gave George another motive for keeping this dispute on an informal level by attempting to minimize the legitimacy of Sanchez's claims and not appearing to take them too seriously.

Also, one needs to account for cultural differences and their effects upon the dispute process. George and Mark were North Americans, outsiders unfamiliar with the Costa Rican culture and the Spanish language. This fact helped the initial creation of the dispute, because of the confusion caused by cultural and language barriers. George and his associates were accustomed to doing business in the United States where they were insiders: they understood the meanings of the transactions they entered into, the identities, roles, and expectations of themselves and the other actors with whom they did business, and, if anything went wrong, they knew how and where to seek remedy.

Clearly, knowing who and what an individual is confronting within a business transaction helps to minimize misunderstanding and mistakes, and leads to a sense of security about the integrity of the transaction. In this case, George and Mark entered into a business transaction—the buying of land—a process they knew something about; however, they knew nothing of the larger cultural context within which the transaction took place. An initial problem was created when they allowed the bill of sale to be printed and read in Spanish. A careful reading of this document reveals that the northern boundary of the property actually *is* two hundred meters inland from the Sierpe River. This might possibly lend some credibility to Sanchez's claim to the rights of possession of this particular piece of land. Thus, George and his North American associates might be considered squatters, because they moved onto and settled upon land already claimed by someone else. Ironically, however, according to Costa Rican land laws and customs, the North Americans now have a legitimate claim to the rights of possession on the land, especially after six years of continuous occupation. It is unlikely anyone will be able to move the North Americans from this land, unless it is left unattended and other squatters arrive to establish a claim.

Finally, this dispute reached the formal authorities only because of an introduction by third parties into the same or similar dispute. Lester and his associates found themselves faced with exactly the same situation and involving the same people; Tom the real estate agent and Sanchez. This is an example of how the sudden appearance of new actors and new alliances can radically alter the dispute process, in this case facilitating access to the formal authorities.

This dispute is actually between two outsiders who claim the same land on the Boca Río Sierpe. Although Sanchez lived in the nearby town of Puerto Cortez, he has visited the Boca only four times in the last six years. Also, he is not well known in the area and Pancho, George's neighbor, was Sanchez's only informal contact among the local residents. Of course, George and his associates were outsiders, who had *no* access to Sierpe's informal social control network. Thus, we see in this dispute the conspicuous absence of any involvement or influence by the informal social infrastructure of the Sierpe community. In other words, the object of this dispute—control of a piece of land on the Boca—was actually fought in two different places by two different groups of people who did not know each other or agree in any way on the meaning of definitions of this dispute. This might explain why attempts by both sides to settle this dispute have been aborted. Eventually, however, the formal authorities "took over" the management of the dispute and used the resources of the state to work on behalf of one of the disputants.

While the formal legal system was rejected by both sides for a variety of different reasons, disputing on the informal level was also limited, because each side did not gain access to the informal social network of the other. Mark, who was actually living on the Boca, did not have access to his *own* informal social network. After George's death, he found himself facing Sanchez on his own, without the immediate support or backing of many of the people most significant to him. For Mark, this fact played a crucial role in his management of the dispute:

> I couldn't do anything! Whenever Sanchez would make another threat, I'd try to get to Sierpe and call somebody or mail a letter. But the phone service was usually terrible and the letters took at least a month to go there and receive an answer. Anything could happen in a month! Sometimes I found myself sitting on the Boca alone, worrying about losing the land or wondering when Sanchez might come to tear down the houses. And the worst part was knowing that nobody in the States knew what was going on. I have never felt so alien and alone, truly a stranger in a strange land. In fact, I was pretty much immobilized; for the first five years of this dispute with Sanchez I did nothing to try to resolve it.

Now, however, with the support of Lester and his friends, Mark has taken this dispute to the formal authorities in Puerto Cortez. While Mark and Sanchez were in Puerto Cortez to give their definitions of the dispute to the council, we discussed the case with Sanchez. He said it was the first time he had heard about how George and his associates had first bought the land on the Boca, and their agreements and understandings made with Tom. He said he now understood the problems of the North Americans. He stated:

> [I am not really against] them, I'm just trying to protect my rights of possession that I have paid for for the last thirty years. The Americans got fooled by Tom and it's too bad Tom can't be here today before the council. Everybody wants to ask *him* a few questions. But these people are on my land. They either have to get off or pay me for it. I'm sorry Tom lied to them, but that has nothing to do with me. They're on *my* land and that's not right!"

These statements by Sanchez reveal a more conciliatory tone than his earlier demands "to tear down the house and get the hell out!" At least there is some dialogue about the dispute, whereas up to this time there were only long periods of silence broken occasionally by threats, demands, and misunderstandings.

In 1987 the municipality determined that Sanchez had "abandoned" the milla maritima—as evidence they cited the fact that all the residents had been living in this zone for over a year, building houses and making improvements. Sanchez lost his rights of possession. The municipality then invited all residents of the zone to make application for formal recognition of their claim to these rights. Despite Sanchez's attempts to sue the municipality and appeal its decisions, in March 1988 the First Appellate Court in San José also decided in favor of the municipality. However, in 1990 Sanchez continued to pursue the issue by claiming to have new, relevant legal grounds for review.

This case serves as a vivid illustration that when an original dispute remains unresolved, secondary disputes may frequently arise. These varied disputes were contested by actors who, using numerous tactics, tried to control the disputes by creating and maintaining definitions of deviance. In general, disputants attempted to maintain or elevate their status or legitimacy by defining other disputants as deviant (cf. Selby 1974; Lauderdale 1984). In addition, the secondary disputes reflect the varying impact of different levels of access to formal and informal social control as well as the factors of time and cost. Moreover, this case also demonstrates how one dispute (in this case a land dispute in a remote area of Costa Rica) can be influenced directly by a dispute occurring in a dramatically different, distant place.

Case 4:
Denouncing the Campesino

In June 1981, Jim, a North American, was granted a concession to mine gold on Violínes Island. The boundaries of this concession included property already claimed by Pablo, the same Costa Rican involved in the case "*Resident or Squatter*"?. Pablo has been a resident of the Boca for almost fifty years and the property he claims is located on the eastern end of Violínes, facing the Sierpe River.

During this same month, while on a trip upriver to the town of Sierpe to obtain supplies, the Sierpe guardia told Pablo that they had received a summons requiring him to appear in the Municipalidad de Osa in Puerto Cortez within the next five days. When Pablo inquired about the nature of the summons, the guardia said they did not know any details. Pablo had to travel to the one public telephone in Sierpe to contact the *municipalidad* to ask about the summons. He was told that someone had placed a denuncia against him, and he was required to go to Puerto Cortez to respond to the charges. A secretary said that all Pablo could be told on the telephone was that the denuncia related to disputed property rights on Violínes Island. Pablo was both mystified and angry—it was the first time anyone had ever placed a denuncia against him. He thought the complaint might have something to do with the recent mineral rights concession granted to Jim, yet he first met Jim a few weeks before and was not aware of any problems or complaints that Jim might have against him.

Pablo returned downriver to his house on Violínes Island and gathered papers pertaining to the rights of possession to his land. The next day he returned to Sierpe, took the bus to Puerto Cortez, and went directly to the office building which houses the offices of the alcaldía and both the criminal and civil judges. Pablo had no lawyer and no witnesses with him, and introduced himself to the appropriate secretary in order to ask about the denuncia. Pablo was told that three weeks earlier Jim had put a denuncia against him claiming that property contained within Pablo's mineral rights concession, including his farm, was actually Jim's. Jim had suggested that Pablo was nothing more than a precarista, a squatter, and had brought three witnesses to Puerto Cortez who testified on his behalf. All the witnesses were Costa Rican citizens who claimed to be living in the Sierpe district. Jim also had two lawyers with offices in San José helping with his case.

Pablo immediately demanded to talk to the judge who handles the civil cases in the Cantón de Osa. After waiting more than an hour, Pablo was ushered into the judge's office. The criminal court judge was visiting the office of the civil court judge, and Pablo asked him to stay and listen to the review of his documents. The meeting was not considered part of the formal court process but rather an informal gathering; the civil judge reviewed the details of Jim's denuncia and asked Pablo for his response. Pablo turned over his papers that included receipts from the Central Bank of Costa Rica for payment of land taxes over the last twelve years, receipts for the payment of taxes on the milla marítima for the last nine years, a survey map of the thirty acres he had claimed on Violines Island, and a formal "recognition" of his rights of possession, granted in 1970 by the Muncipalidad de Osa in Puerto Cortez.

According to Pablo, both judges were surprised at the extent of his legal documentation regarding the property and wondered what possible grounds Jim had for making his *denuncia*. Jim claimed to have had several pieces of heavy machinery on the land for several years, to have cleared part of the land, and to have planted various fruit trees. The judges reviewed the statements made by Jim's witnesses and questioned the credibility of the witnesses. The criminal court judge then told Pablo that he could make a formal complaint against these witnesses, because they had made false statements in an official court proceeding and had signed their names to the statements. The judge commented that, if found guilty, the witnesses might spend up to two years in jail. Pablo refused to press charges, because he knew one of the witnesses personally and did not want to see any of them go to jail, because he felt they had done him no serious harm. The civil court judge then stated that he wanted to see both Pablo and Jim in his office the following week at which time they "could work something out."

One week later, Jim, Pablo, and the civil court judge met in the judge's office in Puerto Cortez. Pablo also described this meeting as "informal." Jim was not formally represented, because the judge had called Jim's lawyer earlier in the week and the lawyer had agreed after hearing the facts of the case that everything should be handled in an "informal manner." Jim's lawyer advised him to show up at the meeting prepared to accept whatever decision the judge made, to "keep his mouth shut, and not make waves."

The judge declared that he considered Jim's *denuncia* to be *incompetencia*—that is, lacking sufficient proof to back up adequately the claims he was making. He also declared as "invalid and possibly criminal" the statements made by Jim's witnesses. The judge then stated that he wanted Jim and Pablo to work out a formal contract in his presence, outlining their responsibilities to each other as related to Jim's intention to work a gold concession on Pablo's property. The judge suggested that Jim pay Pablo 26 percent of all the gold profits, reimburse Pablo for any property damage or the removal of timber, and allow Pablo to mine gold at the same rate of salary as Jim's other workers. Both Jim and Pablo agreed to these conditions and signed a contract before the judge.

At this point the formal denuncia against Pablo was "dropped" and the property dispute was resolved. Pablo said later that he was satisfied with the outcome of the dispute. When Jim was asked what he thought about it, he shrugged his shoulders, laughed, and said, "Ya can't win 'em all." When asked why he made the denuncia against Pablo in the first place, Jim replied that he was misled by his Costa Rican partners, one of whom was a lawyer, who assured him he could win such a case against someone they considered to be "an ignorant campesino in the country." Jim said he was very surprised at the legal control Pablo had over the property and the legal expertise he had exhibited in the judge's office. Jim commented further that if he had known the extent of Pablo's hold on the "rights of possession" he would never have made the denuncia. Asked if the denuncia had been pure fiction, Jim replied that "some of it was fiction, but most of it was true. I had a chance to win only if Pablo could not firmly establish his rights of possession."

The witnesses who had testified on Jim's behalf were all outsiders who had been living in San José. The family of one of them, however, owned property in the vicinity of the Boca Río Sierpe. This person was identified by Pablo and later interviewed. He said that everything Jim mentioned in the denuncia was *pura mierda*, or "full of excrement." He agreed to testify because Jim had given him money and had promised him a share of the gold profits. He justified his testimony against Pablo by saying that "Pablo has a lot of gold on his farm and was doing nothing about it. Costa Rica needs that gold." He thought it would have been better if the land was in someone else's hands who had the desire and the resources to develop it.

Although this particular dispute was resolved, problems between Jim and Pablo continued. Pablo continually complained that Jim was not working his mining concession and instead spent too much time in San José. Also, Pablo heard that Jim discovered an Indian burial ground and "took out a lot of gold objects, worth about $250,000." Jim denied this, however, and he later boasted to friends about finding "a lot" of Indian gold on Violínes Island, which he sold to purchase a new tractor.

In December 1982, Jim stopped working his gold concession. Jim's family in the United States was wealthy and he received monthly checks from a trust fund. Jim confided that he was discouraged with the initial results of his gold mining efforts, saying "there's not enough there to make the work and investment worthwhile." Pablo, however, said that Jim was "looking for elephants and when all he found were sand flies he quit looking." Jim was looking for big pieces of gold and his whole gold mining operation was designed to catch "elephants" with big tractors and bulldozers, a drag line, two eight-inch water pumps, and a long metal sluice filled with large steel riffles. Pablo went to the end of the sluice where the tailings of Jim's gold operation washed away. He scooped up a handful of the dirt, threw it into a gold pan and, under the water faucet of a sink, worked the material until a few tiny pieces of gold were visible. Pablo said that the whole area was filled with such tiny pieces.

In March 1985 it was rumored that Jim had sold his gold concession to another group of North Americans for $600,000 and had returned to the United States. Most local residents know that gold concessions in Costa Rica cannot be bought or sold, and that only the government has the right to grant a mineral rights concessions. Concessions are not sold, but rather are *given* by the government in return for the right to buy the gold from whomever has the concession. Pablo thinks that Jim committed *una estafa*, a swindle, and took the money and returned to the United States. He left behind a small bulldozer, a tractor, one water pump, a diesel-powered generating plant, and a two-story house on Pablo's property on Violínes Island. According to Costa Rican law, Jim was required to pay Pablo for the right to keep his machinery on Pablo's land, but Pablo says that Jim paid nothing. When Pablo was asked what the status of the machinery is now, he replied "They're *mine!*"

In early 1986, Jim unexpectedly returned to Sierpe. He had not sold his gold concession for $600,000, as rumored, but instead had returned to work his claim. He brought three workers from San José and a new machine. He said that he had developed a new process that would recover fine gold and he said, "Our analysis shows that 90 percent of the gold in this area is powder. And I'm going after it!"

Pablo had mixed feelings about Jim's return. He did not want Jim to do any more mining until Jim had made some kind of settlement about the money he owed. On the other hand, Pablo was relieved to see that Jim did not sell the concession, was still in the country, and that he might still pay back his debt.

However, Jim claimed not to have any money, or at least not enough to pay Pablo. Nor did he have enough money to pay his workers; after spending one week on the property, Jim left his workers on the Boca and traveled to San José with no apparent plans to return. Pablo and the workers feel very bitter about this. The workers had to sell some of their personal belongings in Sierpe to pay for bus tickets back to San José. Meanwhile, Pablo still complains that Jim cannot or will not pay him the money owed, and the dispute continues.

In review, it should be reiterated that the dispute was initiated by a formal complaint made by Jim against Pablo without Pablo's knowledge. Conflict initially existed only via the actors in the minds of Jim and his associates in San José, who, by Jim's admission, attempted to use the formal legal system as a means to realize personal, private motives—the takeover of Pablo's property. At this point, no dispute existed, because Pablo was unaware of any breach of expectations in his relationship with Jim. It was not until Pablo was informed of the complaint that a dispute developed. Thus, this case serves to illustrate that conflict can be made "public" but still not be considered a dispute. Disputing is by nature socially defined; that is, *conflict* may exist in the mind of one or more individuals, but a *dispute* has the distinctive characteristic of being a *social interaction*.

Although the first dispute began as a reaction to a formal complaint, the actual management of ensuing disputes was conducted on the informal level. In fact, all ensuing disputes between Jim and Pablo have been managed informally. This pattern began during the initial dispute when all parties, including the formal authorities, agreed to keep the settlement proceedings informal. It was understood that the judge in Puerto Cortez would not invoke the formal legal process as long as the disputants could settle the dispute to the satisfaction of all concerned. The formal and informal law may become so closely related until there is only a fine line distinguishing them. In this case the judge agreed not to act in his formal role, but rather as a citizen mediating between two other citizens. However, his formal identity gave him the power to impose such an informal resolution.

When we consider why people involved in the disputes agreed to informal management of the initial dispute, it is clear that time and cost were important factors. During an interview with one of the judges at the *municipalidad*, we described this dispute between Jim and Pablo, and asked if such informal settlements are common. The judge responded:

It's fairly common with *me*. I try to do it whenever the circumstances are right. There are special times when it's best not to use the law, to let people work out problems on their own, especially those cases that aren't so serious or cases where one person is clearly right and the other is clearly wrong. The law can be too expensive and take too much time; money for lawyers and court costs or official inspections, plus many papers and reports have to be made out and filed . . . It's better to do it clean, easy, and fast. But only if everybody agrees. That's very important. If someone wants to use the law, that's their right and I can't stop that. I have to get into the law. But if everyone agrees to go around the law, then we can go ahead.

The factor of financial cost has continued to bother Pablo in his dispute with Jim and it is one of the main reasons he offers for not "using the law." However, cost in the social sense was also important to Pablo; during the initial dispute he decided not to seek formal prosecution in order to avoid causing serious problems for one of Jim's witnesses who was an acquaintance. In addition, Pablo anticipated a continuing, multiplex relationship with Jim. In essence, Pablo did not want either relationship complicated by the animosity or hostility that typically arises from a formal legal battle. In Pablo's words, "Jim had the gold concession on my land. Not much I could do about that. I wanted good relations because there was a possibility of work for me and maybe some gold. But the main thing, of course, is that the farm is mine and will stay mine, and Jim had to agree to that." Thus, despite the fact that Jim was an outsider and Pablo an insider, they had a *multiplex* relationship, and it has influenced how they continue to manage their dispute.

The social costs for Jim in this initial dispute were much different. Initially, he did not worry about preserving his relationship with Pablo because he does not respect Pablo or value their association; thus their relationship was simplex. Based upon numerous conversations with Jim, it is evident that he considers Pablo an "old superstitious fool," as he remarked on one occasion. The costs for Jim were primarily represented in the form of financial costs, including fines, court costs, damages, or a potential jail sentence. Jim avoided these costs by agreeing to drop his formal complaint against Pablo in return for an informal management of the dispute.

However, Jim incurred other costs as a result of his dispute with Pablo that can be better measured in social rather than financial or legal terms. One measure of the social dimensions of this dispute touches on the insider or outsider status of the disputants. Although by most standards Jim is considered more "powerful" than Pablo in terms of resources and mobility, he is nevertheless viewed as an outsider and did not have access to the informal social structure of Sierpe. Pablo was and continues to be an important member of the local social system and is clearly an insider with regard to social interactions on the Boca and in Sierpe. Also, even though Jim's workers were from San José, they were Costa Ricans and quickly became assimilated into the informal social circle of the Boca. This is significant for two reasons: (1) the complaining by Pablo and Jim's workers led eventually to the social construction of a deviant identity for Jim; and (2) the consequences of this process reveal new insights into the informal social control infrastructure of Sierpe.

To illustrate this process we recall several occasions when Jim had left for San José for extended periods without leaving sufficient food or money for his workers. The workers were forced to borrow from their neighbors—insiders on the Boca Río Sierpe. In explaining their need for food or money, the workers invariably complained about Jim and how stingy, he was. They also mentioned that whenever Jim did spend time on the Boca, his behavior was "crazy" or otherwise erratic from the constant smoking of marijuana. Thus, it soon became known throughout the area that Jim was not a reliable employer. Consequently, Jim can no longer find people in and around Sierpe who will work for him. Jim has complained about this, saying that "These people around here are lazy and don't want to work," adding that this has cost him money because workers from San José generally demand more in salary and often are not as reliable or efficient, because they are not accustomed to living and working in wilderness conditions.

Closely related to the idea of cost, access also played a role in the continuing dispute between Pablo and Jim. Jim initially was able to gain access to the formal authorities in order to bring the denuncia against Pablo. However, Pablo also managed to gain relatively easy access to the formal social control network and was able to make himself heard. Moreover, neither Jim nor Pablo found access to the formal authorities problematic—although disputing within this network was kept at an informal level. Financial cost did limit Pablo's later attempts to access and utilize formal social control, but this can also be attributed to the fact that Pablo's insider status allowed him greater access to the informal social control network. Since he had the support of the local community, Pablo was less likely to continue disputing on the formal level.

Once more it becomes clear how the social construction of reality, in this case a *discredited identity* for Jim, can lead to consequences affecting social relationships and behavior (Downes and Rock 1982; Ben-Yehuda 1985). Furthermore, attitudes toward Jim have led to local support for Pablo's definition of his dispute with Jim. Most residents agree that Jim is a deviant and Pablo has the right to seek "compensation" by claiming ownership of Jim's "abandoned" gold mining equipment and the house Jim built on the gold concession. This means that no one is likely to complain about Pablo's "takeover" of Jim's possessions, or to notify Jim of what Pablo is doing. In fact, Pablo is now attempting to organize a tourist project on his property using Jim's house ("*my* house," says Pablo). Jim has not visited the Sierpe area for several months and it is assumed he knows nothing of Pablo's plans.

It is clear, therefore, that although financial costs may have inhibited Pablo from disputing on the formal level, Pablo will probably continue to dispute with Jim on the informal level of social control where he, as an insider, is assured quick and easy access, and the kind of predictability and control he could not otherwise expect from formal agencies. In fact, it has been part of Pablo's strategy in this dispute to "keep things on a low level," he said, "away from the law. I don't want to alarm Jim or draw his attention to what I'm doing. I have a lot of patience and I can be quiet and wait. I'll get the money he owes eventually—one way or the other."

These comments by Pablo reveal that the time necessary to maintain the dispute is a crucial factor to him. He has displayed a willingness to continue the dispute as long as necessary to satisfy his claims against Jim. Jim, however, seems to act as if his time is a more precious commodity. Consider, for example, his impatience over his initial inability to find large amounts of gold on the property he was mining. Pablo attributes these differences to cultural factors; "I'm a Boruka Indian," said Pablo. "I have learned to be patient. But Jim is a gringo and gringos lose patience if they can't do something right away or if they are not satisfied with initial results. Jim will get bored or disinterested eventually. Then I take over!" Jim has seemed more intent on making a quick profit, whereas Pablo is willing to wait until he receives what he believes he is owed.

This case reveals one process by which disputes may be managed almost entirely on an informal level. While this dispute was ostensibly being contested at the formal legal level, even within this arena it was managed informally. In the original dispute, the judge representing the agents of formal social control kept the most relevant aspects of the dispute on the informal level—bypassing formal adjudication of the case. The case raises the fact that often, as disputes evolve and subsequent conflicts develop, they may remain on the informal level—a formal social control agent such as a judge may use discretion that is legitimately authorized or, as in this case, simply act in an extralegal manner (see Pfohl, 1985). Also, a disputant's insider or outsider status, once again, is a significant factor affecting both the management and development of disputes; insiders may feel compelled to maintain their disputes on the informal level where they frequently enjoy advantages in access and control.

Case 5:
The Fruit of the Land

This dispute involves property purchased by George and his North American associates in June 1979. Circumstances surrounding this case illustrate the changes an original dispute may undergo when a related or secondary dispute arises. In November 1981 George's associate Mark, who had been living on property on the Boca Río Sierpe since June 1980, married the daughter of Pancho, a man who had been living on the Boca for twelve years. Pancho's house was located within the milla maritima (the zone adjacent to a body of water which is considered common land available for use by all Costa Rican citizens) and across a small mountain stream from the house built by the North Americans. Pancho's work included building dugout canoes and working as a fishing guide.

A dispute involving Pancho became public in June 1982, when Andy, another of George's associates living on the same site, crossed the stream to pick avocadoes from two trees about fifty meters behind Pancho's house. Pancho complained to one of his friends about Andy's taking the avocadoes. Mark and Andy received word of the complaint from one of Pancho's daughters, Marisa, who is married to Mark. Pancho was quoted as saying that if Andy wanted more avocadoes in the future, he must first ask permission, because the avocado trees were on Pancho's property.

When Andy heard the complaint, he became quite angry and argued that the avocado trees were actually on the land purchased by the association. Andy suggested that he and Mark have a talk with Pancho.

The following day, Andy and Mark walked to Pancho's house and asked him on what basis he claimed that the avocado trees were on "his property." Pancho explained that about two acres of the milla maritima were "given" to him by Sanchez, a man who claimed the rights of possession to a strip of land occupied by the North Americans and who had also threatened to tear down the houses of George and his associates. Pancho said that Sanchez had given him the land so that he and his family would always have a place to live. Although Sanchez had no interest in selling or farming the land, he nevertheless claimed ownership and control over the land. Pancho called it a matter of pride and family tradition. Mark asked Pancho when Sanchez had given him the land, and Pancho replied that Sanchez had given it to him twelve years ago when he had sold one thousand acres of land on the Boca Río Sierpe to Sanchez for about $125. This property consisted of the land forming the southern part of the mouth of the Sierpe River and extended from the mouth of the river south to Estero Ganado along approximately three kilometers of the Pacific coastline. This land also included the one hundred acres Sanchez had sold to the North Americans for $50,000. Pancho said that at the time he sold the land, Sanchez promised more than two acres of the land would be Pancho's "forever" and would never be sold. When Mark asked if Pancho had any papers proving his claim to the land, Pancho indicated that he did have papers. When Andy asked Pancho to produce the papers, Pancho said he did not have them but that they were in a "safe place."

The dispute eventually became known to George's North American associates after Andy complained to one of them during a telephone conversation from Sierpe. The associates were already worried about threats and claims being made by Sanchez. When they heard about the dispute with Pancho, they demanded that something be done immediately to clarify the issue. Some also demanded that legal action be initiated to get "Pancho off our land!" Mark was an associate and part owner of the property on the Boca and responsible to his other partners due to some earlier financial agreements. At the same time, since Pancho was his father-in-law, he had a strong interest in maintaining good family relationships. Mark said that for him to become involved in a legal action against his wife's father would involve great personal costs.

Thus, Mark decided to take no action against Pancho. Instead, he became a mediator on Pancho's behalf, without Pancho's knowledge or consent, while negotiating with his associates in the United States. Mark attempted to persuade his associates to drop their demands for legal action and accept Pancho's presence "on or near" their property. At the same time, he decided to refrain from mentioning the subject further to Pancho and to allow their relationship to continue without conflict.

In attempting to persuade his associates to allow Pancho to continue living on the Boca property, Mark did not emphasize the fact that Pancho was his father-in-law, although it was common knowledge. He instead stressed cultural and legal factors. He argued that members of the association were strangers trying to develop property in the rural wilderness of a foreign country, and that they needed to learn the language, customs, and "ways of the jungle." More importantly, he said, they needed to establish and maintain good relations among the people of the Boca and Sierpe communities.

It is also important to note that when these North Americans began their association located on the Boca, they initially hired Pancho in the roles of groundskeeper, caretaker, and general laborer. Pancho became acquainted with some of the members of the association who visited the site early in its existence. However, as fewer and fewer of the members came to visit the site and generally withdrew their interest in the association, Pancho's salary was gradually diminished.

Furthermore, Pancho was well known and respected throughout the entire southern zone of Costa Rica. Mark suggested that bringing a lawsuit against Pancho or trying to "kick him off" his land would lessen chances of gaining the friendship and confidence of the community. Also, Mark cautioned his associates against initiating a costly lawsuit that they were not likely to win. He explained that in Costa Rica there were many legal precedents for granting the "rights of possession" to a person who is physically living on, controlling, and working a piece of land—no matter who may claim ownership or have the proper "papers." Since Pancho had built a house and had been living on the same site for over twelve years and had planted cacao, avocado, and banana trees, he had a claim to the land and the Costa Rican court system was likely to acknowledge it. In addition, as one local noted, the court system will take into account the fact that:

Pancho has lived here off and on for almost all of his forty-seven years and usually has no fewer than three people staying with him and at times as many as twelve. Pancho provides for them by fishing, building boats from the trees, occasionally working as a taxi guide on the river, or hire himself out as a guide to other fishermen [sic]. His home was once a church and has a large open area under an old tin roof and for a long time we have seen points of light glowing dimly through the cracked walls. Pancho is part of this area.

In addition, Pancho's house was located within the milla maritima. It was impossible to own this land, and the building of any structures within this zone was prohibited unless one had special permission from the *municipalidad*. Pancho had built his house before the current laws were passed and, thus, his house could remain. If the North Americans assumed that their land began directly behind the milla maritima, then Pancho's house was not on their land and they could not legally remove Pancho from public property. Mark told his associates that if Pancho wanted to think of the two acres behind his house as "his property" there would be no harm done, as long as he did not try to sell or develop the property.

This initial dispute spawned other disputes, most notably those arising among the North American associates and between some of these associates and Mark. While some of the partners were willing to allow Pancho to stay on the property, others were angry or discouraged, fearing that their investments might be lost or diminish in value. Also, in an attempt to save his relationship with his father-in-law, Mark lost the support of some of his associates in the United States. This loss of support usually was expressed in two forms. In some cases, further financial investments were withheld, because the associates felt they had already made a bad investment and were reluctant to lose more. In other cases, his friendships with some of the associates were severely affected, some being stretched to the breaking point.

This dispute has been managed to the extent that there is presently no conflict between Pancho and the North Americans. However, the effects of this dispute, especially the secondary disputes arising between members of the association, have had considerable consequences on cohesion and commitments within the group. The initial dispute was one in a series of similar events which contributed to the eventual dissolution of the association into two loosely connected groups: those who have renounced the project and have withdrawn all support, and those who continue to maintain interest and support.

In review, the multiplex nature of the relationships of the actors involved had a significant influence on the course and outcome of the dispute. As Gluckman (1955) notes, the stronger and more involved the relationship, the more likely a dispute will be handled in a noncombative manner such as negotiation or mediation. That was certainly the case in this dispute. Mark had been living on the Boca since June 1980, at which time he was ignorant of the Costa Rican culture and the Spanish language. However, by the time the dispute with Pancho arose, Mark had become a "marginal" insider partly through his marriage to Pancho's daughter Marisa. This new status offered Mark partial access to the local informal social network, but because he still did not speak Spanish well or fully understand the social character of the local culture he was not considered a "true insider." Nevertheless, his marriage to the daughter of a popular, long-time resident of the Boca gave him limited inroads into the local culture and some understanding of local values and traditions.

The insider or outsider status of the disputants is obviously relevant to the management of this dispute. Pancho clearly was an insider on the Boca Río Sierpe and was well-known, well-liked, and respected. Mark's associates in the United States, on the other hand, were outsiders to the area who had little knowledge of the local culture, including the language, laws, and customs. Because these North Americans sought acceptance within the local community, the desire to foster and maintain good relationships with members of the Boca and Sierpe communities dictated against formally challenging Pancho. Rather than attempt, as outsiders, to challenge the 12-year-hold of Pancho on the disputed land, the Americans chose not to pursue the dispute. One reason for this strategy was to increase their chances of being viewed as reasonable by members of the Boca and Sierpe community, as well as to enhance chances of eventually being accepted as insiders. Another was a genuine concern by some of the North Americans that Pancho be treated fairly and kindly.

When this dispute arose, Mark was faced with the decision of either participating in legal action against his father-in-law or mediating on his behalf with his associates in the United States. Mark chose the latter, because he valued his relationship with his wife and father-in-law more than he valued pursuing the dispute. This decision and the disagreements over the appropriate reaction to Pancho's actions led to secondary disputes among the members of the association. Thus, the dispute underwent a shift in emphasis, from a dispute over control of land to a number of separate disputes involving personal loyalties and responsibilities. In fact, some of the North American associates directed more suspicion and animosity toward each other than toward Pancho. In this case, the circumstances surrounding the dispute—how it was handled and the actors who were involved—actually became more important than the issues raised by the original conflict.

The factor of access also played a role in this dispute. The facts of the dispute suggest that both the formal and informal agents of social control were predisposed toward Pancho in this dispute. Because of his reputation as an insider within the local community, Pancho would enjoy considerable advantages in access to the informal social control network, and because he arguably has a more legitimate claim to the land in question, he would probably also have an advantage in the formal arena. The dispute was not pursued through formal means and eventually was abandoned by the North Americans, therefore it is unclear how significant a role access might have played in an ongoing dispute. Nonetheless, questions of access may have been important in determining how the dispute was managed and in the decision not to pursue the case any further.

The involvement of personal motives and use of privileged information played an additional role in this dispute. Mark gained considerable insight into Pancho's character and personality through direct observation and through interactions with his wife Marisa and other insiders on the Boca. He also learned that Pancho did not want to take his complaints to the level of the formal law for the same reasons Mark did not; to protect his relationship with his new son-in-law. Mark's wife Marisa was the mediator in this dispute and she assured Mark that Pancho wanted to resolve the dispute quietly and on a friendly basis. Thus, the immediate, informal access between Mark and Pancho—with Marisa as an intervening third party—had an important influence on the course of this dispute.

Mark has said that the dispute may have developed very differently if Pancho had clearly been out for personal gain by taking advantage of his role as Mark's father-in-law. Mark, however, was aware that Pancho was not a person prone to this kind of action. Mark continually reminded his North American associates that twelve years earlier Pancho had sold a thousand acres of prime beach property on the Pacific Ocean for only $125.

By his own admission, Pancho has no interest in things which do not contribute directly to his and his family's survival. He is a fisherperson and a boat builder and, in many conversations with Mark, he has indicated that he only wants to live peacefully with very little or no responsibility. On one occasion, Pancho stated to Mark what he called his "philosophy of life"—"I don't want to own valuable things or get involved in business deals because it's too much work. I like taking it easy, and I only work when I have to. It's better to have nothing because then you've got nothing to worry about and nothing to lose." And Mark has reported that for the year and a half before the initial dispute became public, Pancho seemed to live his philosophy. Because of this, Mark felt confident in persuading his associates to allow Pancho to stay where he was. As Mark stated later, "I knew he had no interest in developing the land or in stealing something he thought was valuable. He was simply claiming something that he thought was rightfully his." Mark's North American associates, however, did not understand this—to some of the associates the concept of "private property" is sacrosanct.

Both personal and financial cost played an important role in this dispute. Mark could not allow his associates to institute legal proceedings against his father-in-law without suffering considerable adverse consequences in his relationship with his wife, her relatives, and others in the Boca community. As he explained later, "I had to live with my wife and with the people around the Boca and in Sierpe. Pancho was well known and well liked and members of his family are spread out through the whole area. On the other hand, my associates were three thousand miles away and could not possibly know what was actually at stake. For me, there was no other choice." Thus, for Mark, the interpersonal cost of continuing the dispute was too high.

While the interpersonal costs of disputing were more vital to Mark than the time necessary for attempting to resolve the dispute, time may have played a more important role to his associates in the United States. Because of the physical distance between the Boca and the United States and the difficulty in maintaining the dispute without Mark's support, members of the association may have decided that the investment of their time and resources would be better utilized elsewhere. In addition, they were less likely to spend the time necessary to maintain the dispute considering that the likelihood of success through both formal and informal means seemed ambiguous.

Moreover, the advice Mark gave his associates concerning their chances of winning such a court case appears accurate. Pancho needed only to prove his claim that he had been living in the same place for twelve years and had "improved" the property to establish a legal claim. In addition, virtually everyone in the immediate area could attest to the facts offered by Pancho. Although Pancho may not be able to prove his claim to any property beyond the public property line, it is highly unlikely that anyone would ever be able to "kick him off" his property.

Also, the time factor had some role in this dispute, because of what Mark called "the bad timing" of the emergence of this dispute. Mark's associates were already worried and discouraged about the disputes with Sanchez and Tom, the real estate agent. When they heard about the dispute many became even more upset and more determined to safeguard their investments. This led to strong statements of doubt concerning Mark's handling of their affairs and their insistence about "doing something to get rid of Pancho." Mark's decision to do nothing about Pancho cost him further support of his associates.

This case illustrates some of the processes by which disputes can escalate and expand, as well as how the nature of the social relationship can have varying influences on the dispute process. The multiplex relationship between the locals clearly affected the outcome, or more accurately, the management of this dispute. This case presents conditions under which the continuation of highly valued relationships can become more important than the control of nonhuman resources.

Moreover, it seems apparent that the impact of a simplex or multiplex relationship can be mitigated by other conditions. Although relevant advice in this case was based upon an understanding of the local laws applied to the facts of the case, many of the North Americans continued to concentrate more on what they perceived as their associate's disloyalty and disregard for their interests than on the nature of the original dispute. Mark has been labeled as a deviant by some of his former colleagues, while others refer to him as unpredictable. While the North American investors initially had a multiplex, or continuing, relationship with their associate on the Boca, it is clear that many considered the value of maintaining control of "their land" to be more important than preserving the relationship.

Starr and Yngvesson (1975) contend that when control of a scarce resource is at the foundation of a dispute, the disputants' relationship typically will be sacrificed in order to resolve the problem. Yngvesson's (1978) study of Atlantic fishermen who were disputing the control of land supports her prior research with Starr: "cases involving control over scarce resources are likely to go to court; parties to such cases often seem more interested in winning the case than in muffling a grievance (with a view to maintaining their previous relationship)" (1978: 77). While the land claimed by both the local and the North Americans is one example of a scarce resource in this dispute, it is also likely that a highly valued resource, the large investments of money, time, and emotions, may have a similar impact as a scarce resource on the management of a dispute.

Case 6:
The Sierpe Gift

In 1973 executives of the United Fruit Company, based in Palmar Sur, were worried about squatters who had begun moving onto company land along the edges of the banana plantations. This land was owned by the company but it had not been developed or planted with bananas. In this same year, a managing director in the company offices in Palmer Sur "gave" approximately ten hectares of land to a local Costa Rican, Roberto. This tract of land was located about half a kilometer north of the town of Sierpe and was bordered on one side by the road leading from Sierpe to Palmar, and on the other side by the Estero Azul, a small tributary of the Sierpe River.

This land was given to Roberto in return for his promise to "keep an eye on" company property and keep squatters from moving onto the undeveloped company land which, at that time, consisted of about fifteen hundred acres around the town of Sierpe along the western edge of the banana plantations. Roberto was urged by his friends to have the company give him formal papers legalizing the transaction. The pact, however, remained an informal transaction, a personal agreement between the company executive and Roberto. The executive did not have the authority to give away or sell company property, but both he and Roberto knew that if Roberto stayed on the land for any length of time and developed and improved the land, then Roberto could claim the "rights of possession."

In 1975 the United Fruit Company began selling this undeveloped company property, which was excellent farm land—very flat with loose, rich soil and good drainage. During this time, Roberto had fenced off the land he had been given and had cleared it to make a pasture for the several head of cattle he owned. Then, in 1981, the company sold seven hundred acres to a foreign investor, Sergio, who already owned several hundred acres of rice farms in the area. Part of the land Sergio bought was located across the road from Roberto's farm.

Shortly after Sergio bought the land, he went to Roberto's farm and demanded that Roberto vacate the property because he claimed it was part of the land he had bought from the company. Roberto refused, explaining that the company had given him the farm and that he had lived and worked on the land for the last eight years. Later, Roberto attempted to contact the company executive who had given him the land, but he could not locate him. The company workers Roberto contacted said they knew of his arrangement with the particular company executive, but that they could not give him any information about the land purchased by Sergio or help Roberto in his claim for the rights of possession of the farm. They indicated that since the arrangement had been personal and informal, the company could not become involved formally in the dispute between Sergio and Roberto. At this point, Roberto decided to adopt a "wait and see" attitude regarding Sergio's claim against his farm. He explained to the investigator that he really had no choice. He had no legal title to the land and the only way he could present his claim to the rights of possession was in answer to a formal legal challenge. He therefore waited for Sergio to act.

Sergio's next move, however, was so unorthodox that the repercussions are still affecting the dispute to this day. About six months after Sergio demanded that Roberto vacate his farm, he went to Sierpe bearing "legal papers" he wanted Roberto to sign. He found Roberto sitting at a table in a local cantina and told him to sign the papers. Roberto refused, saying "I'm too drunk to read and too drunk to sign." Sergio persisted and Roberto continued to resist. Sergio then approached the owner of the cantina, Omar, and suggested that Omar sign the papers in Roberto's name. Omar had been close friends with Roberto for many years and has been operating the cantina in Sierpe since 1948. At first, Omar refused to sign the papers. Sergio continued to urge Omar to sign the papers, saying that they were not important, that it was only a "formality," and that Roberto could not possibly get hurt by it. Omar claims later that he was preoccupied in serving his customers and, after gaining further assurance from Sergio that it would not cause problems for Roberto, he agreed to sign the papers. Sergio told him to sign the name that appeared on the papers, which was "Roberto Daley;" however, Roberto's last name is Ortega. Omar said that this further convinced him that no harm could come to Roberto, so he signed the name Sergio told him to sign. Omar admits that he never read the papers. There were at least two other patrons present that day in the cantina and, although they had no idea at the time of the significance of what occurred, they later testified that this sequence of events is accurate.

In November 1982, approximately one year after Omar signed these papers, Sergio again went to Roberto's farm and demanded that he vacate the property. Sergio explained that according to the agreement he and Roberto had signed one year earlier, they both agreed that Roberto would stay one more year on the farm and at the end of that year he would turn over the rights of possession to the property to Sergio. Roberto protested, saying that he had not signed anything of the kind and that he had no desire to make any agreement with Sergio. He tried to show Roberto a copy of the agreement, but Roberto waved him off and said "get off my property and don't come back." As Sergio was leaving, he promised "further action." Sergio then went to Puerto Cortez to bring a denuncia against Roberto.

In February 1983 a formal summons was sent to the Sierpe guardia requiring Roberto to appear before the alcaldía in the Municipalidad de Osa. When Roberto learned of this, he immediately went to Puerto Cortez to speak to the alcaldía. She explained the basis of Sergio's denuncia and asked Roberto how he planned to react. Roberto told her his side of the story; how the company had given him the land, that he had built a house, cleared the land, and had been living there for the last nine years. During this conversation, the alcaldía indicated to Roberto that if he paid her about $100 she would make a decision in his favor. Roberto agreed but said he only had $75 with him; however, he added that had friends in Puerto Cortez from whom he could borrow the rest of the money. He then left the office in search of the necessary $25.

Roberto reports that when he returned about three hours later, the *alcaldía* had changed her mind, claiming that her secretary had overheard the negotiation and she was afraid of jeopardizing her job. She told Roberto that it was better if they continued the case according to established legal procedure and suggested Roberto contact a lawyer. Roberto reports he left her office angry and confused, did not contact a lawyer, and instead returned to his farm in Sierpe.

Three months later, in April 1983, Roberto received another summons to appear in the Municipalidad de Osa. However, he elected not to go, primarily because his health had begun to deteriorate and because he no longer trusted the *alcaldía*. As he said later, "First she offered to decide in my favor if I paid her money, then she changes her mind, then she sends me another summons. I ignored it. I thought she was crazy!"

One week after the date of the summons had passed, Roberto was arrested by the Sierpe guardia and put into the local jail. He spent the night there and, in the morning, managed to persuade the guardia to let him go by telling them he was an old man in failing health (Roberto was seventy years old at this time) and that he was not about to run away. The guardia agreed on the condition that Roberto present himself to the Municipalidad de Osa in Puerto Cortez. Instead, he went to San José where he entered the hospital for two weeks. When Roberto returned to Sierpe from the hospital, he received another summons to appear in Puerto Cortez. As the date of the summons approached, he left town once again and went to Puerto Limón on the Atlantic coast of Costa Rica. He had family (sons and daughters) in Puerto Limón with whom he stayed for about three weeks. In this manner, Roberto avoided the court date in Puerto Cortez for the next eight months.

Finally, in February 1984, an order was issued to arrest Roberto on sight and take him to Puerto Cortez. That same month, when Roberto returned to Sierpe from a hospital visit, he was arrested and taken to the jail in Puerto Cortez. Roberto was required to answer formally the *denuncia* placed against him by Sergio and, after four days in jail, was released. Roberto then returned to Sierpe to Omar's cantina, where he occasionally had been living and working since April 1983. Roberto had been paying a caretaker to stay at the house on his farm during this time.

Then, in May 1984, several of the guardia from Palmar Norte and Puerto Cortez, appeared on the road alongside Roberto's farm. They stood in a loose formation across from the house, all carrying

M-1 carbines. Roberto was brought to his farm by the Sierpe guardia and an officer from the Municipalidad in Puerto Cortez, and was then read a formal order signed by the alcaldía. The order commanded the guardia to remove all people living on the farm, their personal possessions, and any animals on the property.

Roberto started crying, the caretaker's wife was crying, and the caretaker became very angry. The caretaker asked the officer in charge what he was supposed to do with all his personal possessions, pointing out that it was raining outside and he had no other place to go. The officer replied that he was sorry it was raining but that the order had to be followed. He told the caretaker that his personal possessions had to be off the property in the next half-hour and that the caretaker should put his possessions out on the road, rain or no rain.

During the next half-hour the caretaker and his wife, helped by several members of the guardia, moved all their personal possessions out of the house and onto the road. A few members of the guardia were sympathetic, apologizing but saying they had no choice. While this was happening, other members of the guardia opened a gate in Roberto's fence and chased his cows out of the pasture and onto the road. At that time, Roberto had nine head of cattle and about twenty five chickens. During the whole procedure, Roberto sat on the ground, his back against the wall of his house, staring out over his farm, tears rolling down his cheeks. On the road about a kilometer from the house, standing beside a car was a person watching the evacuation. Roberto recognized the car as belonging to Sergio.

After the caretaker had made arrangements with a friend to carry his possessions to Sierpe in a pickup truck, the guardia openly warned Roberto not to return to his house, yet whispered to Roberto that he could move back after they left. About two hours later, the caretaker got permission from a local cattleman to allow Roberto's cows to use his pasture until other arrangements could be made. Various households in Sierpe offered to take care of his chickens.

The next day, Roberto went to Puerto Cortez. He said he wanted to talk to a lawyer, with whom he had done business in the past. While he was in Puerto Cortez, one of Sergio's workers brought a bulldozer onto his pasture and began leveling it in preparation for the planting of rice. When he returned from Puerto Cortez, he reported that the lawyer told him that Sergio had paid the *alcaldía* to decide the case in his favor. The lawyer and one other friend had both mentioned the same amount of money, $500. Roberto said excitedly:

I'm going to win! That woman is crazy! She's screwing me! The lawyer is talking to people in San José. We're going to get her out of there. She's no good. But I'm going to win this case. I'm going to win!

In February 1984 the woman was removed as alcaldía in Puerto Cortez and a new alcaldía was appointed. About a month after the original alcaldía had left, one of the investigators asked Roberto's lawyer in Puerto Cortez about the bribe. The lawyer would say only that money had been paid, but refused to say how much or to comment further on the case.

For the next two months, Roberto continued to live with Omar in the cantina in Sierpe while Sergio planted a rice crop on Roberto's former pasture. Then, in July, Roberto moved back into his house on the farm and brought most of his personal possessions. However, he left his cows on another person's pasture because he was afraid if the cows destroyed Sergio's rice crop he would attract attention to the fact that he had moved back to the house on his farm.

During the next few months, Roberto continued to live on the farm without any problems from Sergio or the local guardia. After Sergio's workers harvested the rice crop in December, he moved his cows back onto the pasture. He was also advised by his lawyer to provide proof to the Municipalidad in Puerto Cortez that he had lived on the land for the previous twelve years. He circulated a petition among the local residents in and around Sierpe and approximately two hundred people signed it. His lawyer then formally submitted the petition in the Municipalidad de Osa in Puerto Cortez in support of Roberto's claim to the rights of possession on this farm. The lawyer talked informally with both the alcaldía and Sergio, telling them that if any further orders were issued to remove Roberto from his farm, the lawyer would take the matter to the authorities in San José. Roberto also said the lawyer told Sergio that if he wanted to claim the land, then he would have to pay Roberto for working and living on Sergio's farm for the last four years and that Roberto would charge 160 *colónes* a month for his services plus 600 *colónes* for the house.

In June 1985, Sergio made another denuncia against Roberto in the Municipalidad in San Isidro, a town 156 kilometers north-east of Puerto Cortez. Both Roberto and Omar received a summons to appear before the alcaldía in San Isidro on July 16. According to Roberto's lawyer, this denuncia claimed that Roberto and Omar had made false representations in the signing of the papers Sergio brought to Sierpe in November 1981. These were the papers in which Omar signed the name "Roberto Daley" even though Roberto's last name is Ortega. Apparently, Sergio claimed that neither Roberto nor Omar informed him the name was wrong and that they, in fact, conspired to sign the wrong name.

Furthermore, in June 1985, the Sierpe guardia, who are sympathetic toward Roberto, warned him that another order was being prepared to remove him from his farm. The *guardia* said that the order would be coming from Puerto Cortez, but when asked how they knew about it, one merely remarked "we heard about it." This time, however, Roberto worked out a strategy with the Sierpe guardia. It was decided that when and if the Sierpe *guardia* received such an order, they would comply and he would be required to vacate his farm. However, since the job of the guardia is to maintain order and protect the citizens of Sierpe, they would then leave and Roberto would simply move back onto his farm. The guardia would be satisfied because they had complied with the order and Roberto would be satisfied because, except for the inconvenience of moving out on the road, he would be allowed to return.

On July 16 Omar failed to make the trip to San Isidro to testify, partly because he did not have the money for a bus ride and Roberto had made no arrangements for him. Omar points out that:

> The law in Costa Rica is the pen and paper and not the steel law of pistol and bullet. This is good and the way it should be. But to get into the law takes money—money makes the law go around. This is too bad, but that's the way it is.

Omar was willing and eager to go, not only to help his friend Roberto, but also to clear his own name in the denuncia. However, Omar's health had also been deteriorating. He is very old (he has no official identification card or birth certificate, but he claims to be over one hundred years of age), and is also suffering from the effects of a broken leg suffered in an earthquake.

Roberto also did not go to San Isidro, because he was in the hospital in Puerto Cortez. He had been there for over two weeks and was reported to be seriously ill. One of the investigators visited Roberto and talked with him in his hospital room. Roberto was thin, weak, and very short of breath. Although he complained bitterly about his health and the boredom of the hospital, he remained concerned about "that damn Italian trying to steal my farm." He said that he had arranged for his lawyer to represent him before the judge in San Isidro and was confident he would win the case.

The court in San Isidro heard the case presented by Roberto's lawyer and accepted as evidence the petition attesting to Roberto's rights of possession to the farm in Sierpe. The judge announced that the final court meeting would be held in three months on October 18. In the meantime, the alcaldía in San Isidro would study the evidence presented by both sides and make an official inspection trip to examine the disputed territory. Omar received another summons to appear at this next court session.

However, in mid-August one of the investigators heard that a number of residents of Sierpe were planning to take over Roberto's farm. These were mainly young people who either lived in the same house with their parents or were living in their own houses on their parents' lots. A number of these people were interviewed, and it was discovered that several large families in Sierpe lived together on the same plot of land—sons and daughters and their families who could not relocate, because they could not afford to buy or rent their own lots. They all said that they liked and respected Roberto, but now it appeared he was dying; they were concerned that the farm could fall under the control of either that "crook Omar" or Roberto's relatives. They seemed well-acquainted with the facts of Roberto's dispute with Sergio, and knew that Roberto had never gained official title to the land. These circumstances, coupled with their redefinition of Omar and the fact that land within fifty meters of any navigable waterway was considered "public territory," convinced these people that they had a legitimate right to take over the property.

The "squatter movement" was highly organized—it even had its own committee of president, vice-president, treasurer, and others—with a quick and efficient system of communication and a list of those most in need of their own plot of land. The plan was to wait for an opportune moment, then move to the farm en masse, divide the land into small lots, and build bamboo huts on each lot. These huts were necessary because any structures built on a plot of land provided one of the requirements for a claim to the rights of possession. These structures would be nothing more than four bamboo poles stuck into the ground with a palm-leaf roof, but their presence satisfied the letter of the law. Roberto died in Palmar Norte at 9 o'clock on the morning of August 7. By noon that same day there were approximately fifty huts erected on Roberto's pasture. Many residents of Sierpe who did not have their own plot of land came together and in an orderly and coordinated "invasion," moved to occupy Roberto's farm. The land was divided into lots thirty meters wide and fifty meters long, and assigned to each claimant on a first-come first-serve basis. The guardia of Sierpe knew what was happening, but did not react. Asked what she thought of the takeover of Roberto's farm, one woman remarked that "no one has made any formal complaint about it and no laws were broken, so what can we do?" The guardia went on to say that they sympathized with the takeover, saying that they thought it was better if Roberto's farm provided lots for people who had none, rather than allowing Sergio a chance to absorb it into his already vast landholdings.

The next day Roberto's relatives arrived in Sierpe from Puerto Limón (on the Atlantic coast of Costa Rica). At first they were quite surprised and upset by the swift takeover of their father's farm, but as one son explained to one of the investigators, they did not have the interest, time, or resources to fight a court battle with fifty families for control of the property. The children then went to the farm with a member of the Sierpe guardia, who was to act as an official "witness," and told the leaders of the takeover that the squatters could remain on the farm and they would not press charges or attempt to regain control of the farm. That same afternoon a representative of Sergio also arrived at the farm and told the squatters that Sergio was also dropping his claim on the disputed land.

In review, the nature of the social relationships among the people involved in this dispute is quite intricate. Sergio and Roberto had a *simplex* relationship. Also, Roberto was an insider in the Sierpe community while Sergio was considered an outsider. However, Sergio had significant access at the Municipalidad in Puerto Cortez (an "insider" at the formal control level) and managed to enlist the cooperation of the formal authorities. It is not clear whether or not this cooperation was gained with bribes, personal influence, or because Sergio's claims are actually legitimate.

On the other hand, Roberto had the cooperation of the rank and file guardia, who ostensibly enforce the orders issued by the authorities in Puerto Cortez. At the time the first order to remove Roberto from his farm was being carried out, for example, two different members of the guardia whispered to the caretaker that after he had moved his personal possessions out on the road and the guardia had left, he was free to return. Here, the formal legal system itself can be viewed as being divided into two opposing *informal* arrangements of relationships; Sergio and the alcaldía on one side and Roberto and the guardia on the other.

On at least two occasions, the Sierpe guardia made arrangements with Roberto allowing him to return to his farm after they evicted him. Some of the rural guardia in Sierpe have become quite integrated into the community—not only are they the formal representatives of state authority, but they are also friends and neighbors who have developed personal allegiances. The guardia in Sierpe had developed a multiplex relationship with Roberto which influenced their official behavior; they attempted to protect their continuing relationship with Roberto. Here, the motives of private individuals behind the public offices has a significant influence on the performance of the official duties and responsibilities of that office.

It is not clear how the relationship of the alcaldía in Puerto Cortez with Sergio can be characterized—both have been unavailable for comment. However, charges of bribery have surfaced during the course of this dispute. We have not been able to verify such charges, but they have been offered with strong conviction. In fact, the belief that influence peddling and the payment of bribes is common in disputes involving the formal authorities is quite widespread among the people in the Sierpe community. In "The Inspection," for example, most people suggested that Mark take matters into his own hands because it was unlikely he could receive a fair hearing given the power, wealth, and influence of the other party. Whether or not these beliefs were justified, is not at issue here, but what is important is that people believe these allegations are true and that such attitudes may have a direct influence on how they will react to some offense or breach of expectations.

When considering access to the formal law, both Roberto and Sergio were offered the opportunity to make an informal agreement with the alcaldía. However, Roberto did not have enough financial resources and Sergio apparently outbid him for the services of the *alcaldía*.

On the other hand, neither Sergio nor the formal authorities had access to the insiders in Sierpe; that is, to the squatter movement. The simplex relationship between members of the squatter movement in Sierpe on the one side and Sergio and the *municipalidad* on the other is noteworthy. Here is a case where a common interest in alleviating the land shortage problem in Sierpe drew the insiders together and allowed them to use the resources of their informal social network to their advantage. Such resources included their combined strength (about one hundred people, including children) and fast and secret communications.

Cost—financial as well as personal—is also a central factor affecting the nature of this dispute. Roberto suffered considerable emotional anguish when he was removed from his farm. Also, Roberto became increasingly ill during the course of this dispute before his death. He had been to the hospital several times and his symptoms resembled a severe case of emphysema; he had trouble breathing and could walk only a few paces before he needed to stop and gulp for air. Under such conditions, Roberto's mobility was limited and a trip to Puerto Cortez or a visit to his lawyer was quite painful and inconvenient for him.

Cost of a financial nature is relevant, because Roberto had believed, as did many of his supporters, that if only he had the $100 to pay the bribe to the alcaldía he would not have had such problems. Roberto constantly reiterated this situation and complained about it. There is also the labor costs involved in Roberto's developing the farm. Roberto was willing to concede that it might be Sergio's land and he said he would leave the farm if Sergio would pay him for his work.

Moreover, time is an important factor in this dispute. Roberto used delaying tactics by planning his trips to the hospital in San José and Puerto Limón to stay out of sight of the guardia and avoid being arrested. In this manner, Roberto was able to delay part of the formal legal proceedings for eight months. The most important aspect of time in this case is related to how long Roberto had lived and worked on the property in dispute. In fact, this forms the entire basis for his defense. He did not have formal title to the land and could not prove that the United Fruit Company actually gave him the land, he could only claim the rights of possession based on the fact that he occupied the farm for over fourteen years and was entitled to some rights, for example, payment from Sergio for working on Sergio's land for four years.

Furthermore, there is also the issue of how to assess the termination of a dispute. This dispute was "formally resolved" at least once when Roberto was removed from the farm by the guardia and Sergio was allowed to plant and harvest a rice crop on Roberto's pasture. However, Roberto gradually moved back onto the land along with his animals and continued to live there as though nothing had happened. Just three months after the rice was harvested, the pasture appeared almost the same as it had previously and Sergio never regained possession or use of the land.

This case offers a clear example of one process by which part of a community became involved in a dispute between two people over the control of land, which in this instance, was a very scarce resource. Apparently, the pressures of a housing shortage in Sierpe prompted some residents to orchestrate a takeover of vulnerable property in the area. In interviews with several of the squatters' leaders, it became evident that Roberto's mounting legal difficulties with Sergio combined with his failing health convinced them that Roberto's farm was the perfect target. Their only problem, they explained, was timing— they did not want to aggravate Roberto by moving onto his farm while he was still alive—on the other hand they wanted to get there before Sergio could take over and before Roberto's children could stake a claim.

The takeover of Roberto's farm was planned in advance and was well-coordinated. On the Monday following the takeover, representatives of the squatters met with members of the Municipalidad de Osa in Puerto Cortez to solicit support by the local government of the occupation of Roberto's property. The municipalidad guaranteed that no action would be taken against the squatters and offered their support and assistance in any way they could, such as moving quickly to install a water pipeline and electricity.

This case illustrates how under certain conditions the local forces of informal social control can assume command over the course and outcome of a land dispute. Unlike the kind of community involvement described earlier in the dispute between Wilson and the Simo family, in which the Sierpe community was used merely as a witness "to stir up the municipalidad," this demonstrates how part of the community became an active participant, sweeping aside informal and formal arguments and managed both the land dispute and a housing problem in Sierpe.

This case reveals new insights into the structure of the informal social control infrastructure in Sierpe, demonstrated, in part, by the organized manner in which the takeover was planned and executed, as well as the success of those who would benefit by keeping the plans secret. As one squatter put it:

"We knew Roberto was dying but, of course, we had no idea when it might happen. This meant we had to be ready to move at a moment's notice and we had to be very quiet about it. If Sergio or Roberto's family or the *municipalidad* knew what was going on, they would have stopped us. We adults could keep our mouths shut, but we had to watch ourselves around the kids; they might not have understood the need for secrecy and could have talked about it to their friends.

When Roberto died (at nine o'clock on a Saturday morning), a friend with whom he had been staying in Palmar called Sierpe and notified Omar, Roberto's friend and partner for many years. The word spread quickly. Those in the squatter movement were informed by a special "messenger" running from house to house. These people dropped whatever they had been doing, rushed to Roberto's farm, and staked out their lot. Before noon the same day, there were fifty lots established on Roberto's pasture, all sprouting crude bamboo structures. The channels of communication in Sierpe can be fast and effective. Also, the takeover was accomplished with precision and discipline. In fact, this event could be described as a kind of peaceful "guerrilla action" undertaken by an "army of local residents with a clearly established objective," an innovative chain of command and the will and the means to take the law into their own hands.

This dispute was finally resolved by third parties who, up to the time of Roberto's death, were involved simply as interested bystanders. After his death, these people took matters into their own hands and resolved both the land dispute and part of the housing problem in Sierpe. Today, fifty families live on the disputed land which was named Pueblo Nuevo (new town). The decision regarding the outcome of the original dispute was thus taken out of the formal court system and settled in an informal manner by a movement within the community. This development expands upon the work that suggests how larger social movements can use the formal court system to promote their goals (cf. Barkan 1985).

This case further exemplifies the problems of prediction in the investigation and analysis of disputes. Previous work suggesting possible influences on the dispute process did not serve to predict the "resolution" of this case. While the dispute process should be observed and analyzed from the perspective of the surrounding social context, this context is usually regarded as a more or less passive background or "stage setting" upon which the passion and drama of dispute would be played out. The direct and decisive action taken by the community, for example, as a form of self-help through collective interaction has not been adequately studied in prior work (cf. Kidder 1980–81; McAdam 1989).

Case 7:
The Absentee Landlord and the Local

In June 1981, three North Americans arrived on the Boca Río Sierpe to inspect land they were interested in buying. They had been directed to the area by Tom, the real estate agent who had sold property to George two years earlier. The land Tom was selling consisted of nine hundred acres he bought from Sanchez—the same land Sanchez had bought twelve years earlier from Pancho for $125. Tom had told the North Americans he would sell them the nine hundred acres for $1 million.

The North Americans asked Pancho, who had been hired by Tom to watch the land and keep away squatters, for permission to place tents next to his house while they examined the property for three or four days. They told him that they were considering cutting the trees and exporting the wood to the United States. They also said they were very interested in mining the gold in the area and that they had available both the necessary equipment and technology. After two days of examining the land, the North Americans expressed disappointment to Tom that he had not told them that there was a substantial area of the property which was low, bog land; very wet and bare of any timber except mangrove trees. In addition, after asking several questions pertaining to gold mining and mineral rights, they learned from Pancho that ownership of the land would not be necessary in order to obtain a concession from the Costa Rican government to mine the gold. They said that Tom had not mentioned this to them either—even though they had told him they were very interested in mining the gold.

On the second day of the inspection, Pancho's friend Jorge, who has a small farm situated in mangrove swamps about one kilometer east of the mouth of the Sierpe River, came to visit Pancho. Jorge was also interested in selling his farm and asked a local acquaintance of the North Americans (who was also a North

American) if he would introduce him to the group of investors. Jorge said that his farm was approximately eighty acres, most of it heavily wooded, with about three acres of avocadoes, bananas, oranges, and cacao. The land also included two freshwater streams that flowed year round and a house in good condition. Jorge said that he wanted about thirteen hundred dollars for the farm. The offer was relayed to the North Americans who expressed considerable interest in the offer. One of them said, "To hear of an eighty-acre farm for thirteen hundred dollars is amazing, especially after looking at the property Tom wants to sell us for one million. Of course we're interested!" The North Americans went with Jorge and the contact to see Jorge's farm. The group was intrigued by the mazelike mangrove swamp which led to Jorge's farm and they liked the privacy and security it offered.

After a brief tour of the farm, the North Americans said that they wanted to buy the property and began to negotiate with Jorge. However, Jorge told them he did not have the legal title, only the rights of possession based upon his having lived and worked on the land for the previous ten years (see Appendix A). He added that he had cut a *carril* around the property—a two-meter wide path cut through the jungle to mark the boundaries of the farm. The North Americans said that they required a formal title and would attempt to legally obtain one. They initially would pay Jorge a down payment of $300 and would pay the remainder of the money when they received the formal title. Jorge agreed to the terms and issued a receipt for the down payment.

Approximately one month later, in July 1981, one of the North Americans, Bob, returned to the Boca. He said they had begun the process of getting title to the farm, which involved hiring a land surveyor to map the property. Bob said the surveyor was due at the Boca in two weeks. The surveyor arrived as scheduled, accompanied by Tom, and surveyed the farm for two days before returning to San José. Over the following weeks Bob continued to visit the Boca with his wife on two- or three-day visits. He reported that the process of acquiring the title was much more involved than anticipated, but that he and his partners had retained the services of a lawyer in San José and were continuing their efforts to secure the title.

In December 1981, Bob said that they had encountered a complication in completing the title process primarily because a conflict surrounding the land had become public. Bob said that Jorge's neighbor, Philipe, had formally protested the granting of a title to Jorge's farm. He reported that Philipe had contested the location of the boundaries of the farm. A necessary element of the title granting process in Costa Rica is that each neighbor whose land borders the land to be sold must agree formally to the position of the boundaries before the title can be issued. Philipe refused to sign the release, which stated that he agreed to the location of the boundaries.

Jorge became quite angry when he heard about the protest and immediately went to Pancho's house to complain about Philipe's actions. Jorge said that he had worked for Philipe through intermediaries from time to time, and that Philipe had never contested the location of the boundaries of Jorge's farm. However, Jorge said that Philipe was a "rich millionaire lawyer who likes stepping on the campesinos. He's a son-of-a-bitch and because he is rich I can do nothing about it!" Asked what *could* possibly be done to challenge Philipe, Jorge replied that he did not know but said that he would need to hire a lawyer to determine how best to proceed, or else he would need to make a trip to Puerto Cortez. Jorge said, however, that he did not have the money to pay for either the lawyer or a trip. Jorge mentioned that a trip to Puerto Cortez would involve a minimum of two or three days to complete, since he would have to either travel by canoe and paddle, or pay for a ride in someone else's boat.

About one year later, in December 1982, while on a trip to San José, Mark called Bob to ask him what the results had been of efforts to acquire title to Jorge's farm. Bob told him that although they were still trying, they had little hope of gaining the title. He said that Philipe had insisted that part of the land claimed by Jorge was actually his and that Jorge had no right to sell property he did not legally own. Bob said that Jorge was required to respond to the legal challenges made by Philipe, if Jorge could not or would not make the necessary response, then the North Americans would not legally be allowed to buy the property and Jorge would forfeit the down payment.

Although the dispute concerns the location of boundary lines, no denuncias have ever been made. Philipe is not trying to alter the boundaries or remove Jorge from the land, but is only attempting to block the sale of the land within the boundaries Jorge claims. Jorge thinks that he retains the rights of possession, but not the right to sell the land. As long as Jorge or members of his family posses the land, Philipe must recognize their rights of possession. However, if the farm is to be sold, the boundaries will need to be adjusted formally to the satisfaction of Philipe. Jorge contends that the boundaries he claims are fair and correct, and have been the same since he has been on the land, but he says he does not have the resources to formally challenge Philipe. Jorge and his family continue to live and work on the farm, Jorge still complains occasionally about Philipe interfering with the sale of the land, and he no longer visits Philipe's farm while Philipe is there. Meanwhile, the North Americans who originally agreed to buy Jorge's farm and paid the down payment have not returned to the Boca Río Sierpe.

In December 1984, when Jorge was asked what had transpired in his dispute with Philipe, he said that they were no longer disputing. Jorge said that both Philipe and a few insiders on the Boca had told him that the "real problem" with the land sale was with the North Americans. Apparently Philipe had told his workers that he never had a disagreement about the location of the boundary lines, that the "trouble was with the gringos; they just didn't know what they were doing." One of the employees on Philipe's tourist project said that Philipe had asked his workers—some of whom are insiders on the Boca—to pass this message on to Jorge.

Jorge said he was relieved to hear there was no boundary line problem with Philipe, and that he and Philipe "have made peace." Jorge now works on Philipe's tourist project.

Philipe, however, apparently had other plans in mind for Jorge's farm. Philipe had already told some of his workers:

> I don't want anyone else to own that farm. My property extends from the Boca Río Sierpe to the Estero Guerra [the mangrove swamps along the eastern edge of the Boca]. There are only three other small farms in this area and they're all surrounded by my farm. I hope to buy these farms eventually and control the whole eastern part of the Boca. Those gringos wanted to buy Jorge's farm and get formal title. This would have ruined my plans. It was a simple matter to stop the whole process and so I did.

In review, the actors in this case include a Costa Rican absentee landlord, a group of North Americans who were relatively inexperienced in Costa Rica, and a long-time local resident of the Boca Río Sierpe. Philipe, the absentee landlord, is a lawyer who lives and

works in San José, but visits his property on the Boca approximately twice a month. Because of his frequent trips to the Boca and the
fact that he now employs about eighteen local people on his tourist
project, Philipe has become a "marginal insider" on the Boca.
Although he is still viewed as an absentee landowner and a "rich
man" who cannot be trusted by many residents of the Boca, he has
established a strong presence in the area and enjoys some access to
the local informal social network. Importantly, Philipe is an insider
in his relationship within the network of formal social control.
Because he is a lawyer, lives in San José, and controls many
resources, Philipe has considerable influence and power within the
formal social control arena. He could have used his knowledge and
resources in attempting to control outcomes of the dispute if Jorge
or the Americans had challenged Philipe over the location of the
boundaries of Jorge's property on the formal level.

All the members of the North American group buying the
land can be considered outsiders on the Boca Río Sierpe. Jorge, on
the other hand is an insider—a local worker who has lived on this
particular farm for approximately ten years. While Jorge is considered an insider by members of the local community, it is unclear
to what extent, if any, he has attempted to influence local opinions and definitions of the dispute. Jorge initially moved to the
farm when asked by the previous owner to act as caretaker while
the owner was away; however, the owner never returned and did
not pay Jorge for taking care of the farm. Jorge remained on the
farm and now claims it as his own. The property has never been
officially recorded in the public registry at the government land
offices in San José and thus has no formal title.

Although Jorge claims that his relationship with Philipe has
always been cordial, he said that he has also felt that there existed
un obstaculo secreto—a secret obstacle—between him and Philipe.
Asked what he thought the barrier might be, Jorge replied,
"[Philipe] is a professional man, a rich man, with cars and boats
and motors and a big house in San José, and I am a poor
campesino—a man of the country. We are not on the same level.
He was always friendly to me, but I couldn't say we were ever
friends." Jorge added that their only meeting was when he was visiting with Philipe's caretaker while Philipe was present. Jorge also
said that although his farm is surrounded on three sides by
Philipe's property, there were no previous disagreements or conflicts over the location of the boundary lines. The nature of their
social relationship can therefore be described as simplex; there

never was extensive personal involvement between the two, and thus never any need or desire to maintain the relationship.

The involvement of this North American group introduces a cultural factor which contributed to the emergence of the dispute. Philipe may have always had doubts about the location of the boundary lines—or secret plans for Jorge's farm—but it was not until the North Americans attempted to buy the farm that a dispute became public.

The fact that Jorge is a "poor campesino" is another important factor in this dispute; he claims not to have had the financial resources to challenge Philipe's claim. Thus, Jorge's involvement in the dispute was reduced to complaining about Philipe's actions. Jorge thinks his only resource is to avoid conflict. Furthermore, it is generally assumed by Sierpe residents that Philipe has the resources and expertise to initiate and sustain any legal actions. The wide disparity in social and economic resources between Philipe and Jorge demonstrates not only the relevance of the nature of the social relationship between disputants, but also the relative strengths and weaknesses of social positions.

The issue of access to mediating parties or formal authorities is an additional consideration in the dispute. Because Jorge lives in the isolated wilderness of the Boca Río Sierpe, far from telephones or formal legal services, he feels he has no other alternative but to "lump it"—that is, to accept the limitations of his circumstances and do nothing. When asked why he didn't seek the help of friends and relatives, Jorge replied, "Because they're as poor as I am." Philipe, however, lives in San José near the offices of government agencies and he has no problems of access to formal authorities. The cost of maintaining a dispute is also clearly a factor that affected the level of access available to Jorge in this case. As Laura Nader (1984b: 962) has stressed poignantly:

> When law is a product, like a product it meets a demand and law viewed as a product is commercialized. Money then dictates who the users of the system are to be. If law is to respond to justice—to human needs and the distribution of rights, opportunities, and remedies—then the manner of practicing law is different. What if the user cannot be a payer?

We want to reiterate that the factors we have discussed, including the nature of the social relationship and social position of Jorge and Philipe, access to the forums of formal social control, as well as cost, are all interrelated and overlap. Jorge could not gain access to formal social control because he lacked the necessary resources. Philipe, however, apparently had no problem with access or cost, because of his vast personal resources. Also, Philipe's status as a marginal insider allowed him access into the local informal social network. He used this access in the management of this dispute by communicating with Jorge and convincing him that the "real problem" in the emergence of this dispute was the North Americans' ignorance of Costa Rican land laws. In fact, Philipe blamed the problem between him and Jorge on the North American outsiders.

Time as a variable affecting the nature of this dispute is relevant primarily with respect to the North Americans. After more than a year of dealing with their lawyer and Philipe, the North Americans dropped their proposal, due to waning interest and a growing sense of futility. They said that while they were waiting for developments in their attempts to purchase the farm, they became involved with other projects in Costa Rica and gradually lost the interest and desire to continue with the title acquisition process. They said that they had been informed by their lawyer that they could answer Philipe's challenge on Jorge's behalf, but by this time they were no longer interested and, according to one of the North Americans, "were simply afraid of getting into a long and protracted legal proceeding which might have cost us more than the farm was worth." Time is also a factor in relation to how long Jorge has occupied the farm. Since he has lived and worked on the property for more than ten years, it appears that he has gained the rights of possession and is relatively secure in his legal control of the property. However, if he should abandon the property, it will once again become "up for grabs," and he may lose the rights of possession to the property.

Finally, there is another aspect of the time factor demonstrated in this case. As time passed, Jorge and Philipe eventually resolved some of their differences and the dispute ceased to be a sharp point of contention. In fact, the dispute simply "faded away." Thus, the nature of their relationship has changed from simplex to multiplex—Jorge now works for Philipe and depends on him for part of his livelihood.

This case traces another process by which the nature of a social relationship can evolve and produce unexpected effects on the management of a dispute. While the changing relationship from simplex to multiplex affected the way in which this dispute was managed, it is clear that other factors may determine whether the case resurfaces in the future. The potential for conflict may still exist, for example, if someone else tries to buy Jorge's farm in the future. The case also points to the importance of extending work, which considers the impact of who uses the law and under what conditions (Merry 1990). People studying the resolution or management of disputes have only recently become systematically informed by focusing upon the advantages, not only of who has the resources to use the law, but who repeatedly uses the law (cf. Nader 1984b).

Case 8:
The Inspection

In June 1982, a North American, Mark, bought a farm near Estero Guerra, a wide, deep channel that winds through the mangrove swamps along the edges of the Boca Río Sierpe. The property consists of thirty five acres with one small house and a freshwater spring. Mark was a stranger when he arrived on the Boca in June 1980, but by the time he bought the farm in June 1982, he was fairly well known in the area and was becoming increasingly familiar with the language and culture.

The facts of this case began when he heard of a local Costa Rican, Juan, who wanted to sell his farm. Mark, Juan, and a local neighbor, Philipe, who had a law practice in San José, met in the farmhouse to draw up a bill of sale. There was no formal survey of the farm; thus, the physical dimensions of the property described in the bill of sale are approximate and include a description of forty acres of land with about three hundred meters of river frontage. The lawyer, Philipe, witnessed the transaction and notarized the paper after Mark and Juan had signed it.

During the next two years, Mark cleared about two acres of land and planted four hundred hybrid cacao trees as well as seventy five banana and plátano trees on part of his farm. Occasionally, he lived and worked on the farm during one- or two-week periods, but most of the time he paid a local Costa Rican to live on the farm as a caretaker.

In April 1984, Philipe went to Mark's farm with several of his workers and put up a fence about two hundred meters inside what Mark thought was the western boundary of his farm. When Mark's caretaker protested the action, Philipe said, "If Mark wants to fight about it, tell him I'll meet him in criminal court in San José." On May 3, 1984, Mark's caretaker traveled to Mark's residence in Sierpe to tell him what happened on the farm.

Mark's first inclination was to tear down the fence. In fact, he received support for this idea from several people he talked to the following day in Sierpe. A local Costa Rican friend who had lived in the Sierpe area for forty years told Mark to "go down to the farm and rip it [the fence] out, throw it away." In response to inquiries about Philipe, Mark was told by several people that he was a "rich man, a lawyer in San José with powerful political connections. For twenty years, he was the Chief Justice of the Supreme Court of Costa Rica!" The general consensus was that Mark would have no chance of winning a court battle against Philipe and he was advised to take action on his own behalf immediately, to tear down the fence so that "Philipe will have some respect for you. Don't be afraid of him. That's what he's counting on. Fight back! Tear down the fence!"

Mark did not want to risk removing the fence, however, without confirmation that his actions would be appropriate. He explained later that, despite thinking that taking down the fence might be illegal, he still had considerable difficulty deciding how to proceed. He had been told by many people to take matters into his own hands, usually with reference to ideas of machismo and self respect. He felt pressure to yield to public opinion, even if it meant acting against his own judgment. Rather than tear down the fence, Mark called Juan, the person who had sold him the farm, told him what had happened, and asked him to come to Sierpe to confirm the boundary line. He told Juan that he would pay all the expenses for the trip and Juan agreed to come to Sierpe in three days.

Juan arrived in Sierpe òn May 10. He and Mark traveled downriver to the farm. They studied the exact placement of the fence, and Juan then showed Mark the boundary line, pointing to a short stake in the ground placed by a land surveyor in 1980. The marker confirmed that the fence was on Mark's land. Mark wanted to tear down the fence but Juan cautioned him against it saying "the fence must have cost much to put up, including labor, and maybe you shouldn't tear it down. You might get in serious trouble. Philipe is a lawyer and knows all the tricks."

Although Mark had sworn to tear down the fence, he hesitated, deciding to take the matter to the local authorities as Juan had suggested. Upon returning to Sierpe, Mark contacted the local guardia and told them about the fence. One of the guardia suggested making an "inspection trip" to the farm, explaining that such a trip was necessary before further legal proceedings could be initiated. They also said that Mark would need to provide a motor-powered boat, gas, and about $25 to finance the trip. He agreed and made arrangements for the inspection to be conducted the following day.

The next day, Mark and two members of the Sierpe *guardia* traveled downriver to the farm in Estero Guerra. The guardia noted the location of the fence and then Mark showed them the stake placed there by a land surveyor in 1980. He explained that the fence was approximately two hundred meters inside the surveyor's marker and that the land now fenced off included all the cacao and banana trees he had planted over the past two years. The guardia ate lunch at the farm and returned to Sierpe the same day. On their return to Sierpe, the guardia told Mark to wait for their decision. They said a member of the guardia would be going to Puerto Cortez soon and would notify the alcaldía about the results of their inspection trip.

After waiting a week without hearing from the guardia, Mark decided to go to their office in Sierpe to ask what had happened. He was told that the guardia had not yet been to Puerto Cortez and he was advised to come back "in the next few days." After waiting another week, Mark returned to the office of the guardia and was told that he must go to Puerto Cortez in order to make a formal denuncia against Philipe. The guardia told Mark that they had related the details of their inspection trip to the alcaldía's secretary in Puerto Cortez and that the secretary was waiting to hear from him.

Initially, Mark did not have enough money to go to Puerto Cortez and had to postpone the trip a week. During the first week in June 1984, he went to Puerto Cortez with his bill of sale and a survey map showing the location and approximate dimensions of his farm. Mark made his formal complaint against Philipe, which consisted mainly of telling his side of the story. When the secretary asked if Mark had any witnesses, he gave the names of three long-term residents of the area who he thought should know the location of the boundary lines. He was told that the witnesses would need to give their statements in Puerto Cortez before an inspection trip could be arranged by the alcaldía. Mark protested, saying that he had spent a lot of money for the inspection by the Sierpe guardia. The secretary shrugged his shoulders and said there was nothing "they" could do, because an inspection by the Sierpe *guardia* meant nothing and that the inspection by the alcaldía would be necessary.

Over the course of the next month and a half, Mark's three witnesses made their formal declarations in Puerto Cortez. Mark was required to pay the expenses (approximately $10) of only one witness, because the other two had made their declarations while in Puerto Cortez on other business. Two weeks after the last witness had testified, however, Mark still had not been notified by the alcaldía and contacted the Sierpe guardia. The guardia said they also had not heard from the alcaldía's office and suggested that Mark call Puerto Cortez. He called the *municipalidad* in Puerto Cortez several times without receiving information regarding his case.

On August 20, 1984, Mark made another trip to Puerto Cortez. After waiting three hours, he was ushered into the office of the alcaldía who made arrangements with Mark to make the necessary inspection trip on August 26. The alcaldía told Mark that he would need to provide transportation for her from Puerto Cortez to his farm and that he should provide her with lunch. Rather than discuss details of the inspection, she said she did not like onions or garlic, and asked that Mark make sure they were not included in the food for lunch. He asked her what would happen if he did not have the money to pay her expenses, and the alcaldía replied that he could wait perhaps another month until there was enough money available in the *municipalidad* treasury. Mark agreed to pay for the trip, because he felt that too much time had already passed.

Approximately three days later, he was visited by a Costa Rican friend who said that he had talked to his cousin, who was the alcaldía in Puerto Cortez. Mark's friend reported that the alcaldía said it was possible for the inspection trip to be arranged at no cost to Mark, because the alcaldía enjoyed fishing and was planning a trip to the Boca Río Sierpe in the near future. Mark's friend would lend the alcaldía his boat and motor, and while she was on her fishing trip, she could stop at Mark's farm to conduct the inspection. Mark agreed to the arrangement and was told the fishing trip would be August 28. On that day, the *alcaldía* arrived in Sierpe with her two children and her mother; they had packed a lunch, brought fishing equipment, and had made arrangements for a boat pilot.

Mark accompanied them to the Boca, but by the time they arrived, the tide was too low for the boat to reach Mark's farm in order to make the inspection. Instead, the *alcaldía* and her family fished for several hours and caught a few fish before traveling on to Mark's farm in Estero Guerra. As Mark's worker fried the fish, the *alcaldía* made her inspection, looking first at the fence and then measuring the distance to the surveyed boundary line. After the inspection, the *alcaldía* told Mark to wait for her decision. She said she would contact the guardia in Sierpe who would then relay the message to Mark.

After one month with no response from the *alcaldía*, Mark made another trip to Puerto Cortez. He was told by a secretary that the *alcaldía* was not there. When Mark asked about the status of his case, the secretary replied that the court process was confidential, but if Mark had a lawyer she could allow the lawyer to look at the file on Mark's case. Mark did not have enough money at that time to hire a lawyer and returned to Sierpe.

Approximately one week later, in the first week of October, Mark returned to Puerto Cortez and contacted a lawyer suggested to him by a friend in Sierpe. He told the lawyer the story, and said he wanted to know what was happening with the case. The lawyer agreed to represent Mark and they walked about three hundred meters from the lawyer's office to the *alcaldía's* office. After reading the file, the lawyer explained that Philipe had formally answered Mark's denuncia, saying that he had paid for that part of the farm in question, giving him a right to put up the fence. The lawyer suggested they demand that Philipe present legal proof that he had bought the disputed part of the farm. The lawyer made a formal request and Mark was then told to wait "about two weeks" before making contact with the lawyer again.

Toward the end of October, Mark made another trip to Puerto Cortez. The lawyer said he was on his way to the *alcaldía's* office and invited Mark to accompany him. They were told that nothing new had happened with the case except that Philipe formally had requested another inspection trip by a land surveyor. Philipe indicated that he could pay about $50 for the services of the surveyor. Mark said he would not trust any surveyor Philipe might hire, especially for the amount discussed. The lawyer explained that Philipe had the right to request another inspection, but that the court could provide an impartial surveyor. Mark was told that after the inspection trip was organized and the *municipalidad* had hired a land surveyor, he would be contacted so he could accompany them on the inspection. Mark asked when this might happen and was told in "about three weeks or so."

In the first week of January 1985, he was told by his worker that Philipe had made his inspection trip accompanied by the alcaldía without a land surveyor. One month later, Mark took another trip to Puerto Cortez and was told by the secretary that a decision had finally been made on his case in favor of Philipe. He was told that if he wanted to pursue the case any further he would need to contact a lawyer who could explain his options and represent him formally.

Mark has done nothing further regarding the case. The fence remains in place and the various cacao and banana trees Mark planted are maturing on the contested property. He reports that he has no intention of allowing the case to end. He is planning another trip to Puerto Cortez to talk to the lawyer about alternatives available to him, yet he concedes that so much time has already passed that he is no longer infused with the anxious indignation he once felt. He is weary of continuing the fight with Philipe, because it is a continuing drain on his time and financial resources. He says he cannot allow Philipe to win, however, especially since no land surveyor has ever been consulted. He plans on going to Puerto Cortez in the future to demand that a land surveyor be consulted and that the *municipalidad* pay for it.

As part of this investigation, Philipe was asked for his side of the story. He became very agitated as he said that Mark had no right to put a *denuncia* against him; that no one had ever put a *denuncia* against him in his life. He said he was a well-respected lawyer, knew the law, and always lived within the law. He said Mark's problem was with Juan, because Juan had lied to Mark about where the boundaries were located. When Philipe was asked if he had made any challenging remarks to Mark's worker when he put up the fence ("Tell Mark I'll meet him in criminal court!"), he said he had not. However, several of Philipe's workers were also interviewed and each one remembered Philipe making the remark. Philipe was then asked why a land surveyor had not been consulted in a dispute over a boundary line. He replied that *he* was not going to pay for a land surveyor, and that if Mark had wanted a surveyor he could have hired his own. The dispute was handled in the formal Costa Rican court system and can be said to be resolved legally. However, Mark does not accept the decision and is planning further action.

An analysis of this case reveals that the nature of the social relationship of the actors in this dispute is "simplex." Although

Philipe and Mark are neighbors on the Boca Río Sierpe, they have never entered into a continuing, personal relationship, nor are they likely to anytime in the future. Mark reports, however, that before Philipe put up the fence, their contacts with each other had always been cordial and, on occasion, they had done small favors for each other. In addition, since the building of the fence, Mark has been told about several instances when Philipe has made similar actions against other neighbors. Keeping in mind Mark's description of the discussions and exchanges of damaging information, which took place on the street corners and in the taverns of Sierpe:

> Crime brings together upright consciences and concentrates them. We have only to notice what happens, particularly in a small town, when some moral scandal has just been committed. They stop each other on the street, they visit each other, they seek to come together to talk of the event and to wax indignant in common. [Durkheim. 1964: 102]

Durkheim's observation seems particularly relevant in this case, because Philipe is regarded as a marginal insider. He lives in San José where he maintains a lucrative, successful law practice, and comes from an old, well-established, and wealthy family. Although he has several large landholdings in the area, makes regular trips to Sierpe, and enjoys some access to the informal social system, his social status is mostly outside the social context of the Sierpe community. Throughout the course of the dispute, Mark's conversations with the people in Sierpe served to further arouse his indignation against Philipe and bolster his resolve to fight Philipe in the courts.

This case was handled in an informal, almost casual manner by the formal authorities in Sierpe and the municipalidad de Osa in Puerto Cortez. Consider, for example, the meaningless inspection trip made by the guardia in Sierpe. Mark said that in this instance, he thought the guardia were simply taking advantage of his ignorance of Costa Rican legal procedures and his anxiousness to get the inspection completed. The only people who profited from the trip were the Sierpe guardia, who, by their own admission, divided the money Mark had paid them and had a "fiesta" in the local bars. In addition, the "formal" inspection trip made by the alcaldía while on a fishing holiday with her children and her mother seemed informal and ineffective. The alcaldía merely looked at the fence, considered the area where Mark said the boundary line ought to be, and noted the boundary marker placed in the ground by the surveyor in 1980. The alcaldía is not a land surveyor and, therefore, was unaware of precisely where the boundary line was located.

In this case, private identities conflict with official or public positions; however, it is not clear how these identities affected the course and outcome of this particular dispute. When Mark went on the first inspection trip with the Sierpe guardia, for example, he thought he was in the company of official representatives of the government who were performing their duties according to the law and regulations of the state. He had already rejected the advice of his informal "advisors" to take matters "into his own hands," because he lacked the knowledge and resources to respond effectively to Philipe's challenge, at least on an informal basis. Instead, he sought to introduce some measure of control and predictability into his management of the dispute by appealing to the formal legal process. The Sierpe guardia, however, had personal motives unknown to Mark. Also, while the alcaldía was, on the one hand, simply a private person on a fishing trip with her children and her mother, at the same time she was ostensibly acting in her official capacity as the alcaldía, which is regarded as a powerful and responsible position in the legal organization of the Municipalidad de Osa. In essence, such formalism often breeds "professionals" whose social statuses are a function of power they exercise over individuals and resources (Abel 1982a).

Although a decision was handed down in this case in favor of Philipe, there is no clear evidence available that would indicate that sufficient evidence existed to make a decision on the formal, legal level for either side. This dispute centers upon the location of a boundary line, and despite the fact there were three inspection trips made to the disputed area, no professional land surveyor was ever consulted. Furthermore, Mark has been unable to determine how or why a decision for Philipe was made in this case, because he must retain a lawyer to get access to the official file.

Thus, in exchange for the state's services in dispute management, Mark has had to give up a large part of his control of the dispute. The authorities took over management of the dispute according to the rules and dictates of the formal law, and Mark generally was not allowed into these legal proceedings except during the highly controlled legal rituals. Specific examples of these rituals included the rules controlling approach to the formal law, making a complaint, producing witnesses, inspection trips, and courtroom proceedings. In this sense, Mark complained bitterly about being "dependent" on the formal authorities:

> They told me what to do, when to do it, and how to do it. And I had no choice but to comply. Mostly, they told me to wait. I spent months waiting for the *municipalidad* to do whatever they had to do. Also, I couldn't get access to any information on my complaint unless I was accompanied by a lawyer. This was supposed to "protect" both parties from any personal interference. But all it did for me was to shut off all information about what was happening to my own complaint. I felt powerless, like everything was out of my control.

This illustrates an ironic twist in the process of the rationalization of law in Costa Rica. In an attempt to ensure legal equality by separating the formal law from political, moral, or economic interest, other consequences ensue—such as adding time and expense to the legal process—resulting in conditions allowing for unequal access and representation.

Therefore, it is obvious that the variables of time and cost have had an influence on this dispute. Consider, for example, the instances where Mark had to wait until he had the money to make the trip to Puerto Cortez, to pay for the travel expenses of his witnesses, or to pay for the services of a lawyer. He said that the money he paid to the Sierpe guardia was "money down the drain." He added:

> You get what you pay for. The trip didn't cost me anything, but that's just what I got; nothing. The main point of the trip was fishing, the "inspection" was treated as a side excursion. This was the first time I started feeling suspicious and uneasy about the whole process. Here was the alcaldía of the Municipalidad de Osa in shorts, raincoat, and big, floppy hat on a fishing holiday with her kids and mother. I couldn't help thinking of the worthless inspection trip by the Sierpe guardia. I didn't think she was taking my grievances very seriously and this scared me. I didn't know what the hell was going on.

Philipe, on the other hand, had considerable resources at his command, evidenced especially by the large "tourist resort" project he is currently building and financing himself on the Boca Río

Sierpe. Also, Philipe has two cars and a telephone, and is not hindered by the kind of transportation and communication problems Mark experienced. Philipe did not have to pay for the services of a lawyer, since he represented himself.

Inequality of personal resources had an important effect on the management of this dispute. Despite Philipe's advantage in resources, he did not have to spend much time and money during this dispute, simply because he did not make any formal complaints. He had already accomplished what he wanted by putting up the fence, which remains standing to this day. He seemed unconcerned with how much time had gone by, since he was not required to produce witnesses or make repeated trips to Puerto Cortez. Mark, however, *did* make a formal complaint and it was up to him to prove the validity of his claims. This is where the difference in personal resources played an important role; Mark could not sustain contact and access to the formal authorities and, in effect, "dropped" his formal complaint. He vows that if and when he gets more money, he will appeal the decision by the *alcaldía* and take his case to the next highest jurisdiction.

Meanwhile, Mark continues to complain about Philipe's fence, but his complaining is now restricted to the informal level. This brings us to another aspect regarding the time factor in this case. When the conflict with Philipe first arose, Mark was still something of an outsider in Sierpe and thus, Mark said, "I had very little help or support from the local people; I couldn't communicate that well and not many people knew me personally. During the first part of the fight I felt very alone and lost, totally dependent on the *municipalidad*." But as time went on, Mark became more integrated into the local social system and was regarded eventually as an insider in most social interactions, allowing him access to the informal social control infrastructure in Sierpe. This provided him with what he calls "a sense of belonging." He commented:

> As I got more proficient in Spanish and made more friends, I received some sympathy and support for my problem with Philipe. In fact, as I got more and more discouraged with the formal authorities, these friendships seemed to fill the gap in my frustration and anger. It provided me an outlet and a way to get my claims understood and validated. But I must admit, it hasn't done much to help me get rid of that damn fence.

This last statement reflects another point concerning this case that also relates to previous cases. Although informal social control may provide a kind of "compensation" for those unwilling or unable to manage their disputes on the formal level, the effects of the informal law in settling these disputes has been minimal. One explanation is because the informal sanctions available to the people of Sierpe (including shame, ridicule, or avoidance) could be most effective only if applied to other members of the same informal social structure. In fact, information we have concerning theft of personal property among local residents—that is, insiders against insiders—would seem to verify this. However, outsiders, such as persons from a different culture or absentee landlords, are rarely affected by such informal sanctions.

Thus, this case also illustrates that in disputes involving insiders and outsiders, insiders may often have a significant advantage in gaining support and validity for their claims among members of their informal social network. Clearly, the process of social solidarity is often more an attempt to control the definition of a dispute and deviance within the informal social network than an attempt to bring about resolution (Inverarity 1980). This factor is especially important from the point of view of our study, since the majority of the cases involved disputes between insiders and outsiders. This reaffirms our position that emphasizing the process of dispute *management* may be more useful for further studies than a continued emphasis on dispute *resolution*. Indeed, the majority of the cases we have examined are unresolved and continuing. Furthermore, we suspect that many similar cases that appear resolved on the formal level, for example, are unresolved at the informal level or may resurface again at the formal level in another form or under a new label (see Fitzpatrick 1988).

Case 9:
The Rainy Season

In October 1984, during the Costa Rican rainy season, Lopez and his partner, both of whom are long-time residents of the Boca Río Sierpe, were searching for gold in one of the many small spring-fed streams that flow through the low hills on Violínes Island. They were using shovels, gold pans, and a crude wooden sluice box. They searched for gold by shoveling material from the stream into the sluice, which was placed so that the running water from the stream washed the dirt, gravel, and other materials over the small wooden riffles at the bottom of the sluice. While working along a short, flat stretch of the stream, the men discovered a rich deposit of gold. Lopez said that the gold was located toward the bottom of the stream under about three to four feet of loose gravel and dirt, lodged against the bedrock. (Gold will usually work its way down through layers of lighter material until it reaches bedrock.) During the week following their initial discovery, the two prospectors found approximately one pound of gold.

Lopez and his partner then traveled upriver to the town of Sierpe for more provisions with plans to return to Violínes that afternoon to search for more gold. Lopez wanted the discovery to remain secret, at least until they could return to working the rich deposit found in the stream. However, Lopez's partner became drunk in a local cantina and boasted loudly of the large quantity of gold they had discovered. He did not reveal the exact location, but divulged that it was in a stream along the southern slopes of Violínes Island.

The story spread rapidly throughout the town of Sierpe. In a short time, Lopez's partner was surrounded by members of his family—two cousins and a brother. He invited these family members to return to Violínes Island to help him and Lopez dig out more gold. Lopez was displeased but eventually agreed to allow his partner's family to share the additional gold they might find. Lopez later explained that he did not mind if his partner wanted to help out family members. "And besides," he said, "there's enough for all of us and, if the deposit runs out, I know where I can always find more."

The five men left later the same day and paddled downriver to Violínes Island. Shortly thereafter, several local residents also traveled downriver in the hopes of finding their own fortune. One person stated that he had no idea exactly where Lopez had discovered the gold, but that he hoped to follow Lopez and his partners to the particular stream that had yielded the rich deposit. Asked if he expected to have problems with Lopez and his partners, or if he might be intruding on a personal gold claim, the person answered that all minerals in Costa Rica were equally available to each Costa Rican citizen and therefore Lopez had no special claim over the gold deposit. On the other hand, if Lopez had been formally granted a mineral rights concession, he could prohibit others from searching for gold in the same area.

Six days later, Lopez and his partners returned to town, took a bus to Palmar Norte and traveled by taxi to the town of Golfito, one of the largest towns in the southern zone of Costa Rica. The prospectors traveled to Golfito to sell their gold illegally, primarily because of its size and because Golfito is an ocean port visited by merchant marine seamen from around the world. The men hoped that these factors would allow them to receive a higher price for the gold and to be paid in U.S. dollars.

After returning from Golfito two days later, Lopez said that he and his four partners had mined another pound of gold from the same stream. It had yielded about $700 for each member of the team, which was comparable to about seven months' salary for many campesinos in the area. However, they had been working in the stream for only five days when Fernando, a Costa Rican absentee landlord who claims the rights of possession on several hundred acres on Violínes Island, arrived at their campsite in the hills of Violínes accompanied by three members of the rural guardia from Puerto Cortez. Fernando demanded that Lopez and his friends vacate the area immediately, claiming that they never asked permission to be on his land and that their presence was "upsetting" Fernando's cows and pigs on that part of the island. The guardia, from the office in Puerto Cortez, did not have a formal order from the judge or the alcaldía, or any other formal documentation. However, they said they were present to insure that Lopez and his partners complied "with the wishes of Fernando" and abandoned their gold mining operation immediately.

Lopez and his partners argued that as Costa Rican citizens they had the right to look for gold anywhere, providing they did not use any machinery. The guardia replied that while this was correct, they still needed to secure the permission of the landowner, and since Fernando did not want them there, they would have to leave. The gold prospectors continued to argue their case, demanding that Fernando present proof of ownership or his rights of possession before they would comply with his wishes. Fernando became quite angry and insisted that the prospectors leave, shouting loudly and threatening them with arrest. The guardia, who were armed with pistols or M-1 carbines, watched and listened to the exchange and remained silent. Lopez said that while Fernando did not actually use violence, he felt that the threat of violence was obvious. Subsequently, Lopez and his partners gathered their tools and camping gear, and left the area.

Lopez appeared angry as he told the story, and his partners in the gold mining enterprise confirmed the basic sequence of events.

When asked why the guardia were on hand to support Fernando's demands, Lopez replied that because the guardia had not presented official orders and since Fernando had not made any formal denuncia against them, that Fernando had probably bribed the guardia to secure their help. Asked if he was certain, Lopez answered that he was not absolutely sure of the allegations. However, he had been told by friends in Sierpe that the day after Lopez and his partners had come to Sierpe, Fernando also returned with the same members of the guardia. The guardia were reported to have had two large pigs tied up in the bottom of the boat. The pigs were then loaded into Fernando's truck, and he and the guardia left Sierpe in the same truck. Lopez said he believed that Fernando might have bribed the guardia with the pigs. Asked what he was going to do about it, Lopez shrugged his shoulders and said "What *can* I do about it? Fernando is a big man in this area and there is certainly not much we can do legally. But I know what I can do secretly." He explained that he would simply wait "until things cooled off" then secretly return to the same location and continue to mine the gold. This incident demonstrates that informal justice has the potential to expand the net of social control by supplementing formal apparatuses rather than replacing them (Abel 1982b).

Fernando was approached and asked if he was willing to answer questions about the dispute, but refused. However, his wife was willing to talk and said that the caretakers on the Violínes ranch had reported that many people were seen on the property and that Fernando "did not like it." Asked why, she replied that "We've had problems in the past with people sneaking over to Violínes and stealing our pigs or killing cows." She also said that the caretakers had called Fernando by shortwave radio and asked for help, saying there were "a lot of people walking around with shovels." Asked how Fernando had enlisted the help of the guardia, she replied that her husband had simply "called the police" reporting trespassers on his property, and "like good police everywhere," they responded to the plea for help.

One of the guardia from Puerto Cortez who accompanied Fernando to Violínes was asked about the incident. He said the *guardia* "knows Fernando well and all the problems he has on Violínes Island." Asked specifically what the problems are, he replied that "people have been stealing his pigs and cows and the coconuts along the beach; he uses them for pig food." He said that Fernando had established his rights of possession to the satisfaction of the guardia a long time ago, and that whenever he needed help with people trespassing on his property, the guardia would respond. When this member of the guardia was told that there were people in Sierpe who believed Fernando had bribed him and his colleagues with pigs, he laughed and said, "No, Fernando gave us no pigs." He said the law "was with Fernando because Fernando was right"—Costa Ricans can search for gold by law anywhere, providing they have the permission of the landowner. Since Fernando did not want anyone on his property he had the right to "kick them off."

In review, the nature of the relationships in this case is simplex; Lopez, his partners, and Fernando know one another, but the relationship is not highly valued and revolves around this single issue. Also, Fernando is regarded by the residents of the Boca to be an outsider, while Lopez has lived on the Boca for many years. There was no attempt to settle this dispute through informal mediation or negotiation; neither party had access to the informal social control system of the other and therefore could not utilize informal social control mechanisms to effectively attempt to end the dispute.

Although this dispute was not referred directly to the formal court system, representatives of the formal law—the Puerto Cortez guardia—were used to enforce Fernando's demands to remove Lopez from his land. Since Fernando did not make a formal complaint and the guardia acted without court orders, there is some question whether the actions of the guardia were in accordance with the formal regulations intended to govern their behavior. When questioned about the matter, one of the guardia involved in the incident at Fernando's property said, "Fernando's farm is well-known to us because he's had a lot of problems down there. We've seen the survey of the farm and all his papers, so he doesn't have to continually prove his property rights. If he has any more problems on Violínes we will respond and we don't need court orders or formal denuncias. If we had a similar relationship with you, you could expect the same kind of service."

When asked who had paid for the trip, he said, "Fernando paid, of course. The guardia do not have a boat and motor, and the *municipalidad* has no money so what can we do? If Fernando has the money, a boat, and a motor and wants us to check out his complaints, then he provides everything. This is not bribery, but the normal thing to do. We don't get anything out of it." When asked what might happen if a person with none of these resources wanted the guardia to investigate complaints, he answered, "They would have a problem, I admit. They can wait until the guardia have the money or ask a friend to help. This is a bad situation. But the Costa Rican government just doesn't have the money to finance better legal services. This might favor the rich over the poor, but what can we do?"

A legal secretary at the municipalidad de Osa was asked if formal rules had been followed in this particular case. "Yes," he said, "formal *denuncias* are made for special cases like property damage or invasion by squatters. But in a case where a landowner is well known and has already presented his papers, he only has to ask for assistance in case of trespass, and we will help him. Fernando is well known here and we know about his problems on Violínes, so anytime he needs our help we will give it."

These statements by the guardia and the legal secretary suggest that Fernando was within his rights to summon the guardia without making a formal complaint, and that the guardia could act without formal court orders. They also indicate that although Fernando was an outsider on the Boca, he was an insider at the *municipalidad*, regarded with respect and familiarity—giving him easy, almost casual access to the formal authorities.

It is interesting, however, that Lopez and his friends were certain that some "mysterious deal" had been made between the guardia and Fernando—that Fernando had bribed the guardia with the pigs. Fernando's outsider identity among the locals, combined with a general belief that the local formal legal system is corrupt, led Lopez to define the actions of Fernando and the guardia as based on personal, private motives rather than upon the dictates of formal, rational law. Thus, the interpretation and definition of the "resolution" of this dispute was influenced directly by a peculiar social construction of reality among Sierpe residents. In fact, more than one resident has offered details of this particular dispute as an example of local corruption. Such attitudes might weigh heavily in the decision of how and when to respond to conflict and dispute. In this particular case, for instance, Lopez and his partners simply "gave up" and left Fernando's farm because they saw themselves as "underdogs" in a power struggle with Fernando and the guardia.

Recall Lopez's observation, "What could we do? Fernando is a big man in this area and there's not much we can do legally." Lopez believes that the formal law was closed to him as a means to respond to Fernando and this was already *expected*. In fact, in the opinion of Lopez, this dispute was managed on an informal level primarily because of Fernando's alleged influence over the guardia. However, Lopez did not criticize the overall formal legal system in Costa Rica—only specific parts of it. And although he seemed angry over the initial outcome of this dispute and what he saw as the "questionable" circumstances that preceded it, he was confident in the knowledge that he could "beat" Fernando on a different level, a level in which *he* had fast access, control, and predictability—that is, among *his own* informal social control network.

Thus, in a sense, both parties achieved some of their objectives in this dispute. Fernando was successful in removing Lopez and the other prospectors from his property. And while Lopez initially complied with the guardia's orders, he later continued to mine gold on Fernando's land secretly. Lopez was asked recently how many times he has "trespassed" on Fernando's property since the incident with the guardia. "Quite a few times," he said, "about twenty five I took some good gold, too. But I had to be careful and only went over there when I knew Fernando was in San José. People traveling on the river told me where he and his workers were and when he was expected in Sierpe or coming downriver. So there wasn't much chance of getting caught." Lopez said recently that he is working a different, steady job now, and has not been to Fernando's property since December 1985.

Lopez knew, therefore, that each time he went to Violínes Island he was acting in conflict with Fernando's interests. Fernando, however, presumably knew nothing about Lopez's clandestine gold mining trips to his property, or if he did, he did not choose to admit it. Thus, although there may have been conflict between Fernando and Lopez, there was no actual dispute unless Lopez was caught trespassing.

Also, the local informal social control network was one of Lopez's main resources in this dispute. For instance, Fernando's attitude about people trespassing on his property is well-known among the local residents of the Boca. This is mainly because the land Fernando claims includes 2.5 kilometers of palm-lined beaches—several of the locals have attempted to recover the coconuts from the palm trees to make coconut oil for cooking. Fernando, however, claims that the coconuts are his and that he needs them to feed his pigs. There have been many disputes in the past between Fernando and the local residents over these resources.

These residents have frequently complained to one another and have arranged to help each other arrange secret trips to the island to take the coconuts. Although the locals are certain that they have the legal right to take the coconuts—claiming that all beach property in Costa Rica is, by law, public—they prefer to resolve the dispute by resorting to informal social control tactics. This is mainly because the formal social control agencies are seen as expensive, time-consuming, and often ineffective. Thus, Lopez had little trouble finding support among the local residents for helping him in his clandestine gold mining trips.

Cost also played a role in this dispute because Lopez and his partners did not believe that formally challenging Fernando's claims would be fruitful. According to Lopez, the trip to Puerto Cortez and "all the time and expense of making a formal complaint was not worth the bother," particularly since he could manage the dispute much faster and easier by himself. Thus, Lopez and other insiders on the Boca manage their land-use conflicts on Violínes Island with Fernando by using self-help tactics, including amplifications of deviance (Douglas 1966).

The time factor has not played a significant role in this dispute, other than the fact that the insiders have lived in the area for many years and are well acquainted with secret or concealed pathways into Fernando's farm. Nonetheless, recent reports in the newspapers in the capital of Costa Rica may make time a more relevant factor in the near future. The reports include provocative articles on new "gold discovery" trips being planned for the Osa península as well as limited information on the procedures necessary for mining gold. Some of the information claims that access to mining the gold is usually not problematic, however. People interested in more extensive control including "ownership" of the land must conform to Costa Rican regulations that include provisions on time of possession.

This case emphasizes some of the potential consequences of being an outsider in a dispute, and the effectiveness of informal social control among insiders (see Williams 1986). Although disputants may have more resources at their command, they may be insufficient or inappropriate to control actions within the informal social system. Thus, while there may exist, for example, a close relationship between a disputant and representatives of the formal legal system, the effect of the informal system of social control may be to counteract or diffuse the formal power of the state to shape the outcome of a dispute. In addition, the case demonstrates how it is possible for both parties in a dispute to achieve many of their objectives without actually resolving or "winning" the dispute, and yet not define the situation as a compromise (cf. Perez Vargas 1988). Both parties, for example, may be successful in controlling definitions of the dispute within their own informal social control network and decide to bypass the formal legal system.

3 An Analysis of Dispute Management: The Absence of Resolution

The analysis of disputes includes an exploration of findings that extend our understanding of the more fundamental aspects of social control, including the management of disputes. In this chapter, we examine the struggle for control by analyzing the various dimensions of the dispute process focusing upon the nature of the social relationship, access, time, and cost.

It is apparent that these general factors are interrelated and differ primarily in degree of influence. A Boolean analysis of the variables did not produce additional insights, but it revealed the crucial impact of our operational definitions and the need for more precision in future research. Furthermore, even a superficial analysis shows that a single dispute can quickly reverberate into other ongoing disputes or can create additional disputes. The complexity of social conflict and the dispute process obviously requires a more comprehensive approach than the dichotomous schemes or policy perspective used previously (cf. Abel 1982b; Merry 1990). Carefully describing the ostensible facts of a given case can be surprisingly difficult. And reaching beyond the descriptive level in an attempt to uncover some of the underlying processes that create the definitions of social reality is imbued with problems, which are not easily corrected. The following discussion, therefore, focusing upon general factors, is not an attempt to order the findings according to levels of influence or importance, but instead to provide a strategy for future theory and analysis.

The Nature of the Social Relationship

The evidence in the cases reconfirms that the nature of the social relationship between disputants is only one indicator useful in attempts at understanding or predicting the course or outcomes of a dispute (a related argument can be found in Miller and Sarat 1980–81: 547). In addition to being considered in relation to the other variables we have already discussed, the nature of the social relationship in the dispute process needs to be reconceptualized. It is important to include relationships other than those among the disputants; for instance, the social relationships within the particular informal social system of each disputant, and the surrounding social context, including the relationship between the agencies of informal and formal social control (cf. Blumer 1969; Greenberg 1981, 1989; Nader 1990a).

Simplex/Multiplex

One of our strategies for examining relationships within the cases was dependent upon whether the relationships are considered to be "simplex" or "multiplex." Of the cases studied, a few disputes involved "multiplex" or continuing relationships, and this factor had an important influence on how these disputes were managed (cf. Van Velsen 1967). In "The Fruit of the Land," the dispute between Pancho, Mark, and his associates, did not reach the level of the formal court system, primarily because Mark and Pancho both wished to preserve their relationship. The dispute was diffused, in effect, by being transformed into an internal dispute among the associates in the United States. Also, in "Resident or Squatter?", Pablo did not make a formal complaint against Jim or his witnesses, because he thought he would have a continuing relationship with Jim and did not want the relationship complicated by animosity or hostility arising from a formal legal battle.

The evidence in those cases is consistent with our expectations of how people in multiplex relationships will likely manage their disputes. Disputants typically avoid bringing disputes involving multiplex relationships to the formal level of social control. "The Fruit of the Land," however, also illustrates how these relationships may shift or may be mitigated by other factors. Mark's multiplex relationship with his wife and father-in-law became more important to him than his other multiplex relationship with some of his associates. In addition, some of the North Americans were willing to sacrifice their multiplex relationship with Mark in order to attempt to gain control of land they felt they rightfully owned. This finding supports work by Starr and Yngvesson (1975), which suggests that relationships will typically be sacrificed where scarce resources are at issue. Nonetheless, a fruitful topic for future work would include an analysis of the conditions under which one multiplex relationship will take precedence over another.

In the other cases, the disputants had "simplex," or single issue, relationships. In most of these cases, the dispute was referred for adjudication to the formal court system and no particular efforts were made to protect or preserve the existing relationship. In essence, because disputants did not value their relationships highly and did not plan to continue their interactions, they were willing to risk sacrificing further interactions for the sake of pursuing their disputes.

A point related to the willingness of disputants to sacrifice relationships is that the nature of relationships may obviously undergo changes during the course of a dispute. In "The Absentee Landlord and the Local," for example, the relationship between Jorge and Philipe shifted from a simplex to a multiplex relationship, when Jorge became employed by Philipe. Jorge subsequently ceased disputing with Philipe. However, Philipe appears to be less committed to the multiplex relationship and may have the ability to terminate it more easily due to his varied resources. Although the remaining cases were not referred to the formal court system, there were still no obvious attempts to minimize damage to the relationships. In fact, in each of the simplex cases, part of the management of the dispute involved a rupture of the relationship and the avoidance of any further social contact.

The findings within the multiplex/simplex categories are basically consistent with prior research, yet other factors obviously influenced the course of these disputes. There are other aspects concerning the nature of social relationships that merit further consideration. We have seen, for example, that the relationship between each disputant and the surrounding social context can have a strong influence on the course and outcome of a dispute, particularly involving insiders and outsiders.

Insiders/Outsiders

The designation of insider or outsider refers to the relative level of acceptance of disputants within the local community and their perception of their position (see Vidmar 1984). This concept incorporates the individual's relative position inside or outside the particular cultural and social context. Clearly, these insider/outsider identities are social constructions which reflect how disputants are viewed; thus insider or outsider status can also evolve over time and disputants may be defined as insiders to a greater or lesser extent within the community. Philipe, for example, was considered to be a "marginal" insider on the Boca Río Sierpe; while he is a Costa Rican citizen who is frequently seen on the Boca, his status as a "rich" absentee landlord, and his aggressive actions create a sense that he is not an insider with respect to many social interactions. Other absentee landlords, however, were perceived as so far removed from the community that they were considered outsiders with respect to all social interactions.

Related to the social negotiation of an insider/outsider role is the fact that the course of disputes may be affected by desires to achieve insider status or, at least, minimize outsider status. In "The Fruit of the Land," for example, one reason the North Americans did not pursue their dispute against Pablo may be because they wished to gain the favor of the local residents. Rather than continue the dispute against a well-liked, well-respected insider, they chose to let the matter "drop." While other factors obviously impacted their decision, there was some consensus among these outsiders that abandoning the dispute might help how they would be perceived with respect to future interactions.

Virtually all the cases involve disputes of insider(s) versus outsider(s). The disputes involve disagreements, for example, between insiders in the district of Sierpe and outsiders within Costa Rica or outsiders from entirely different cultures—such as North Americans coming to Costa Rica for a variety of business or personal reasons. Each dispute consists of a unique combination of social relationships and these combinations frequently have a decisive influence on the course of the dispute. About half of the cases involved disputes of North Americans with Costa Ricans. In a few of these cases, the North Americans were absentee landlords living in San José, Costa Rica, in dispute against Costa Rican insiders. In these cases, however, we see a different type of insider/outsider relationship. These landlords are Costa Ricans living outside the district of Sierpe, but because of a shared cultural heritage and increased centralization of political authority in San José, they often have inside access to the country's power centers.

While we have discussed insider/outsider status primarily with respect to disputants' position within the informal social network in and around Sierpe, we also have examined disputants in terms of their insider or outsider status within the *formal* social control network. From this perspective there are at least two distinct levels of insider/outsider status depending on whether the arena of social control is formal or informal. Disputants therefore can be considered inside/insider; inside/outsider; outside/insider; or outside/outsider. A disputant such as Philipe may become a marginal insider on the informal level as well as an indisputable insider on the formal level. Or, for example, some of the North Americans are clearly outsiders on the informal level as well as outsiders on the formal level in Costa Rica. While insider status on the formal level may often be difficult to gauge, this distinction is nonetheless potentially useful and should be pursued on a more systematic level (cf. Perez Vargas 1988).

While many of the Costa Rican absentee landlords in our cases enjoy insider status on the formal level, as is the case with Philipe, they often achieve, at best, only marginal insider status on the informal level. This marginal status usually includes the establishment of contacts or allies among members of the Sierpe population allowing them some access to the local informal social control network. This allows for more predictability and control in social relations than most foreigners achieve. Miller and Sarat offer additional insight into the importance of access expressed in terms of "institutionalization of remedy systems," which refers to "well-known, regularized, readily available mechanisms, techniques, or procedures for dealing with a problem" (1980–81: 563).

In one case, the landlord had the support of the local residents and thus gained some access to the local informal social control system. In the other cases, however, the absentee landlord was not integrated within the social context of the Boca Río Sierpe and did not garner support among most of the residents. In two cases, "Resident or Squatter?" and "The Rainy Season," we see how an outsider status has affected disputes with the locals. Fernando, for example, has had frequent disputes with his neighbors on the Boca Río Sierpe, involving mostly land-use conflicts on Violínes Island. Because of the way Fernando manages these disputes, he is known locally as a "tough" man who is not above using threats, including physical intimidation. Fernando's reputation and social identity on the Boca influence the way residents respond to him. In most cases, rather than confront Fernando directly, residents will "help themselves" by trespassing on Fernando's property or by making thinly veiled personal attacks in an attempt to raise their status relative to him.

In "The Rainy Season," we see this social control process illustrated clearly. Lopez was part of the local conspiracy among residents to trespass on Fernando's farm. Fernando, however, had other resources, including a close relationship with the authorities in Puerto Cortez. In this particular case, Fernando was successful in persuading the guardia to remove Lopez from his farm, but on only one occasion. Since then, Lopez has made many trips to Fernando's property without his knowledge.

We see this same informal social control process in "Resident or Squatter?," in which Pablo also cooperates in the local conspiracy against Fernando by allowing gold miners to enter Violínes Island through his farm. In fact, Fernando is "losing" both these disputes on the informal level. The residents continue to trespass and, as one said, "What Fernando doesn't know can't hurt him or us." Moreover, it is possible Fernando believes he has won the informal dispute because he has not caught anyone trespassing for the past year and a half.

However, in this case, Pablo is the only Boca resident to have become involved in a formal legal battle with Fernando. According to Pablo, this is because "the offense is more serious. This is not a fight over coconuts and gold, but ownership and control of property. I've been here for over fifty years and that's *my* land!" Although Fernando may lack control and predictability on the informal level, his relationship with the authorities in Puerto Cortez has augmented his formal management of this dispute. Thus, despite Fernando's advantage in resources, his outsider status and the fact that he is not well-integrated into the Boca Río Sierpe community has been a definite disadvantage for him.

In the other case involving only Costa Ricans, "The Absentee Landlord and the Local," the social identities are similar to those in the cases involving Fernando, but the nature of the social relationships are quite different. In this case, Philipe, the lawyer from San José, is involved in a dispute with Jorge, a local campesino who has lived for twenty years on the Boca. Although Philipe is considered only a marginal insider, he is more thoroughly integrated in the Sierpe community than Fernando, and enjoys more local support. This is primarily because he has been one of the largest employers in the area; for the past two years Philipe has had more than fifteen full-time employees working on his tourist project on the Boca. Also, Philipe makes more frequent trips to Sierpe than other absentee landlords—at least twice a month for three or four days at a time. Thus, he is an anomaly; an absentee landlord who has been able to gain considerable access to the local informal social control system.

The nature of social relationships in "The Absentee Landlord and the Local" is further complicated by the involvement of third parties in an alliance with Jorge; North American outsiders want to buy his farm. Because of their limited ability to converse in Spanish and unfamiliarity with the Costa Rican culture, these North Americans had limited access to the local informal social control systems, but they had the resources to hire bilingual lawyers and interpreters in San José.

However, Philipe used his advantage on the formal level by stalling the sale of Jorge's farm to the North Americans, who after a year of battling in the formal court system, lost interest in the transaction and withdrew from the dispute. Meanwhile, Philipe managed the dispute with Jorge through the informal social system on the Boca Río Sierpe. Thus, despite Philipe's social identity as an "absentee landlord," his limited acceptance on the Boca has allowed him some control and predictability in local disputes.

Throughout the discussion of these disputes, it has been demonstrated that slight variations in the nature of social relationships can have an important influence on the dispute process. These variations involve not only simplex/multiplex relationships, but also insider/outsider relationships—especially in relation to the degree of integration within a specific formal and informal social control system. Also, there are other aspects concerning the nature of social relationships warranting attention that influence the dispute process—for example, the nature of the relationship among disputants as well as the larger social context which impacts upon Sierpe and Costa Rica (Vargas 1989).

Social Context and Social Relationships

The concept of social context is elusive (cf. Short 1986). In this analysis we have concentrated on the specific social context of the Sierpe area, yet it is clear that events outside Sierpe influence the amount and type of social control within Sierpe.

For instance, the sudden withdrawal of United Brands Company from the southern zone of Costa Rica has resulted in a concerted effort by public and private investment sectors to find alternative methods of using the natural and human resources in the area. This change has led to an increase in government resettlement programs and private development projects in the Sierpe district, which has resulted in increased land values, as well as new conflicts and disputes (Vargas 1989).

Also, the larger social context is relevant, including the political, economic, and strategic importance of Central America within the international power structure. Some of the people coming to Sierpe are refugees from disputes in El Salvador Panama, and Nicaragua. In fact, in the past ten years some four hundred thousand refugees have crossed the borders into Costa Rica. These refugees not only represent potential cultural conflict, but also have been accused of "stealing" jobs and land from Costa Ricans. Moreover, there are Costa Ricans arriving in the southern zone who have left their homes and farms on the border area with Nicaragua because of military tensions and refugee problems. One of these displaced people described the southern zone as "the last frontier, a wilderness area still open to settlement and exploitation." Thus, political pressures on the international level also affect the amount and type of social control in Sierpe (Vargas 1989).

However, there are other social contexts that have a more immediate and direct effect on the dispute process; that is, the various informal social systems *within* the larger social context of the Sierpe community. These are the small networks of interpersonal relationships based on symbolic systems of shared meanings and expectations about one's social identity; normative and deviant behavior; values and beliefs; and the disputants "ideology" regarding legal and extralegal procedures and outcomes (see, for example, Merry 1987; 1990).

We have examined some of these informal social systems and their impact upon the dispute process; for example, the local conspiracy among Boca residents against Fernando, or the Simo family and their supporters' actions against Wilson. The most significant influence involving small, informal social systems occurred in "The Sierpe Gift". The events in this case demonstrate the problems of prediction in the study of social control, and illustrate the need to examine less visible levels of social control.

This case was followed avidly by most residents of the town of Sierpe because it involved two long-time residents, Roberto and Sergio, and also because it was highly visible and dramatic. The case included allegations of bribery on both sides, the eviction of Roberto from the farm by armed guardia, the plowing of the pasture for the planting and harvesting of rice, and Roberto's eventually retaking his farm. However, while Roberto and Sergio used many of their resources in managing this dispute, an entirely different view of the dispute emerged from the landless people in

Sierpe. From their perspective, this dispute was no longer a question of ownership between Roberto and Sergio, but an opportunity to partially alleviate the housing and land shortage in Sierpe. This small, informal "social context"—now referred to locally as the "squatter movement"—organized quietly and secretly, waiting for an opportune moment to act. The years of conflict and dispute were settled when this small group of people unexpectedly emerged to take control of the dispute.

In this case, for example, the social pressures involved conflicts over land use and control. The squatter movement arose out of an acute social need for more land for those local residents who lived in unhealthy or overcrowded conditions and who were unable to find or afford suitable property. Thus, small, informal social systems—including collective interaction groups and nascent social movements—can often have a more dramatic effect on the dispute process than more remote levels of social control (see McAdam 1989). This extends the idea of social context; that is, not only does it encompass a general social "field" around the dispute process, but also it includes a multitude of informal social systems, some of which may become involved in social conflict and dispute.

Moreover, because access to a disputant's informal network is usually not problematic, systems such as the collective interaction that gave rise to the squatter movement offer crucial resources to people in dispute. Typically, there is a relatively high degree of control and predictability via high levels of social solidarity and close communication. These systems can help to define disputes as well as protect and defend disputants' identities. Thus, these informal social systems can often come into direct conflict with the formal law, or penetrate and vitiate the formal law, or, operating alongside it, supplement the formal law (see Dennis 1976 for an analysis of how peasant landholdings affect intercommunal conflicts and social organization).

This brings us to a consideration of the nature of the social relationship between networks of informal and formal social control. By analyzing a number of cases involving the same North American, Mark, we see how the nature of the social relationships and insider/outsider status can evolve and change. Mark held a different social quality than all other people in this study; he was not an absentee landlord, nor was he initially an insider. Because of his few, often misunderstood encounters with his neighbors, at first he had no social identity other than "the gringo;" however, he was slowly assimilated into the local culture. As we trace these disputes, it is apparent how slight variations in the nature of social relationships can have a considerable impact on disputing. Also, the importance of the time factor emerges, especially as it relates to integration into the community and the ability to successfully manage disputes.

Mark had been living in Costa Rica only six months when the first dispute involving him began in December 1980. The dispute also involved Sanchez, a Costa Rican absentee landlord. At the time "House without a Home" began, Mark said that he felt virtually alone, cut off by both language and culture from the local residents, and also out of touch with his informal social network in the United States. This lack of support was an important factor in determining how he was unable to manage this dispute effectively. During the initial stage of this dispute, the only activity by local informal or formal social control agencies was through manipulation by Sanchez. Mark had no access to either formal or informal apparatuses. Thus, this case remained at a quiet stalemate for several years, flaring occasionally when Sanchez made threats or intimidations. It was not until December 1985, after Mark had become experienced in disputing in Costa Rica, that this case finally came to the attention of the formal authorities (Vargas 1989).

By the time "Fruit of the Land" developed, in June 1982, Mark had come to be considered a "marginal" insider, primarily because he married the daughter of his neighbor Pancho, an insider on the Boca Río Sierpe for many years. Through his wife Marisa and her family contacts, Mark gained partial access to the local social system, but because he initially spoke little Spanish and could not understand fully the social nuances and character of the local culture, his access was limited and usually unpredictable. Consequently, Marisa became the most important link between Pancho and the North Americans, because she carried messages and acted as a mediator. Meanwhile, Mark found himself between two cultures; on the one hand responsible to his associates in the United States as the caretaker of their property; on the other hand bound by family loyalty to his new relations in Costa Rica. This web of intergroup conflict eventually caused the deterioration of his relationships with associates, but it allowed him to maintain good family relations (see Simmel 1955; Sherif and Sherif 1969). As this case illustrates, the number of parties involved in a dispute and their relationships may change considerably. Thus, allies can become enemies and opponents can become friends (Felstiner et al. 1980–81).

The last case in this analysis, "The Inspection," began in May 1984, when Philipe, a Costa Rican absentee landlord, put up a fence on land Mark considered to be his property. By this time, Mark had a better command of Spanish, had become well-known in Sierpe, and was regarded in most informal interactions as an insider. While this status considerably improved his access to the local informal social system, he still had no experience in managing disputes on the formal level.

Conversely, Philipe was well integrated within the formal social control system and had considerable access to the informal system. To reiterate, Philipe is a lawyer who maintains an office and home close to the Supreme Court Building in downtown San José. He is reputed to be a "rich" man with considerable political influence. Because of his involvement in prior land disputes in Sierpe, he is known personally to the authorities in Puerto Cortez. He therefore enjoys considerable informal access to the formal law. Philipe's social identity among the Sierpe residents has a "larger-than-life" quality about it, which illustrates how the social construction of reality can influence relationships and behavior. To emphasize the extent of Philipe's power, several residents mentioned the same "fact" about Philipe; "He was Chief Justice of the Supreme Court of Costa Rica for twenty years!"

Although Philipe had been only a lower court judge for a few years, the residents created a social identity for Philipe that places him far outside the social realities of Sierpe and gives him more power and status than he may actually merit. At the onset of a dispute, socially advantaged and experienced individuals such as Philipe are usually better able and more likely to pursue their interests on the formal level. Nader (1984b) refers to these individuals as "voicers"; people most likely to take their cases to the formal court system, where they enjoy sufficient resource advantages to maintain control over the management of their disputes. In some instances they may utilize formal social control agents; however, they may also choose to avoid incidents that have the potential to generate disputes because the cost of maintaining the dispute is high or the chances of success are low (Miller and Sarat 1980–81). This attitude led several of Mark's informal contacts to decline his requests for assistance, claiming that no matter what he did, he would lose eventually. Nevertheless, because he had become integrated into the local culture by this time, he took a more active role in this dispute on both the formal and informal levels.

These cases suggest that as perception of disputants' insider status evolves, there is a corresponding increase in ability to manage disputes. However, since we have typically regarded insider status in terms of the informal social control system, these advantages may be gained disproportionately on the informal level. On the other hand, if disputants gain insider status on the formal level, they may be more likely to achieve success on that level of dispute management. This shift in status involves social characteristics that follow a logical progression from one to the other; language and meaning, cultural integration, social solidarity, and increasing predictability. Thus, these characteristics offer an analytic guide to assess the degree of integration within a specific social context and to determine how variations in integration might help explain and predict the dispute process (cf. Black 1989). We will see the value of identifying and describing these variations from one social context to another in the following discussion of the other cases involving North Americans.

In these cases, the North Americans demonstrated that they had the resources and information to initiate the management of their disputes within the Costa Rican formal legal system. However, the fact that they typically were successful only at the initial stages and were seen as outsiders on the Boca Río Sierpe had important implications on the course of their disputes; precisely because they lacked access to local informal social control networks. Two of these North Americans, Wilson and Jim, had become partially integrated into the Costa Rican culture; they had hired interpreters and bilingual lawyers, and thus had some measure of control and predictability in their social relationships—at least in San José. In the Sierpe district, however, they had very limited cultural and social integration, and had almost no predictability or control in their relationship with local residents. Wilson and Jim had easy access to the formal authorities, but no access to the local informal social system. This variation in the nature of social relationships had a considerable influence on the course of these disputes.

In "Resident or Squatter?" Jim was a North American considered an outsider making a formal complaint against Pablo, who was thought of as a Costa Rican insider. Although by most standards Jim could have been considered more "powerful" than Pablo, he was trapped outside the local channels of communication and did not know Pablo had resided on his property on Violínes Island for many years. Also, he did not know that Pablo has had a history of land-use conflicts on Violínes and that he was experienced in the management of disputes. In fact, Pablo gained informal access to the judges in Puerto Cortez in this case, primarily because he is so well-known as *un hombre puro pleito*—a man full of disputes. Prior research suggests that a small number of individuals may repeatedly bring disputes to the level of formal social control and that these disputants may gain considerable advantages including knowledge of the requirements and procedures entailed by the formal system (Nader 1984b). Thus, even though Jim had more resources in terms of finances and mobility, he could not sustain the validity of his complaint, and Pablo gained control of the definition of this dispute. However, this was only the initial phase in what has turned out to be an ongoing adversarial relationship between Jim and Pablo. Throughout their disputing, Jim's outsider status and lack of access to the local culture has been a definite disadvantage for him, especially in terms of financial costs.

In "The Colorado Camp," Wilson also had the resources to manage his dispute against the Simo family in the Costa Rican formal court system. However, he was regarded by most residents of Sierpe as an outsider and, because of his past activities and the local popularity of the Simos, he was not particularly well-liked. These social facts directly affected the course of this land dispute and indirectly affected Wilson's gold mining and tourist activities. In addition, because of Wilson's outsider status and discredited identity, the Simos could generate the support of their friends and neighbors in their dispute with Wilson. Sometimes support simply was lending a sympathetic ear to their complaints.

Moreover, in part, because Wilson and Jim were considered outsiders in dispute with insiders, there was more involvement in these disputes by the local social system than in the cases involving Mark. The differences in the nature of social relationships offers insight into the informal social control infrastructure in Sierpe. Not only did the increased involvement by the local social system influence these disputes, but it also provided an alternative resource in dispute management for the Costa Rican insiders. The informal system offered them more control, predictability, and recognition than did the formal level of social control. Most importantly, however, the local informal social control system allowed the insiders a chance to "win" the dispute before an audience of their peers, thereby maintaining their reputations and protecting their social identity. This kind of compensation may offer an important outlet for the frustrations and angry sentiments often associated with formal legal battle or social conflict in general.

In those disputes between Costa Rican absentee landlords and Costa Rican insiders, we also see a high level of involvement by the local social system. In these cases, however, we again see the different type of insider/outsider relationship introduced earlier. These landlords are Costa Ricans living outside the district of Sierpe, but because of a shared cultural heritage and increased centralization of political authority in San José, they are thought to have an insider access to the country's power centers. Also, unlike the North American absentee landlords, these Costa Rican "outsiders" usually have strong contacts, or "allies," among members of the Sierpe population, giving them some access to the local informal social control network. These are people with whom they may have close personal or working relationships, and with whom they have a common national identity and cultural tradition. This allows for more predictability and control in social relations than most foreigners would ever expect to achieve (Vargas 1989). These absentee landlords were not integrated fully within the social context of the Boca Río Sierpe; however, apart from their allies they did not enjoy social support among most of the local residents. In essence, while they may have more support in the formal social control arenas than inside/insiders, that relationship may be mitigated by other aspects of the social context.

Access and Social Context

It is obvious that the nature of the social relationship between disputants is important to the dispute process, and that more emphasis should be placed on the *social context* in which the dispute occurs and the relative social position of each disputant within this social context. In addition, the nature of the relationship between the formal and informal social structures of the community is also a significant factor.

We have seen from analyzing the cases that cost, time, and cultural characteristics are important in the dispute process, yet they are all closely related with the factor of *access*. Access is a key consideration in the study of the dispute process—especially the informal inroads of access to the formal law. The cases reveal that the conditions under which a private conflict becomes a public dispute are varied and usually involve contacts made among those in a person's informal social network. In every case, conflict between disputants quickly expands along channels of formal or informal social control into the surrounding social context. In some cases, the disputes were referred to the formal legal system, but in all cases specific parts of the informal social structure became directly involved.

When analyzing formal and informal social control, the boundaries of the formal law are comparatively easy to discover and describe; they include the written legal codes and constitutional limits that define specific powers. Portions of the Appendix B of this book outline some of the formal boundaries of Costa Rican law. It reads like the organizational chart of many bureaucratic structures. On the other hand, the informal social structure is a subtly organized and essential element of community life, cutting across the boundaries of formal law. The boundaries of informal control are much more difficult to discover and to trace. There may be a multitude of systems of informal social control within the boundaries of the same society, ranging from the circle of close friends and relatives of those in high positions of authority to the intimate friends and relatives of the local residents in the district of Sierpe. In other words, there are those who, because of social circumstances may be much closer than others to the informal inroads of access into the formal law. What are some of these social circumstances? Who is likely to be included, and who is likely to be excluded?

Power in this context must include the factor of access to the formal and informal agencies of social control, the nature of the social relationship between disputants, the social position of each disputant within the social context in which the dispute occurs, and the factors of cost, time, and cultural characteristics. While power includes the ability of disputants to manage their disputes successfully on both the formal and informal levels of social control, it is useful to distinguish between informal power and formal power.

Our findings do not reveal much unexpected information about access to the informal and formal agencies of social control. We do, however, specifically want to point out that our analysis of the cases demonstrates that other factors relating to the dispute process seem to coincide with respect to the question of access— especially access to the formal authorities. Access, for example, is directly related to a disputant's insider/outsider status, command of financial and other resources, proximity and relational distance (e.g., personal ties) to the formal or informal social control agents, and position in the overall community power structure. Thus, access is one pivotal point in the dispute process, and as such it merits more thorough analysis than it has usually received. Future research might proceed by defining access as existence of a channel that makes it possible to approach a mechanism of control.

Since the state exercises a monopoly on formal social control over disputants within national boundaries—up to and including the right to imprison and execute its citizens—access to the *formal* authorities becomes crucial. In Costa Rica or the United States, all citizens supposedly have an equal right and opportunity to use the formal law in the management of their private disputes. In return, citizens are usually forbidden from taking the law into their own hands, relinquishing control of their formal dispute to the state, and ostensibly agreeing to conform to whatever final, "formal rational" solution is imposed.

This is a theoretic ideal, however, and although it reflects accurately one ideal relationship between a democratic state and its citizens, it bears little resemblance to the complex realities of socioeconomic organization and human interaction. An irrevocable fact about social experience is that it is changing constantly, with an ongoing creation of new social norms and nuances. Corporate structure is not immune to the effects of this process (Thomas et al. 1987). Thus, formal institutions can provide structure and identity, but actors and actions also are shaped by the influences and pressures of informal social control (see Collier 1973 on social and legal changes).

Furthermore, the exclusive nature of the formal law is at once its strongest and weakest attribute (see Lauderdale 1988a). On the one hand, such exclusiveness is at the heart of a nation's identity and legal authority; few internal powers can rival those of the sovereign state. On the other hand, this exclusivity turns the formal law into a scarce commodity; access is strictly controlled and the enforcement and administration of the law is reserved primarily for legal professionals (Abel 1982a, 1986; Nader and Serber 1976). This exclusivity places a high degree of value on access to the formal law, yet it renders the formal law vulnerable to manipulation by private citizens and special interest groups who often compete for its attention and favor. Moreover, such competition involves struggles over the power necessary to manage disputes successfully on both the formal and informal levels. In this sense, power is not only a commodity of the state but also a product of informal social relations.

Thus, the impartiality of state authority has been weakened by the establishment of numerous and unequal informal inroads of access into the formal law, resulting in a legal process responsive to the exercise of disproportionate power as well as formal rationality (Lauderdale 1988a). If, for example, disputants lack the ability to gain either formal or informal access to the formal law, the strength or "objective rightness" of their legal position becomes irrelevant on a practical basis. At this point, the rational character of formal law becomes eroded and other variables come into play, variables related to *informal* social control, such as position or status in the social structure, level and extent of resources, and proximity to the formal and informal social control systems (see Fitzpatrick 1988 on the limits of formalism).

Although access to the formal authorities by the residents in the district of Sierpe was often very difficult, access to their own highly organized informal social control network was usually unconstrained. This ease of access can be attributed, in part, to the closely knit, homogeneous nature of the community, including the numerous interrelated family networks. However, because of the peculiar arrangement of physical and social circumstances, the impact of such informal social control on the formal management of land disputes was minimal. For one thing, the informal sanctions available to the people of Sierpe for reacting to what they defined as deviant behavior could be most effective if applied to other members of the same informal social control network— these sanctions include shame, ridicule, or avoidance. The information we have gathered concerning disputes arising from theft of personal property among the local residents—that is, insiders against insiders—generally supports this conclusion. However, an outsider, such as a person from a different subculture or an absentee landlord living outside the district of Sierpe, typically could not be affected seriously by such informal sanctions, because they are not applied by significant others, or because such sanctions simply could not reach the outsiders. Thus, since our cases involved people in relationships of the insider/outsider type, informal social control inside the district of Sierpe was limited.

On the other hand, as we might expect, in secondary disputes occurring among outsiders, definitions of deviance and application of informal sanctions again became important. In "House without a Home," for example, a portion of the dispute was managed through the creation and maintenance of deviance definitions. In this case, a group of North Americans attempted, among other things, to elevate their status within their informal network by defining one of their colleagues, George, as a deviant. This process began by informally referring to George as a greedy outsider.

In general, the people who tried to utilize informal social control in Sierpe usually did not have the resources to gain informal access to the formal authorities. In "The Colorado Camp," for example, informal social control tactics on the part of the residents of the district of Sierpe managed to have a limited impact on the formal process of the law. In this case, the Simo family resorted to a self-help strategy in the takeover of Wilson's fishing camp. Nevertheless, this display of civil disobedience did not have much of an effect on the formal authorities; the legal process seemed to have accelerated somewhat a few days after the takeover attempt. Also, it did seem to arouse the interest and indignation of the local residents in their reactions to Wilson, but, as we have already noted, such indignation or resentment did not have much of an impact on Wilson because he was viewed as an outsider. In the final analysis, therefore, this informal attempt influenced the formal law, yet it was not a decisive factor in the overall management of this particular dispute. The emphasis of this case, however, did shift from a dispute with Wilson to a dispute between the Simo family and the formal authorities. One instance where there was a more successful attempt by informal actors to affect the formal law occurred in "The Sierpe Gift," where an organized group of squatters took over Roberto's land immediately after his death before any formal legal action could be initiated. This informal group preempted Roberto's opponent, Sergio, from using the formal legal system to gain access to Roberto's farm.

Although access to an individual's own informal social control network was generally not problematic, disputants used these informal networks in varying ways. In all cases that eventually reached the formal court system, the dispute was first responded to in some informal manner—for example, complaining to friends or associates, seeking affirmation that an opponent was deviant, or asking for advice about how to manage the dispute. During interviews with these insiders, it became evident that the involvement of family and friends was considered a common part of disputing; these significant others frequently offered economic and moral support, advice in dispute management, a sympathetic forum in defining the dispute and recognition of the validity of the disputant's grievances. Also, even though a dispute may have been referred to the formal court system, this did not result in an abandonment of the dispute on an informal level; on the contrary, informal social control generally continued concurrently, usually in the form of more complaining to friends or associates, or in the management of the dispute through self-help methods or other extralegal means (see Yngvesson 1984).

In addition, when disputants were unsuccessful at the formal level, they often continued their disputes either entirely or predominantly on the informal level. In "Resident or Squatter?," for example, Pablo was unable to achieve his objectives on the formal level, but rather than abandon his dispute entirely, he shifted his efforts and resources primarily to the informal level. Because he is an insider on the Boca, Pablo was thus able to achieve a ready audience for his dispute through his immediate informal social control network.

Moreover, even when a dispute reached the level of formal social control, there was no assurance that it would be handled by the dictates of the formal law. In "Denouncing the Campesino," while the dispute reached the level of the formal court system, the judge involved in the case kept the dispute on the informal level. In fact, this entire dispute remained on the informal level.

Also important in this informal process was the informal channels of communication. Informal communications have generally been fast and reliable in this area, primarily because there are limited alternative means of communicating. Indeed, the informal social systems in Sierpe can be likened to a closely woven spiderweb which spreads by interconnected threads to the far corners of the district; touch the web at any given point and vibrations usually ripple throughout the whole. The varying accounts used to describe disputes and disputants were constructed and reconstructed through informal group affiliations and the related informal networks of communication (Simmel 1955).

We have seen how access to this informal communication system was a decisive factor in several disputes, allowing the residents at least limited control in the management of their disputes—in fact, they usually had more power from means, such as informal communication, than through the formal legal system. The communication function and informal social support, for example, were an essential part of the Simo family's strategy in their takeover of Wilson's mining and tourist operation. Also, in those disputes involving Fernando—the absentee landlord with land on Violínes Island—the informal social control network allowed numerous insiders to trespass secretly on

Fernando's farm by passing on information about Fernando's whereabouts and the movement of his workers.

In the majority of cases, however, the informal social control network was important because it provided the opportunity for insiders to "win" disputes before an audience of their peers. Those who had immediate access to this network could, for example, manipulate public opinion to their advantage, while outsiders did not have access and could not present their side of the dispute. Although such support and recognition usually did not have much of an effect on the formal legal process or formal outcome of the dispute, its importance as a unifying force in community solidarity cannot be underestimated, especially its relationship to the definition of moral boundaries and the defense and protection of personal identities (cf. Douglas 1966; Erikson 1966; Blumer 1969; Ben-Yehuda 1985, 1990).

Thus, on the one hand, insiders frequently had an advantage in shaping and controlling the definitions of events within their informal social control network—including notions of "right" and "wrong" and the truth or falsehood of conflicting claims. Conversely, outsiders typically had considerably greater ability to gain both formal and informal access to the *formal* legal system. Access to the formal authorities by outsiders, such as absentee landlords, for example, was facilitated because these individuals had better relational distance or physical proximity to the formal legal process located outside the district of Sierpe. Also, recall that by local standards, these individuals are viewed as "rich and powerful people," who travel in new cars, have several people on their payrolls, and finance extensive projects on the land they own or control. The absentee landlords tend to occupy social positions of high status, similar to the prestige and position afforded to legal professionals in Costa Rican society. In fact, Philipe, the outsider with extensive land holdings on the Boca Río Sierpe, had a long career as a lawyer and a district court judge. Thus, because of factors such as relational and physical proximity to formal authorities and command of extensive resources, these outsiders enjoy a significant advantage in gaining access to the formal law.

Many outsiders also did not encounter significant barriers in gaining *informal* access to the formal law. In several of our cases there were allegations of bribery and other extralegal activities on the part of outsiders in their relationships with the formal authorities. Although some of the allegations have proven very difficult to verify, many disputants firmly believed that such secret manipulations of the formal law did occur. In "Resident or Squatter?", for example, Pablo ceased his formal attempts to manage the dispute because his personal investigations of the case revealed that Fernando had been paying bribes to the local authorities. In explaining why he ceased managing the dispute on a formal level, Pablo said, "If it comes down to who has more money, then I can't compete. I'll have to fight some other way." In "The Colorado Camp," the Simo family charged Wilson with making personal agreements with the formal authorities and, in fact, during the Supreme Court proceedings Wilson was reprimanded for "pressuring" the local alcaldía into helping him remove the Simo family from his mining and tourist operation (see Appendix B for a discussion of the relatively new code which focuses upon an improved procedure to guarantee impartiality in such decision-making, and see Perez Vargas 1988). Members of the Simo family claim that such "pressure" came in the form of a bribe. In "The Sierpe Gift," the dispute was formally managed when Roberto was evicted from his farm by orders from the *alcaldía*. However, Roberto claimed such orders were the direct result of a bribe of $500 made to the alcaldía by Sergio, his opponent in the dispute. In "The Rainy Season," it was alleged that Fernando inappropriately enlisted the cooperation of the local guardia in evicting the gold prospectors from his farm on Violínes Island by bribing the guardia. Here, informal access to the formal authorities was facilitated by relational distance, including sharing a similar level of position or status in the social structure, and by physical proximity to the formal law.

The ultimate power to create a final definition of a dispute usually resides in the authority of the state, which "loans" a part of that power to its citizens through the institutions of the formal judicial system. Thus, the representatives of state authority and power in Costa Rica, in this case including the judges and *alcaldía* in Puerto Cortez, are made available to the citizens of the district of Sierpe ostensibly as objective third parties who decide and settle disputes and apply formal sanctions when deemed necessary. As demonstrated by some of our cases, however, there are informal inroads of access into the formal agencies of social control; that is, some private citizens can disproportionately access and use the power and authority of the state by bypassing or manipulating the formal rituals of the judicial system and by making informal agreements with the state's representatives. Moreover, when disputants cannot gain or maintain access to the formal law, they may be at a disadvantage in the control or management of the dispute. Such a disadvantage may not be related simply to the strength or "rightness" of their claims, but to other social factors, such as status or role in the social structure, the level and extent of resources, as well as the proximity and relational distance to the formal authorities.

An examination of the formal written law in Costa Rica reveals that it is characterized by legal equality; that is, laws are based on intellectually calculable rules and procedures (i.e., Weber's concept of rationality) that are designed to protect citizens from legal decisions made purely on the basis of political or economic interests (see Lauderdale, 1988a). Furthermore, because of Costa Rica's traditionally agrarian economy and culture, attempts at rationalization of the law have been evident in land management and reform programs—ostensibly moving toward more equitable land redistribution as well as increasing productivity in the national and international market systems. And because narrowly defined legal boundaries are imposed on the management of land and other disputes, there is ostensibly a high degree of predictability and some measure of control for each disputant (cf. Silliman 1985: 283–86). It is also true that the formal law consists in a special language created, interpreted, and administered by legal professionals. But formal, legal terminology and procedures may often seem strange or "secret" to most citizens. For instance, most residents of Sierpe regard the formal law as some aloof social force with special powers and prerogatives beyond the average citizen's control or influence.

In addition, the formal rational legal system is represented primarily in the written laws and codes that form part of the infrastructure of state power and authority. However, the key word in this definition is "written"; it exists on paper as a formal guide in the organization and management of relationships among citizens. Whether the formal law is applied impartially is problematic. As we have already seen, the residents of the district of Sierpe experienced many problems with both formal and informal access to the formal law, while absentee landlords were accused of having made informal agreements with the formal authorities. Although the apparent facts of the cases suggest that such agreements often had occurred, we cannot be certain of the extent of such agreements, since many involved secret arrangements. There is, nonetheless, ample evidence in the cases to suggest that the ideal functioning of the law and the actual application of the law are very different processes; although the formal law may provide for legal equality, the administration of the law often ignores the tenets of legal formal rationality. As Pablo, the pioneer in the Sierpe area suggests, "the problem with the law in Costa Rica is not the Constitution or the legal codes, but with the people who enforce it."

In fact, virtually every Sierpe resident claims that self-interest by formal, as well as informal, social control agents plays an important role in the management of the formal law in Costa Rica. The residents refer to this process as *chorizo*, a word that translates literally "sausage," but which has a much broader meaning that includes the granting of personal favors in return for political or economic advantages. The concept of chorizo is ingrained within part of the Costa Rican culture and is applied not only to political corruption on the formal level, but also more broadly to informal corruption. Although most residents disapprove of chorizo, they nevertheless strongly believe that it is practiced widely and has an important influence on the formal law. As one resident put it:

> Chorizo is widespread in Costa Rica, especially among politicians, lawyers and police. We don't like it but how can we stop it? After all, these are the people who make and enforce the laws. Can we expect them to report and arrest themselves? Of course not. We can only hope to elect honest people to stop this corruption. But because *chorizo* is a secret and private business, it will always be very hard to find and punish the guilty ones.

The significance of chorizo for this discussion relates to the nature of the social relationship between private citizens and public officials. The ultimate power to decide the final formal definition of a dispute resides with the state, which offers citizens the ability to utilize the institutions of the formal judicial system. Thus, the representatives of state authority in Costa Rica—in this case including the rural police, judges, and "mayors" in Puerto Cortez—are available, albeit arguably on a highly differential basis, to the residents of the district of Sierpe. The inherent objective in this arrangement ostensibly is to advance the ideal of justice—including fair and impartial consideration before the public forums of the formal legal system. However, many residents think that the law does not operate as intended. A statement made by one resident is representative of local attitudes:

> The law is like a marketplace and the lawyers are the merchants. If you want the law you have to go to the law-market.

But because the law is so damn sensitive and confusing, the state has a monopoly on it. This means you can't shop around or look for a better deal. Also, if the market's closed or too expensive, you can't buy any law.

Because of the concentration and formalization of law as one means of legitimizing state power, there is danger that the law will serve only those who can reach it or those who are the highest bidders. As Nader (1984b: 962) emphasizes:

> One cannot understand or develop a user theory of law, a theory which states that a law drifts in the direction of its dominant user, without an understanding of the relationship between law and the socioeconomic order. An understanding of the different modes of dispute resolution will only be possible if dispute resolution structures are seen as a subset of a larger system of control.

Despite written codes and regulations discouraging manipulation of the law, there may be informal, *unwritten* laws that override the formal rules and allow for various forms of interference. Informal social control can penetrate and subvert the formal law, allowing for legal decisions made on political or economic grounds. Nonetheless, informal social control is not some detached, alien force invading the formal law. On the contrary, informal social control is a common process in daily life; it influences social identities and plays an intrinsic role in the regulation and organization of social relationships. Thus, with the power of formal decision-making comes the ability to abuse that power for instrumental gain through informal processes, such as tacit personal agreements. For instance, in "The Inspection," Mark appealed to the guardia for help in his dispute with Philipe, believing he was dealing with representatives of the state who he expected would behave within formal rational boundaries. However, the guardia ostensibly used their position for instrumental purposes. Also in this case, the alcaldía performed an official inspection while on a personal holiday with her children and mother. In "The Sierpe Gift," this same alcaldía ordered the evacuation of Roberto's farm, not as a result of impartial consideration of the legal circumstances, but allegedly in return for a secret payment. There were other allegations of misconduct or bribery in our cases—such as Pablo's "missing" documents in "Resident or Squatter?". Because of a combination of particular social circumstances, informal inroads of access are more available to some than to others (Merry 1990). In almost half the cases, the outsiders involved were accused of having made informal agreements with the formal authorities.

In essence, why do the residents of Sierpe not enjoy the same informal access to the formal authorities? An obvious answer is because the local residents were actually outsiders, partially due to their relational distance from the formal authorities in Puerto Cortez. They were outsiders not only in the sense that they were located far from the Municipalidad de Osa, but also because of their limited understanding of and interactions with the formal law and the agents of the formal law. Most of the population in the district is made up of field workers, small merchants, independent fisherpersons and farmers who do not often associate with others outside their immediate informal social network. Also, the socioeconomic level of the people in this district ranges from lower-middle to the lowest class—most of the individuals would be defined as part of the bottom sector of the lower class within Costa Rican culture. According to the official Costa Rican census, the Cantón de Osa is the third poorest area in the entire country in terms of family income and production. The majority of the people in the district of Sierpe lack the resources that are usually necessary to gain both formal and informal access to the formal law.

Informal inroads of access into the formal law is significant to any study of the dispute process and social conflict in general. This fact has clear consequences for disputes that are evaluated before the public forums of the formal legal system.

The term "public" is key because it refers precisely to the notion that such forums are *open* and *exposed* to the criticism and scrutiny of all citizens; that is, manipulation of the law is discouraged and attempts are made to render such machinations impossible. Understanding the manipulation of law is crucial to analyses of the dispute process and social conflict, and becomes especially important whenever secret access or manipulation is at issue. The general process by which specific information or issues are manipulated so that they do not appear in public or on the appropriate agenda is an important part of the study of law; however, most related work has overlooked the seminal insights by Bachrach and Baratz (1963). Studies concerned with the extent to which law on the books is applied as law in action are obviously significant, but following Bachrach and Baratz, we need more systematic information on the methods used to suffocate or ignore crucial issues of law (cf. Lincoln and Lauderdale 1985; Walker and Associates, 1986).

Another relevant aspect of the rationalization of law in Costa Rica and the nature of social relationships in the dispute process is the role of informal social control as an alternative or supplemental force to the formal law (see Appendix B). There are numerous examples in the cases where, because of access, as well as cost and time factors, the formal law was unavailable to one or more of the disputants. In fact, evidence in the cases reveals a bitter irony in this regard; in an attempt to make the formal law more fair and impartial, strict requirements have been created that actually make access to the formal law even less equal. As a result, the availability of informal social control played a very important role in the dispute process, offering, at a minimum, an immediately accessible source of advice, assistance, and sympathy—especially in the protection and defense of social identity and reputation.

In Sierpe, for example, the process of "complaining" entailed more than the airing of accusations or resentments; it also involved language related to character and honor (cf. Miyazawa, 1987). Disputants seemed determined to convince friends and relatives that they had not committed an offense and that they were either defending rights or taking what was rightfully theirs. This process allowed disputants to gain support for their definition of the facts and rightness of their position, irrespective of what might be happening on the formal level. Thus, a disputant might "lose" the case in the formal court system but still "win" before an informal group of his or her peers. Furthermore, such recognition and support seem to partially compensate for the "failings" of the formal legal system. And, importantly, they offer a relatively safe and locally accepted means for venting the anger and resentment often associated with social conflict.

This process illustrates how informal and formal social control offer elements of control and predictability. The formal law includes written laws and regulations, as well as the legal chain of authority and responsibility. However, informal social control also offers elements of control and predictability. Control exists because informal social control allows a disputant the advantage of regulating or censoring information received by supporters, and predictability occurs, in part, because the definition and placement of identities are related directly to further social interaction and continuing relationships. Decisions and judgments are often made on the basis of familial ties, friendships, loyalties, and related emotional factors. Therefore, in regard to control and predictability, informal and formal social control have more in common than prior work reveals (cf. Friedman, 1985).

In essence, based on our cases, Costa Rican absentee landlords enjoyed better access to formal power because of a combination of social circumstances including proximity to forums, mobility, and personal resources. However, access to informal social control is typically less problematic than access to formal control, because people are already part of some informal social network, although their position in the social hierarchy obviously is influential. In addition, informal access to the formal law may depend on where in the social hierarchy a person's informal social network is located. Some Costa Rican absentee landlords, for example, have better *informal* access to the formal law than do insiders. It is also important to note that more general social conditions in Costa Rica impact upon the land dispute process in the district of Sierpe. For example, the combination of the influx of refugees from conflicts in El Salvador and Nicaragua, as well as more pervasive world economic conditions, contribute significantly to inflated land values and the decrease of land available for development (Harris 1985; Vargas 1989). Thus, any land dispute is likely to be seen as more serious and may result in a stronger commitment by a disputant to resolve the dispute using informal social control, as well as formal social control.

In summary, the factor of access is a central element in the dispute process. Numerous factors relating to dispute and social conflict coincide when it comes to gaining access to formal and informal social control. Furthermore, since disputing is a social process that usually involves the participation of many individuals other than the principal disputants, and since most people are part of some informal social structure, access to informal social control is usually not problematic. However, access to the formal law may depend on many of the factors we have examined, especially those related to social hierarchies (Lauderdale 1988b). Although equal access to the law for all citizens is ostensibly a part of most democratic states, the realities of socioeconomic organization and informal social relations often result in a formal, legal organization that is structured, sometimes by subtle and other times by obvious factors, so that access is disproportionately available.

Time and Social Context

Time has various influences on the dispute process. In the district of Sierpe, the time spent in traveling to Puerto Cortez, for example, and the amount of time it takes to contact the formal authorities are significant. Also, the time involved in managing a dispute on the formal level has proven to be a decisive factor in some cases, adding to the cost of disputing and forcing some disputants to abandon the formal management of their dispute. In "The Inspection," despite the fact that Mark believed in the legitimacy of his grievances and wanted to continue disputing them on the formal level, he was forced to withdraw from the formal court battle after a year and a half because he said that he could no longer afford to invest his time and resources. In the dispute between Wilson and the Simo family, time was a major factor; the Simos eventually resorted to extralegal self-help tactics to dramatize their frustrations over the slowness and indecision of the court system.

In at least two cases, however, the time factor had a somewhat different impact. In the cases involving Mark, we see how his ability to manage disputes increased as he became gradually more integrated into the local culture. In the dispute between Roberto and Sergio we see a more complicated influence of time. As this dispute continued, the gradual deterioration of Roberto's health coincided with a local community crisis involving an increase in population combined with a land shortage. Although Roberto's dispute with Sergio had been continuing for many years, it was not until Roberto's health problems intensified that those seeking land in Sierpe saw an opportunity to take advantage of the ambiguities and uncertainties surrounding the case, and took action. After Roberto died, they resolved both problems at once by taking over Roberto's farm and using their combined strength to convince the formal social control agents to support their takeover and protect them from any further claims by Sergio.

Interestingly, perhaps the most striking feature regarding the influence of time in this study is the fact that disputes continue over many years. In some instances, the formal disputing had been discontinued or "resolved," but the informal disputing continues. One possible consequence of disputing over long periods is the emergence of secondary or related disputes that can aggravate the original dispute and often diminish chances for resolution of any of the disputes.

There are many examples in the cases where secondary disputes arose as a result of maneuvering or nonaction by various disputants and their supporters in the management of the original dispute. Perhaps the most conspicuous example of this process occurred in "The Colorado Camp," the dispute between Wilson and the Simo family; the Simos initiated several related disputes—on both the formal and informal level—designed to retaliate against Wilson and disrupt his tourism and gold mining activities. Moreover, many of our cases involved secondary disputing to some degree.

One reason for the emergence of such secondary disputes is related to the time factor and the peculiar social character of the Sierpe district. The social structure in this area has a distinct homogeneous quality, which is evidenced, for example, by the fact that family members typically live in and around Sierpe for their entire lives and because there is little social mobility. There are many opportunities for the building of "grievance portfolios"— that is, the accumulation of damaging information. Disputants often find themselves living close to their opponents, seeing each other on the streets of Sierpe, passing on the river or associating with common acquaintances. In essence, relatively detailed information about the opponent may be passed on and may be used in the management of disputes or in the creation of new disputes.

In addition, the factor of time combined with the tightly knit informal social networks may lead to the eventual involvement of "marginal actors"; these are people who are not initially involved in a dispute, but because of their interest or allegiance to a particular disputant or issue, they are often obliged to "take sides." Thus, a dispute with one member of a group may be regarded as a dispute with *all* members of the group. This involvement by marginal actors increases the chances for the emergence of other disputes among the supporters of those disputants involved in prolonged conflict.

There is another important aspect related to the homogeneous characteristics of the Sierpe area and the time factor. As disputes continued over the years, disputants often became locked into "mechanical dispute relationships." We suggest that these relationships are characterized by prolonged conflict, the close physical proximity of the disputants, and intense involvement by third parties including the informal social relations of each disputant. In these cases, the disputants search extensively for any new or imagined offense by their opponent and often take any opportunity to complain and to denounce their opponent, demonstrating the superiority of their own position and discrediting the motives of the other (see Garfinkel 1956: 421–22)

Moreover, there is the sense that resolution of these types of disputes is very difficult, if not impossible; in fact, the disputants may continue the dispute because too much damage has already been done and no restitution or forgiveness is expected. The management of these disputes is often characterized by high emotional intensity, and the language used in complaining eventually transcends the circumstances of the conflict and centers instead upon the personal character and integrity of the opponent. When Pablo described, for example, his dispute with Fernando, he said, "my troubles with Fernando will never be over. He is too much a bad man. We are now enemies. And no matter if I win or he wins, we will still be fighting." Asked what it would take to resolve their differences, Pablo replied, "when Fernando leaves this part of the country, or by a bullet to Fernando's head." In discussing the dispute between him and Philipe, Mark appeared upset and angry when he said, "the land Philipe cut off from my farm includes all the chocolate trees I planted. I planted those trees myself, on my hands and knees. Philipe might be a rich man and a lawyer, but he's a thief! I can never forgive him for that and will fight him as long as it takes to win my land back." Philipe, on the other hand, also became upset when asked for his view of the dispute; "Mark has no right to put a *denuncia* against me. There's never been a *denuncia* against me in my life! Who does he think he is? He is a foreigner and a fool. I'm a well-respected lawyer, I know the law and always live within the law." The point here is that such relationships evolve over time and that the disputants have so offended each other by focusing upon personal issues and attacks that settlement becomes very difficult.

Finally, there is one other aspect regarding the time factor that is particularly relevant here; how and when can a dispute be said to have been resolved? Only one of the disputes, "The Sierpe Gift," can be considered fully resolved and that was largely because one of the disputants died. In all other cases, the disputants continue on either the formal or informal levels of social control, and usually both. There have been a few cases where the formal legal system imposed a resolution but where the "loser" has rejected the court's decision and vowed to continue disputing. A formal resolution of a case rarely terminates such conflicts.

We asked several disputants in Sierpe when a dispute could be considered resolved. Responses invariably included one or more of the following conditions: when a disputant (or disputants) either dies, leaves the area, or gives in to an opponent's demands. When one or more of these situations occurs, the solution to the dispute is least problematic and is often self-evident; however, most said that waiting for an opponent to die or to leave the country is an undesirable alternative, because it is too ambiguous. All agreed that the "best" solution was represented by a mutual desire to reach a collective understanding and by a sincere effort to abide by any attendant agreements. In view of this, a dispute can generally be considered settled or resolved only when the disputants agree that the issue in question has been settled and no further disputing is anticipated or expected. In the opinion of the disputants, however, these conditions are also considered unlikely; already existing animosity and ill-will between disputants typically make a resolution of this kind unlikely, and in some cases, unimaginable. In fact, all disputants expected their respective conflicts to continue. Some also added that even if the disputes are "manipulated" or managed on a formal level, they will never be satisfied. As one disputant stated, "I can never trust that guy and could never be his friend. But if there are no more troubles, maybe we can live in peace."

As we have seen in analyzing the cases, the impact of time on the management of disputes is significant. Time may affect the ability of disputants to initiate or maintain a dispute. In addition, as a dispute continues over an extended period or as secondary disputes arise, it is often less likely that there will be a resolution to the dispute. Indeed, only one of the cases we analyzed was resolved and that was related to the death of one of the disputants. Taking these findings into account, we suggest that in the future it may be useful to focus *less* on the factors that may affect resolution of disputes and instead to concentrate attention on the complex, dynamic factors and social processes that impact upon *management* of the dispute process (cf. Nader and Todd 1978: 3).

Cost and Social Context

Access to the formal law depends, in part, upon the resources of the disputants, including property and money, as well as formal and informal contacts with the formal social control agents. These resources partially determine the relative ability of people to manage the varying costs of disputing. One disputing cost encountered by most residents of Sierpe, for example,—especially those living on the Boca Río Sierpe—is the cost entailed by the trip necessary to make initial contact with the formal authorities in Puerto Cortez. Other costs may include the expense of traveling to formally initiate the dispute, the cost of travel to and from the formal social control agencies, as well as costs of transporting witnesses and social control agents during the course of the dispute.

Another example of cost occurs in instances where there are those who can no longer afford the expense of managing their disputes formally and are constrained to continue on the informal level. In this sense, cost is an element in the exercise of power; that is, it affects the ability of disputants to manage their disputes successfully. An obvious example from "The Sierpe Gift" involves the dispute between Roberto and Sergio. The facts of the case suggest that Sergio purchased the use of the formal power of the state by outbidding Roberto for the services of the alcaldía. In this case, however, the efforts of both Sergio and the formal law were overpowered by the formal political strength of the squatter movement. Sergio eventually lost considerable money, as well as potential ownership and control of the farm where Roberto had lived for many years. On the other hand, in the disputes involving Mark and Pablo, we see how the lack of personal resources needed for managing a dispute combined with the time factor led to withdrawal of the formal management of their disputes. Both continued disputing on the formal level, but without access to the power and sanctions of the formal law, they did not enjoy this advantage in the course of the dispute.

Cost is related to the exercise of power on both the formal and informal levels of social control. Such power is not a matter exclusively of money or status or state authority, but may also involve informal social networks, such as "grass-roots" movements that may exercise different types of control (cf. Barkan 1985; McAdam 1989).

Cost in a sociopsychological sense also played an important role in the dispute process. In a small homogeneous community like Sierpe—where almost every person is known to everyone else—the creation, maintenance, or negotiation of personal identities and reputations is a common part of daily life. Also, the level of effectiveness of the informal communication system determines, in part, the extent to which conflict and dispute become a topic of local conversation—for example, where groups of people discuss the personalities involved and speculate on the outcome. Even a slight offense or grievance may be taken seriously within this context and in an agrarian-based economy such as in Sierpe, land disputes are regarded even more seriously, since they usually involve a threat to scarce resources or survival.

Furthermore, residents of Sierpe regard ownership and control of property as a measure of worth and self-esteem. Thus, a threat to control or ownership is also a threat to a person's honor and integrity. Land disputes, therefore, involve not only legal questions and levels of social control, but also sociopsychological factors. In many cases, for example, complaining by disputants involved protecting and maintaining personal identity. The disputants tended to become angry and upset as they discussed the course of their disputes. They had been offended personally and equated land ownership or control with a part of their identity; that is, a part of who they are and their status in the community. The emotion and extent of the "self-feeling" was apparent in the declaration, "this land is *my* land!" When speaking of his dispute, Jorge Simo said, "our fight with Wilson is a fight for family pride and honor. My family has lived in this area for over fifty years and we're well known and respected. No way will we allow him to take away what is ours." It is evident that people in such situations are not likely to give up their dispute or ignore the actions of their opponents.

Sociopsychological cost is partially exemplified by the level of emotional intensity evidenced by the disputants, and these strong emotions can provide the motivation and energy to continue disputing. Further, it is this factor that often leads to self-help or other extralegal tactics in response to the frequent slowness, unresponsiveness, or corruption of the formal law. There were a few disputants, for example, who threatened physical violence against their opponent—a form of self-help—as a way of defending their character and "proving" their control and mastery over what they call theirs.

This aspect of cost introduces an element of unpredictability into the study and analysis of disputes. Emotional response varies from individual to individual, and although its expression may be tempered by formal and informal social pressures, there are sometimes instances when passion blinds reason and behavior becomes "unaccountable." And even if action is well-planned and well-coordinated, the emotions leading to action may take others by surprise, such as the mass takeover of Roberto's farm. In this case, strong emotions, including feelings of desperation and frustration, motivated a group of people to take the law into their own hands, thereby bypassing control by the formal rational law.

Although sociopsychological cost may be difficult to identify and describe, it should be recognized as an integral part of the dispute process and as such, it is a variable influencing social behavior. Thus, inquiries need to be made to gauge the depth and intensity of emotion in an attempt to account for the occurrence of unpredictable or "irrational" events (Giddens 1987).

Thus, the cost factor has had an influence on the disputes we studied in two ways; cost in gaining access to informal agents of social control, and sociopsychological cost. These two aspects of cost were related in the sense that the perceived seriousness of an offense led to a decision about how best to manage the dispute. Despite their obvious symbiotic relationship, we have examined them as distinct elements and discuss them separately.

4 Conflict and the Struggle for Control

Our study has described elements of the distinctive culture and environment in and around Sierpe, Costa Rica. In this chapter we will expand this part of the analysis by focusing upon four interesting factors: tide-time, the milla maritima, private/productive property, and nonviolent disputing. Then we will present more encompassing issues.

Cultural Dimensions

Tide-time

Our cases take place in remote areas of the Sierpe district where there are few roads, no electricity, and only one telephone (which is located in the town of Sierpe and thus not immediately available to 90 percent of the district's residents). Travel and communication in the district of Sierpe are based primarily on water transportation on the River Sierpe, the surrounding mangrove swamps, and the Pacific Ocean. The direction and time of travel is determined most often by the movement of the tide, and provides the basis for a concept we call tide-time.

One important consequence of a social system revolving around the ocean tide is the perception of time. The sense of time in the district is measured by the movement of the sun and by the motion of the tide (and the movement of the moon). Tide-time is determined by watching the current and level of water in the river, in the mangrove swamps, and on the beaches. Thus, tide-time might be considered to be a more "natural" time than the "invented" time of clocks and watches.

Time around the Boca is measured in days and nights, and the changing of the tide. This natural time is orderly but includes another element as well—insiders note that every tide is always a little higher or lower than the previous tide and occurs forty to fifty minutes later than the previous one. Time in this sense is not linear and precise, but rather approximate and sensual. Such a perception of time seems to lead to a relatively slow-paced lifestyle and often to the development of patience. People must wait for a favorable tide before traveling on the river or moving through the mouth of the river to the ocean. Sometimes people wait for hours, for the changing of the tide occurs every six hours. At other times, such as in the case of passing through the river mouth and into the ocean, people have to wait for days. This often occurs when the moon is full. The full moon causes the undercurrent and wave action in the mouth of the river to become more unpredictable and powerful, making travel at such times dangerous. The local residents are well-adjusted to such waiting and regard it as natural and necessary.

There have been occasions, however, when foreigners traveling through the district have become quite upset and impatient at having to wait. Usually these are tourists dependent on local transportation—that is, boats piloted by Sierpe residents. On one occasion a tourist did not want to wait (or did not know enough to wait) and piloted his boat into the mouth of the river at a dangerous time; a big wave hit the boat, the boat overturned, and the man was killed.

Tide-time influences the disputing process in direct ways, such as in the communication of news and information. In "The Inspection," for example, Mark's caretaker had to wait one day before paddling to Sierpe to bring the news that Philipe was putting up a fence across Mark's farm. And Mark had to wait another day before traveling to view the fence, since it was necessary to wait for high tide to enter the mangrove swamps where the farm is located. By that time the fence was already completed and Philipe had returned to San José.

Also, in the same case, when Mark and the alcaldía went to inspect Mark's farm they had to wait on the Boca for several hours for high tide before they could reach the property—at low tide people are confronted with two hundred meters of soft, deep mud that is almost impossible to traverse. It was during this waiting time that the alcaldía went fishing with her children and mother. Mark felt the alcaldía was not taking the inspection seriously and he eventually lost faith in the legal process.

In "The Colorado Camp," Wilson's caretaker had to wait for a day before traveling to Sierpe to call Wilson and advise him of the takeover. Wilson moved quickly, but the extra time allowed the Simo family to consolidate their hold on the fishing camp and make plans and arrangements for their escape. In the rainy season, local residents routinely use the high tide to their advantage in making secret forays to the beaches to gather coconuts. During high tide it is possible to enter small, hidden canals on Violin Island, allowing for clandestine arrival and departure.

These are examples of cases in which tide-time had the most effect, mainly because time was an important element in the cases and the disputes occurred in an area accessible only by water. Another dimension of the culture that has a relatively significant effect on the disputing process is the milla maritima.

Milla Maritima

The existence of the milla maritima leads to confusion and dispute. It is a fairly new law, which stipulates that a certain and ambiguous number of meters of beachfront property (which vary, according to the tide) are to remain available to public use.

The law is administered and governed by the local municipality, not by the central government in San José. Thus, while privately owned land must be registered in the Registro Civil in San José, possession of the milla maritima—adjacent to or part of the same land— must be registered in the local municipality. Officials in the Supreme Court of Costa Rica note that few lawyers in San José know anything about the milla maritima or the rules governing it.

This situation can lead to serious misunderstandings and problems, as in "The House without a Home". When a dispute does arise involving land within the milla maritima, people who know the law can use the legal resources of the local municipality in managing relevant disputes. If, for example, the dispute had been on "privately" owned land—the land behind the milla maritima—there might have been many more problems; George and Mark would have had to provide their our own lawyer, engineer, and land surveyor for required inspections. However, because it was the milla maritima, the local officials were obligated to mediate the dispute and make a decision, thus eliminating court fees and lawyer's costs.

Private/Productive Property

In general, the local residents do not view property with a speculative or investment value, rather they regard it as a means of livelihood. Most landowners in the Sierpe district own only one farm or parcel of land, and it is often the major source of their sub-sistence or income. Land is not regarded merely a possession, it is a place of identity, self-esteem, labor, and production.

Very few farms are not worked. Of those relatively large farms that have not been put into production all are owned by out-siders with other means of income. These farms are used by their owners as a place of recreation, for vacations, or as an investment, to retain with a view of selling them in the future for a profit.

There is a common attitude toward the ownership and use of property: people should use the land, rather than allow it to sit idle. Pancho, one of the insiders from "The Fruit of the Land," echoes the sentiments of most insiders:

> To own land and not use it or let anyone else use it is a sin! This is a poor area and we are poor people. We must work hard for our money. And to see a big landowner sitting on his farm, not working it, putting out a sign with "no trespass-ing," this is a crime, a moral crime! They should lose their land, the government should take it away from them and give it to someone who will use it.

The rules governing the milla maritima seem to reflect this attitude of "use it or lose it." Within the land controlled by the municipality, if one who owns the rights of possession should abandon the land and not use it or cultivate it, she or he is in dan-ger of losing the land; someone else could legally "squat" on this land, begin using it, and therefore eventually gain the rights of pos-session. The analysis in "The House without a Home" illustrates this process explicitly.

Nonviolent Disputing

There is a notable lack of violence in our study. Costa Rican culture has a tradition of nonviolent social relationships, including those involved in disputes. This tradition includes verbal abuse and harassment; it is considered very bad taste to raise one's voice or to use foul or threatening language.

There were no incidents of physical violence in our cases, despite the fact that all disputes were emotionally charged and considered quite serious. In the takeover of "The Colorado Camp," for example, the Simo family did not steal or damage any of Wilson's property. Also, Wilson's caretaker reported that the

Simos treated him "gently" as they kicked him off the property.

In "Resident or Squatter?" there was no physical violence. Pablo has said occasionally that what Fernando needs is "a bullet between the eyes," but never to Fernando directly, and such comments were usually made in the heat of passion and not taken seriously. When asked if he would ever really do such a thing, he answered that no, he would not shoot Fernando, because "it would only make things worse for me."

In "The House without a Home," Sanchez threatened several times to come to the Boca and kick Mark out, and also to tear down the house. Such threats, communicated usually through third parties, typically came from a local Costa Rican who also lived on the Boca Río Sierpe. Although no violence occurred, the threats of such violence had an emotional impact—outsiders became quite upset and frightened. The threats also influenced their management of the dispute, asking for advice from insiders and talking to a lawyer, costing them time and money. However, when there was no other consequences from the threats, they were regarded eventually as nothing more than harassment—a tactic in Sanchez's disputing style—and so they were ignored.

In "Denouncing the Campesino," Pablo was confident of the outcome of this dispute, because he had the documents and receipts giving him right of possession of the land. Jim tried to intimidate Pablo, but when he was unable to manipulate the court system, he retreated to complaining to the other outsiders. Thus, this dispute entailed few emotions and threats of violence did not occur.

In "The Fruit of the Land," there was also no violence nor any threat of violence. However, Mark and Pancho view the dispute as a very serious issue, and both of them comment on it from time to time. For Pancho the ownership or control of this land is a point of honor and future livelihood (he wants his children to inherit it). Nevertheless, there has been no violence and no threat of violence.

In "The Sierpe Gift," Roberto and his caretaker were removed forcibly from the farm by the guardia. The removal resulted from the order signed by the alcaldía. The members of the guardia carried batons, pistols, and M-1 carbines. In this case the threat of violence was made by the formal agents of social control as they intervened in a dispute that was initially between two citizens. After Roberto died, the takeover occurred. A group of local citizens marched en masse to Roberto's farm and staked their claims. One of the leaders of the "squatter movement" stated specifically that they had taken precautions to eliminate the possibility of violence. They pledged themselves to secrecy so that Roberto's children would not be alerted to the plan and try to defend the farm. They also enlisted the support of a sympathetic local guardia to ensure that they would be protected from any reaction by Sergio.

In "The Absentee Landlord and the Local" there was no violence or threat of violence. Jorge disputed in a very peaceful, non-violent manner, and Philipe presented himself as a highly respected lawyer who uses the law frequently and successfully.

In "The Inspection," when Mark, a North American, who at the time was acquiring insider status, discovered that Philipe had put up a fence on his property, he said that he would tear down the fence immediately. In fact when he first went to the farm he brought with him a crowbar and hammer to "rip the fence apart." He was counseled by his Costa Rican friends not to do this; they said this action would only aggravate the problem and also "it wouldn't be right."

The dispute in "The Rainy Season" is only one part of a series of ongoing disputes between Fernando and the local residents of the Boca. Fernando does not want trespassing on "his" beaches, but the insiders feel they have the right to collect the coconuts on public property. Fernando employs caretakers (or guards) who roam the beaches occasionally to keep out trespassers. These caretakers are supposedly armed, but no resident has ever reported that they were threatened overtly with such arms or with violence.

Some of these caretakers are insiders or acquaintances of insiders, and informal relationships exist that allow some residents secret access to the beaches. That is, the guards let certain people move freely on the beaches—as long as Fernando is not around and does not know about it.

We also observed that in disputes concerning theft there is no violence. People complain to acquaintances, friends, relatives, and possibly to legal authorities, but they do not confront the alleged thief in any violent way.

The majority of the rare incidents of physical violence seem to occur in and around the cantinas, when old resentments and animosities resurface, quickly leading to fist fights. Many of the incidents are related to old "private" disputes that ostensibly were resolved. Usually, friends and drinking companions break up the fight without personal injury.

In most cases, a person with a grievance rarely confronts the other person in a direct manner. Complaints are made to third parties who are then expected to "pass the word" to the offender. Insiders as well as most Costa Ricans tend to avoid social situations that are likely to be unpleasant or emotionally tense, and confrontation among principals rarely occurs.

Encompassing Issues

Our study also has attempted to raise other encompassing conceptual issues. Clearly, one focus has been to emphasize the processes involved in *dispute management* rather than *dispute resolution*. In the present context, management is simply a heuristic concept. By management, we have referred to the various social forces that impinge upon the control of a dispute. Obviously, we do not think it is wise to use other definitions of management in this context, since they often prematurely refer to who or what should be controlled. From our perspective, disputes and attendant conflicts can be viewed as one subspecies of crises. Parts of the social structure that remain obscured or hidden in most settings have emerged when analyzed in the context of crises (Offe 1972; Balbus 1973, 1977; Trubek 1977; Christenson 1986; Perez Vargas 1988; Olson 1989).

Having considered the interrelated factors of the nature of the social relationship, access, cost, and time, it is also clear that a number of other factors are not only relevant to the study of disputes, but can be usefully integrated into future analysis. Conceptualizing the different stages in the process of the disputing ordeal, for example, into negotiation, mediation and adjudication, may be a worthwhile strategy in some instances. Nonetheless, an exclusive reliance on such concepts is often very misleading in the context of an examination such as this one. In addition, we should explore other relevant factors that typically influence the amount and type of social control created in the disputing process with the caution that these are only another set of useful departure points. These factors include: (1) the varying types of actors (e.g., individuals, groups, organizations, and larger collectives); (2) the *number* of actors involved in a dispute; (3) the corporateness of the actors (i.e., the extent to which individuals have an organizational structure that exists independent of them and the extent to which the structure persists over time); and (4) the institutional forces that shape the context in which disputes can be recognized, much less pursued.

Moreover, what Yngvesson (1984) has identified as structural variables—including, for example, political autonomy, and presence or absence of exchange relations between groups—are contributing factors to the escalation or containment of a dispute. However, the way in which these variables are defined, and how they are distinguished from the analytic concepts (dyads, triads) are problems that need to be addressed. For a more accurate understanding of dispute processing in general, it is necessary to "explore perspectives other than the official one" (1984: 258).

Obviously, our analysis of the multitude of informal perspectives reveals sharply the problem of using analytic dichotomies. Prior research that has focused upon dispute resolution versus conflict is very misleading for precisely this reason. Most prior analyses have structured our thinking such that most people are searching for the point at which disputes are resolved. However, our analyses demonstrate that dispute *management* rather than *resolution* is the most common feature of conflict among disputants. We think that a reanalysis of prior research and, more importantly, future analyses should include this emphasis on *dispute management*. The fabric of everyday life contains numerous conflicts and disputes, some of which are transparent while others are opaque, and at some level most people are aware of the ongoing evaluation of these problematic social relationships. In essence, even in those instances when we think a dispute is resolved and that we have "won," we often find later that the dispute has either simply changed its form, is being reevaluated using new criteria, or is being reassessed by new or different arrangements of power (Lauderdale 1988A; Elster 1989). In essence, it is important to determine *under what conditions disputes emerge*. Felstiner and associates (1980–81) suggest that antecedents to disputes are as interesting and problematic as the disputes themselves. They describe, for example, why many disputes do not occur, because problems are either internally avoided or externally controlled (also, see Kidder, 1980–81, for a related discussion of the importance of antecedent conditions, especially those conditions where a structural imbalance already exists, and see Kirp et al. 1986).

Modes of Dispute Management

Following an analysis that seeks to reduce the emphasis on dispute resolution, Black (1987, 1989) presents five modes of conflict management that provide a heuristic framework for further research. The modes of management are *self-help, avoidance, negotiation, settlement,* or *toleration.* Black suggests that a particular mode will emerge based on the social context of a dispute. The social context, for example, where self-help will likely emerge is called a "stable agglomeration," such as where a "code of honor" exists. In analyzing most dispute cases, and especially the Sierpe cases, it is apparent that disputes may shift from one mode of management to another.

The social context that influences the management of a dispute needs to be explicated and Black's framework delineating five modes of conflict management is a very useful strategy. A specific management mode such as *self-help, avoidance, negotiation, settlement,* or *toleration* evolves from a particular social setting. Vengeance, for example, is an extreme form of *self-help* that is likely to emerge under varying conditions of equality, social distance, functional independence, organization, and immobility. Self-help can also take the form of discipline and rebellion. Thus, for example, a master-slave relationship is characterized by inequality, elongated cultural and relational distance, functional unity, vertical segmentation, and immobility.

It should be noted, however, that Black does not argue that each variable is present to the same degree, only that these variables are useful in predicting when a particular form of self-help will be employed. The social context determines which variables are most relevant and how the variables interrelate. Therefore, while it is argued that as inequality between disputants increases, discipline and rebellion is likely to vary accordingly; it does not follow that inequality has a greater impact or is more important than the other variables.

Avoidance, the second mode of dispute management, can range from permanent severing of interaction to a brief reduction in the type or frequency of interaction. Avoidance is most likely to occur under conditions of minimal or no hierarchy, social fluidity, social fragmentation, functional independence, and individuation. This mode of management usually emerges where these unstable aggregations are present. The typical predictor of avoidance may be the fluidity of the relationship, the ease with which they are initiated or terminated. However, Black notes that avoidance is often difficult to identify, because the obvious signs of conflict such as a complaint may be absent.

The handling of a conflict by mutual agreement, negotiation, is another primary mode of dispute management. This type of management does not involve intervention by third parties except to represent groups, such as families, organizations, or nations. Basic factors relevant to negotiation include equality, cross-linkages, organization, homogeneity, and accessibility. Relative equality between disputants, for example, usually results in negotiation, and this mode will likely be found in a tangled network.

Settlement, the management of a dispute characterized by the encompassing presence of nonpartisan third parties, represents the next category in the typology. Settlement includes forms such as mediation, arbitration, and adjudication. Each form of settlement is based on relative levels of authoritativeness. In each form of settlement, the third party involved in the dispute must be sufficiently nonpartisan to create the trilateral construction that typifies this form of dispute management. Settlement in its most extreme forms—adjudication and repressive pacification involving violence—is characterized by inequality, relational distance, heterogeneity, and organizational asymmetry. The ideal climate for settlement is referred to as a "triangular hierarchy."

Identified by the relative inaction of the disputants, toleration is the last mode of dispute management presented by Black. In essence, toleration is a mode characterized by the adage "live and let live" (Black 1987: 37). Toleration has not been viewed typically as a form of conflict management, yet it is the most commonly chosen means of handling a grievance. An example of toleration is "unilateral peaceableness"; the practice of diffusing conflict before it escalates. Extreme examples of toleration are found, for example, in the high degree of social acceptance offered to superiors by "underlings," as well as where there are high levels of intimacy between disputants.

Black's framework is a useful departure point for explicating, as well as expanding, the research we have begun here (also see Horowitz 1990). We also suggest some initial steps that may be useful for rethinking tradition and context. From our perspective, this process includes analyzing and, in particular, rethinking the fundamental processes of social control. In essence, the study of control in this context entails a description of basic social processes and suggests a method for understanding social order or disorder (see Meier 1982). We are not pursuing a reconstruction or revisionist interpretation of the processes; the more inclusive literature related to our proposed analysis includes attempts to avoid such problems and encompasses relevant insights from varying perspectives (cf. Kierkegaard 1968, 1983; Habermas 1979; Derrida 1982; Bataille 1985; Ashley 1986b). While those insights are beyond the scope of this study, they should prove useful in analyzing more encompassing processes of social control, and, for the present they suggest that we, at a minimum, need to reconsider some of the key concepts in the study of social control. Black's concept of avoidance, for example, points to the problematic nature of describing, much less measuring, some crucial forms of conflict. How many conflicts are not heard or seen simply because of the silence of disputants?

Social Control and Deviance

Our study of disputes and conflicts also suggests that prior work has focused disproportionately upon what might be distinctive to deviance rather than the factors that create more or less control.[1] We examine how disputants come to be seen as deviant or legitimate, and how deviance is frequently socially negotiated. From our perspective, social control is the process of defining and reacting to deviance. Deviance is a definition created by particular disputants or agencies to refer to action that should not occur. The successful application of a deviance label to another person or collectivity can be, among other things, one mechanism used to transform identities and maintain or increase not only social solidarity but also *social mobility* (Matza 1969; Lauderdale 1980; Christenson 1986).

An analysis of the processes involved in creating, maintaining, and applying deviance labels reflects the thrust of much recent work in this area (cf. Pfohl 1985; Ben-Yehuda 1990). Deviance is inextricably linked to the study of status hierarchies and stratification, with the deviant often occupying the lowest position in a hierarchy (see Lauderdale et al. 1984). In addition, in times of crisis, those individuals or groups who are labeled deviant often find themselves placed entirely outside the social boundaries (see Selby 1974 on "social expendability"). The analysis of the manipulation of deviant categories and deviants has much in common with the study of social mobility, not only how deviants may overcome their stigma and become more upwardly mobile, but how others use the stigma for their own social mobility. The study of the human struggle for social mobility and social change is part and parcel of the study of social control. Thus, from our perspective, the study of social control is inherently the study of social conflict and law.

Arguably the most important contribution made by sociologists and anthropologists to theorizing about law is to identify the structural conditions and processes that appear to give rise to particular kinds of law and to their related systems of justice. Thus the works of Maine, Durkheim, Weber, and the Marxist sociology of law found a tradition of theorizing which transcends the universalism of those natural and positive law philosophers (Aristotle, Hobbes, Austin, Kelsen, Hart) and questions the universalism of intractable functionalists (Llewellyn, Hoebel, Bredemeier), all of whom assume that there are irreducible components of legal systems common to all societies (Henry 1983: 1).

Our approach has relied on an integrative sociology of law perspective which focuses upon social conditions and related processes that lead to particular kinds of social control.[2] This approach emphasizes some of the important similarities in the work of Durkheim, Marx, and Weber, as well as the misguided attempt to characterize them as simply conflict or consensus theorists (see Inverarity et al. 1983; Turner 1986; Lauderdale et al. 1990; Turner, 1991). In Durkheim's classic analyses of the division of labor, as well as the relationship between the normal and the pathological, for example, he used central concepts of social conflict and control to examine some of the basic elements of social life. Deviance was not a tangible object but a concept used to explore the social structure, and it led him to central discoveries, for example, about social solidarity and punishment. We have used the same basic idea of employing central concepts as a means to understanding the structure and dynamics of disputes.

The role that the labeling of deviants can have in a society, particularly with respect to solidarity, was clearly relevant to people involved in our study. As with many disputants in our study, Pablo, one of the first settlers in the Sierpe area, was frequently concerned with who was and was not being cast as deviant. On one occasion when he was reflecting on his own disputes, he commented on the larger dispute surrounding "the land." "My problems are not so large. Costa Rica is always trapped by someone into a dispute. Look at the conflict now between us and our brothers and sisters in Nicaragua. They are now seen as devils by many people but we helped them get free just a few years ago. They are really the same people and so are we. There is something bigger going on and we don't have control of it."

It is clear that the process by which deviance is created or defined exists on several levels of analysis.[3] On the individual level, disputants may frequently attempt to elevate or enhance their status by attempting to label other people or their actions as deviant. And, as the quote by Pablo suggests, attempts to control definitions of deviance extend to include larger groups, organizations, institutions, or nation-states. These deviance definitions are constantly being renegotiated and redefined such that an individual or collectivity initially seen as "normal" can be redefined as deviant, and these definitions obviously may vary depending on the social context. Thus, descriptions of the Sandinistas have varied in particular contexts from that of a group of "freedom fighters" to the "devilish" depiction reported by Pablo.

This reflection by one of the disputants reveals not only the importance of studying the creation, maintenance, and changes in definition of deviance, but also the management of conflict. Pablo's observation can also be placed in the context of broader developments. As we noted earlier, Costa Rica is a relatively stable, democratic country that is regionally bound by political, economic, and military instability. This instability and the more encompassing disputes occurring throughout the Central American region have a significant impact on the process of dispute management in Sierpe and throughout Costa Rica (Lincoln and Lauderdale 1985; Perez Vargas 1988). Developments in the area are determined, in part, by the involvement or interference of more technologically developed countries such as the United States. These outsider actors, who often offer a variety of military and nonmilitary aid, can change significantly the social and cultural landscape of the region.

A fundamental question concerning our study is: What have we learned about the dispute process that may help us to understand the larger picture of conflict and dispute in Central America—indeed, anywhere in the world (see Miyazawa 1987)? One of the obvious findings from our cases is the subtle but organized nature of the informal social structure. This structure, including its informal channel of communication into the formal structure of state law, serves as a primary alternative source of power. Our study also highlights the role and perspective of persons central to the social control process relative to marginal actors. Marginal individuals have little input into how a dispute is conceptualized and, consequently, how it is ultimately resolved. In addition, the *language of disputing* is important; that is, whose language is used or is dominant in the process, and how do specific definitions influence the outcome? (Williams 1986 examines this issue and its implications with regard to Australian Aboriginal and Euro-Australian principles of land tenure.)

The language of social control influences the processing of disputes in predictable ways. Analyses of various forms of *discourse* are essential to the study of social control. Omar, one of the long-time residents of Sierpe, remarks:

> The police talk about theft but *we* know that when something is missing, it may only be a question of borrowing. Maybe the person only forgot to tell the other person that a knife or boat was borrowed? Even if you take something for a long period of time, it may not be stealing. Who knows, maybe it will be returned? Of course, some people do the wrong thing, but we usually know how to take care of that (by talking it out).

More generally, a relationship exists between the language of social control in a society and the social structure in which it is embedded (cf. Kidder 1980–81; Mather and Yngvesson 1980–81; Erikson 1986; Goode 1986; Zelditch 1986; Lauderdale et al. 1990). Obviously, often the "true" meaning of a dispute is not reflected by the "surface facts" of the conflict. When disputants avoid further conflict, for example, by becoming silent, the concept of facts becomes quite problematic if not a conundrum. Or, as we mentioned earlier, when social control agents create an agenda by selectively omitting particular information, the factual basis for a case may be hidden indefinitely. And, more generally, underlying issues become masked by the way the dispute is defined. Understanding the definitional process clearly has crucial implications for the basis and sustenance of the "official" social order and the social structure, and for any further work relating to dispute management (see Ashley, 1980).

Epilogue
Justice and Social Control

I am somewhat perplexed at the way people of the United States take our action in Nicaragua. I confess that it worries me a great deal. I cannot understand how any intelligent, patriotic citizen can remain silent without protesting, while our President is carrying on an unauthorized and indefensible war against Nicaragua. We are establishing a precedent down there that will some day plunge thousands of our young boys into war and bring about untold bloodshed, for certainly, if the President of the United States can carry on war in Nicaragua, without the consent of Congress, he can do the same thing with many other countries.

This excerpt is from a letter written by a U.S. citizen to J. Nevin Sayre who represented The Fellowship of Reconciliation in New York. The message seems relevant to numerous issues debated by governments, by the media, and by citizens and interest groups throughout the world in the 1980s. Yet, the quote is not from a letter written to express opinion about a recent social issue, such as continuing aid to the Contras, but from a letter written on *February 4, 1928*. The quote dramatically reintroduces the following question: If we do not take the time to understand the lessons of history, are we resigned to repeat its mistakes (see Harris 1985:235–49)?

We approached the study of dispute management, deviance, and social control in a small, isolated area of Costa Rica with the goal of attempting, in part, to answer this and other equally important questions. We were interested initially in examining basic factors that affect the management or outcomes of interpersonal disputes and more pervasive social conflicts. We found that the primary sources of many conflicts are difficult to detect, since they emerged from complex forms of dependency and domination relationships. A dispute such as "The House without a Home" reveals that as the secondary conflict emerged, the primary source of the conflict became obscure, even the history of the rights of possession and the legal status of the *milla maritima* were difficult to document. Nader (1990a), for example, notes the complexity of the historical roots and development of dispute management in Zapotec culture. The "harmony" model they espoused was adapted in different ways: traditional elites as a means to maintain status quo relations, peasants as a strategy for using the court system as means to present their conflicts with various forms of dominance. Thus, despite the fact that many researchers have associated a "harmony" model with a hegemonic culture (via developments such as the imposition and proliferation of Christianity), Nader suggests that harmony also can be used to resist the domination of outsiders, insiders, or colonizers who operate as both outsiders and insiders. Her suggestion fits the mode of resistance in disputes such as "The Sierpe Gift" and "The Inspection".

In a similar vein, Scott (1985) reveals the processes by which peasants use everyday forms of deviance such as defiance as a means to confront or resist authority (see Lauderdale 1980, 1988a). Unlike Zapotec culture, in Sedaka, more informal and indirect methods are used by peasants to resist authority. The peasant struggle is not only over property and material gains, but also an ideological one, manifesting itself in "low-profile" deviance such as false compliance, feigned ignorance, and slander. These forms of self-help (Black 1984) also take other forms as is evident in disputes such as "The Colorado Camp" where collective action replaced the law, as well as the official owners of the fishing camp. While Scott feels that his study disconfirms Gramsci's "theory" of hegemony, we view Scott's study and our own as an indication of the ability of disadvantaged people to possess contradictory consciousnesses—a sophisticated ability to articulate how advantaged people sometimes work in their behalf either intentionally or serendipitously, and at other times how they dominate them for a variety of reasons.

The complexities involved in the forms of struggle described by Nader (1990a) and Scott (1985) are not easily discernable. Not only must researchers contend with their own ethnocentrism in their interpretations of what they observe in other cultures, but also activities that occur at levels of analysis that researchers are not aware of or allowed to observe. It is obvious from both Nader's and Scott's work that while a dominant culture is present in both communities, hegemony, as Gramsci described it in the 1930s in Italy, is not as omnipresent or as consistently diffused, since peasants appear to try to resist or use the dominant culture to their advantage (cf. Augelli and Murphy 1988). In both studies, peasants practice a form of resistance which is not apparent or observable at a single level of analysis.

Clearly, we need to examine disputes and encompassing conflicts at different levels of analysis and use different degrees of abstraction as a tool to develop a theoretical framework (Lauderdale et al. 1990), as well as to develop appropriate questions such as: What means do people use to enjoy advantages in the formal and informal arenas of social control? Under what conditions can ostensibly "powerless" people gain access to the formal agents of social control, and when might they be successful in managing their disputes?

Our decision to focus upon the politics of social control was informed by the historical relationship among politics, conflict, and control (cf. Benney, 1983; Gibbs 1989). As Foucault (1977:168) so aptly remarks, "It may be that war as strategy is a continuation of politics. But it must not be forgotten that 'politics' has been conceived as a continuation, if not exactly and directly of war, at least of the military model as a fundamental means of preventing civil disorder." The takeover of Roberto's farm in "The Sierpe Gift" was politics of this genre and the military model has become more visible in recent years as Army Corps of Engineers from other nations construct bridges and establish basic components of communication in the remote jungle area under the banner of progress and modernization. Yet, the local people refer to this activity as building bridges for surveillance—what might also be referred to as establishing part of the infrastructure for war.

The study of the politics of social control in Costa Rica entails an examination of dependency relationships and various associated forms of legitimate assistance or atavistic domination (cf. Perez Vargas 1988). Rationalization is a concept closely linked with the activities of groups or nations who are ostensibly offering developmental aid to less technologically developed nations. These attempts at rationalization may often be partially in response to political or economic instability in a region and may include attempts to increase predictability and stability. However, by offering increasing levels of economic aid, technology, and military assistance, increased destabilization, as well as nascent or continuing dependency relationships, may result.

Furthermore, in attempting to "modernize" a less technologically developed country through the introduction of various assistance programs, ostensible benefits are often discussed in terms of "progress." The emphasis upon progress in the study of dispute resolution is also quite pervasive, yet some of the most enlightening work in related areas suggests that we carefully reexamine such concepts (see Lévi-Strauss 1955; Koch 1974; Kozolchyk and Greenberg 1988; Goldberg 1990.) These dependency relationships are part of the overall process of dispute management and serve typically as one mechanism to maintain or increase social control.

Much of the common knowledge within the study of one form of social control, punishment, for example, implies that society progresses by allowing deviants to serve time rather than be punished in other, supposedly "less humane", ways. Deprivation of freedom often is seen as a more progressive form of punishment. However, time can also be viewed as one of the most precious commodities of human experience, and depriving people of their use of time can be viewed as a severe penalty. One of the disputants in our study, Omar, in reflecting upon the sanctions that people in Sierpe endure, remarked, "all we really have is time and I want to use what little is left for me to feel the freedom of life." As has been clearly noted from one anthropological perspective:

> Anthropologists who work in other cultures often return to their own culture and society with a perspective that makes them question the obvious and see things . . . they might never have seen. [Nader 1984a:951]

In general, our study of related areas, such as punishment, suggests that we proceed with caution when we hear of the benefits of "progress" or "civilization" (see Ryan 1987 on the concept of property).

The potential side effects of attempts at rationalization and modernization are clearly related to the study of authority, legitimation, and domination. Building upon the perspective offered by Weber (1978), we need to examine more closely the processes by which people or groups are dominated, including the conditions that result in people seemingly "allowing" themselves to be dominated. Weber began this latter analysis by focusing upon situations where people allow themselves to be dominated because they believe authority figures have legitimacy, because they do not question the legitimacy of particular rules, or because they fear the consequences of challenging authority. Variations on this theme are evident in many of our cases. In "The Inspection," for example, a disputant, following the advice of other insiders who noted that it would be dangerous for him to engage in self-help, decided to defer to the official inspection and the state authorities. Most people rarely question the source of the authority's legitimacy or the rules, and consequently, they believe that it is their duty to obey (Augelli and Murphy 1988; Bauman 1989).

A potentially interesting extension of such an analysis could include an examination of instances where authority figures attempt to gain or succeed in achieving legitimacy by claiming, "I am only doing my job." The study of conflict management can potentially augment work on the conflict embedded in social movements and protest by providing us with useful answers to questions such as: Under what conditions does the management of a dispute lead to protest, the birth of a social movement, or the growth of a movement (see McAdam 1989)? Under what conditions do people obey because they are only doing their job, or because they simply believe it is "appropriate," or because they fear the unknown or known power of the authority?

Recently, the study of law has embarked upon one interesting aspect of the formal law which explores various patterns of domination. Nader's (1984b) analysis focuses on the extent to which law is reflected by its dominant users referred to in other writings as the advantages of the repeat users of law, (cf. Galanter 1974). This analysis is relevant to our study because it partially explicates some of the conditions under which the legal system may have been structured so that it often either cannot or will not respond to broader concerns with justice, concerns which include access to the development of political agendas, availability of essential legal resources, and clearer interpretations of legal terminology and reasoning (despite, as we noted in the introduction to the cases and Appendix B, the attempt by legal scholars to solve these problems; also see Kaplan 1983:110–14, for clarity in legal analysis).

Nader's examination of the dispute resolution movement in the United States suggests the inadequacy of simply creating more opportunities to use the law. Within the alternative dispute resolution centers, for example, as with the more traditional institutions of law, the disadvantaged typically become the defendants rather than the plaintiffs. The disadvantaged in most of our cases had meager economic resources, little if any knowledge of legal procedures, and usually no familiarity with legal definitions attached to the central issues such as the milla maritima. Nader suggests that one alternative for the disadvantaged is to become plaintiffs. It is unclear, however, how that transformation might occur or what affect it might ultimately have upon the patterns of domination currently embedded in the law and throughout the social structure (cf. Turk, 1976; Abel 1982b; Friedman 1985, especially pages 23–27 and 100–155; George 1989).

While the notion that justice will be served by transforming nonvoicers into voicers within the legal system may be appealing, it may be problematic given other considerations. Our analysis in chapter 3, especially the section on social context and access, suggests that in this particular study the transformation often led to catharsis rather than a catalysis for legal change. In general, even good intentions and well-meaning solutions often become larger problems. Some of the policymakers and entrepreneurs who called for the creation of alternative dispute resolution centers may well have had the welfare of the disadvantaged in mind. However, as Nader has also alluded to in her work, in practice, the centers often create situations that mirror the more institutionalized court system, where "resource dominators" are able to maintain or increase their advantages. In a related vein, Stone (1975:100) has suggested that we run a great risk by unleashing the regulators, their view of law, and the creation, fine-tuning, and detailing of laws as an "end in themselves, a cumbersome, frustrating, and pointless web for those they entangle."

In Kafka's *The Trial*, there is a clear image of such a possibility. Joseph K. has been convinced that law is accessible to everyone, yet in his pursuit of justice he encounters a legal system of endless waiting and bureaucratic nightmares. K. discovers that the (in)efficiency of the system is circumscribed by the duty of each functionary and that the system has become so specialized that law has only bureaucratic meaning (see Inverarity et al. 1983). The way in which the legal functionaries manage his case, he finds it impossible to pursue the case in any understandable context (Auerbach 1983).

The relevance of continuing to focus upon understanding the processes of dispute management rather than indiscriminantly applying resolution strategies to disputes is again apparent when we recognize the considerable force of social structure, especially as it relates to contours of history:

These true believers in the power of social/political ideology and of individual faith not only believe that they can move mountains (and put them down where they want instead of where the advancing glacier does), but that their social ideology and individual faith is *the* active ingredient (the motor force as Marx put it) in defining the course of history. They take any denial of this view to be treasonous consorting with the forces of evil, which they consider to be as voluntarist as themselves. Populist incarnation of any of these forces through the charisma of a leader who is a great communicator will of course generate a force to contend with even if the leader is better at creating the illusion of being able to move mountains than at moving them or the course of history. [Frank 1984:148]

If we define law as governmental social control (Black 1976) rather than as more narrowly concerned only with the activities of formal law, then the alternative dispute resolution perspective and related ideologies have supported policy that leads to the creation of conditions that result in more law. Yet, it is possible that more law, given the structural inequities of society, will only result in more, or a different form of, domination.

Sweeping declarations of the need for more law from legal experts without an understanding of its impact on underlying inequities are misguided and usually reflect narrow policy agendas and ahistorical perspectives (cf. Deloria, 1973). Braudel (1979) suggests that such problems as "civilization, society, economy, the state, the hierarchies of 'social' values should present themselves at the level of the humble realities of material life, proves in itself that history is present at this level too. . . . No sooner has one approached even the simplest aspect of life than one finds customary complexity there too."

How then do we examine situations where political agendas are being created in silence or secret? While the decoding of primary events that shape everyday life is beyond our scope, we want to create a framework for future work that will focus upon the contradictions embedded in social control, including the control of both the powerful over the powerless and the various controls that limit the powerful (see Bachrach and Baratz 1963; Ekland-Olson 1984). In our unraveling of the dialectical process of social control, it has become clear that the obvious forms of control are often intricately interwoven with the unexposed ones. The currently fashionable attack on the mass media and its control of definitions and events, for

example, is a reflection of critics' abilities to once again identify more of the symptoms of control rather than the sources.
The focus upon the process of creating, sustaining, and
changing central definitions of reality can be tedious; however, the
work by Geertz (1973) on the things we "take for granted" is illu-
minating. In the study of disputes and conflict we may need to
reassess some of the basic ideas and concepts that have been taken
for granted. Ashley (1986a) notes that concepts such as rights, contracts, private property, nationality, national territory, duties, and
responsibilities of the state are used routinely by international
lawyers, yet seldom questioned in terms of their varied purposes or
the political boundaries they help construct. This uncritical acceptance is a conundrum in terms of fairly recent global trends:

> A widely echoed tendency toward the "privatization" of
> social policy (even foreign policy); the tightening of labor dis-
> cipline in capitalist states; the intensification of surveillance;
> the rationalization and "economization" of education and
> political practice; the sustained if not increasing emphasis on
> big and highly centralized sources and systems of energy pro-
> duction and distribution; the transgovernmental rediscovery
> of the Soviet menace; the rhetorical reduction of the Third
> World developmental alternatives to an opposition of
> "authoritarianism" versus "totalitarianism," the transgov-
> ernmental reification of Third World "turbulence" as a fear-
> some and emerging force; the reinvigoration and dissemina-
> tion of "antiterrorism" and "antianarchism" as a near univer-
> sal rhetoric of state practice; the militarization of the state;
> the orchestrated use of violence against Third World socialist
> movements; and the glorification of war and preparation for
> war, even nuclear war, as an ultimate crucible of national
> identity and human purpose. [Ashley 1986a:90]

The encompassing issues raised by Ashley point to the
fact that the people who are involved in the disputes in Costa
Rica are directly and indirectly affected by a variety of dependency and domination relationships. There is a pervasive, yet
subtle relationship between economic dependency and other
forms of domination, including those emerging from various
forms of conflict or cohesion. Emotional dependency is one
area of investigation that calls for additional study, not only at
the sociopsychological level but also at the level that appears

most impenetrable to examination—the institutional level (Lauderdale et al. 1990; von Werlhof 1991).

Studying the processes that create disputes and their management may reveal basic elements of law, deviance, social harm, and social justice. The study of dispute management can provide the impetus for understanding basic facts of social life, rather than more atheoretical approaches to the study of deviance and law. We need substantive theories based on bodies of knowledge which provide, at least, explanations of nonintuitive actions, emergent properties—social phenomenon that are more than the sum of their parts—and the contradictions embedded in current concepts of social control. In light of recent confirmations of the fragile state of our environment and existence, we have no choice (von Werlhof 1989). This understanding may contribute to a body of knowledge that enables us to free ourselves from undue conflict or cohesion, and encourage us to constantly examine the meaning of social control and its relationship to the pursuit of justice (also see Grinde and Johansen, 1991).

We conclude this study by reflecting on one of our own contradictions as we quote from a remarkable former "administrator," Fernand Braudel, chief administrator of the Maison des Sciences de l'Homme:

> Books . . . run away with their authors. This one has run on ahead of me. But what can one say about its waywardness, its whims, even its own logic, that will be serious and valid? Our children do as they please. And yet we are responsible for their actions. Here and there I would have liked more explanation, justification, and example. But books cannot be expanded to order, and to encompass all the many and varied constituents of material life would require close and systematic research, followed by much synthesis and analysis. All that is still lacking. What the text says calls for discussion, addition, and extension. [Braudel 1979:559]

We should be so fortunate.

Appendix A
Agrarian Reform in Central America

Introduction

Prior analyses of land reform and who has the legal or extralegal rights to land in Costa Rica suggest that we study these aspects of property within the broader development of rights within the Central American region and the world system (Hall 1984; Lauderdale 1986b; Ramirez 1987). There are a number of useful empirical studies of agrarian reform (de Janvry 1981; Vargas 1989), and further theoretical analysis of reform from an encompassing law and society perspective can provide new and provocative agendas for future research.

The institutional development of rights such as citizenship, public education, and social welfare is an important aspect of the legitimation and expansion of the modern state (Meyer and Rowan 1977; Boli-Bennet 1979; Ramirez 1987; Thomas and Lauderdale 1988). Most institutional perspectives focus upon the state's incorporation of areas such as citizenship, education, and welfare within the broader context of organizational and world structures (Meyer and Scott 1983; DiMaggio 1988; cf. Zucker 1983). From this perspective the state is not simply a coercive force operating in isolation from its world context. The state's claim to legitimacy has also rested upon providing people with rights that are now taken for granted as part of "modern" life (Meyer et al. 1987).

We extend the institutional perspective by examining the relationship between state authority and the emergence and expansion of land reform programs within Central America and in the context of the world system. This examination contrasts with earlier comparative work on the structural conditions that ostensibly facilitate reform (cf. Moore 1966; Wolf 1969), as well as the growing body of research based on the emergence of the resource mobilization approach (Snyder and Tilly 1972; Tilly 1975; Barkan

1985).[1] Instead of asking under what conditions can the peasantry overwhelm other interests and gain control of the state or produce reactionary responses from it, we pose other largely unexplored questions. Why does the state offer land reform when other methods of control are available? Under what conditions does the state attempt to co-opt land reform movements (cf. Basu 1987)? And when does the state initiate rather than respond to demands for land reform? These questions are especially relevant, not only because they have not been addressed but also since there is wide variation in the actual implementation of land reform programs.

The foundations for land tenure and reform programs were established with the emergence of Central American countries as political entities in the nineteenth century. Much of their incorporation into the world system was predicated upon the expropriation of products from their land. Land tenure and reform programs and the technization of agrarian production are part of the more encompassing rationalization of world and state polities.

Rationalization and Land Reform

The emergence and expansion of land reform programs throughout the world system is a basic component of the institutional establishment of state jurisdiction and the more encompassing process of societal rationalization. We expand upon the perspective that citizen rights and national institutions are incorporative by conceptualizing land programs as part and parcel of the rationalization of authority and society. The rationalization of state and society around collective purposes includes the construction and mobilization of individuals through land programs.

Rationalization is the general process by which authority and exchange are brought within the purview of intellectually calculable rules inherent in the capitalist world system. Authority comes increasingly to be characterized by an impersonal, intellectually calculable, formal legal order with concomitant levels of bureaucratization, centralization, and incorporation. Increased rationality leads to authority systems that are simultaneously individualistic and nationalistic, with authority becoming increasingly impersonal and grounded in the legal order. Traditional (local) authority is mediated by individualism at one level and nationalism at another. Similarly, the rationalization of exchange incorporates local markets into larger national and international markets. Exchange becomes more predictable and includes processes such as monetarization, commercialization, and bureaucratic planning within the dynamics of an impersonal world market; exchanges come increasingly to be monetarized and legal. The process of rationalization also includes the creation and expansion of the commodity markets of land, labor, and money. Concepts of economic development and growth such as gross domestic product, energy consumption, national income, and percentage of the labor force in agriculture reflect the rationalization of the accounting system. In general, as rationalization continues, expanding economic development necessitates increasing levels of centralization and formalization, which further increases the likelihood of adoption and expansion of these programs.

The World-Polity Perspective

The rationalization of economic exchange and authority has increasingly taken the form of incorporation into the world political-economic system. When countries establish land reforms in order to gain legitimacy in the world system, they often foster symbolic formalization in order to gain assistance such as international loans or aid. The state may also implement various land programs as an attempt to mobilize society and control traditional groups or meet new problems. Such events are seen typically as crises that confront the state. Consider, for example, agrarian revolutions. Dramatic social change in land tenure and reform is typically viewed as a response to crises such as war, economic depression, and natural disasters such as drought, famine, or flooding. The magnitude of these crises makes it difficult for local structures to resolve them adequately, thus reinforcing or increasing the centralization of state authority and leading occasionally to the transfer of all authority to the state (Thomas and Lauderdale 1988).

Some researchers address such crises in terms of how the state manages problems of production, typically capitalist production, and labor control. Stinchcombe (1983) presents an analysis of the legal legitimation of advanced capitalism through its use of incentives; for example, he explores the control of labor through the incentive of "career" versus hourly wage. Other research programs focus more abstractly upon the general processes involved in social crises (cf. Lauderdale and Associates, 1984). Although the substantive topics in the research vary from work on deviance (Erikson 1966) to war (Gouldner 1970) to class structure (Offe

1972) to social movements (Gamson 1975, 1982 et al.), a common theme is the differential impact of crises from internal and external threats on the state (Thomas and Lauderdale 1987).

The expansion of the state apparatus and the further integration of society into the world system is fueled by many crises such as economic depressions. An institutional examination of a crisis such as the economic depression in Mexico in the 1980s underscores the role of the world system and the process of rationalization. In the 1970s Mexico obtained substantial increases in wealth, particularly from its petroleum export earnings. These earnings underwrote a varied and ambitious welfare expansion (Michael Lauderdale 1986). Mexico also borrowed heavily from external sources and collateralized the loans with anticipated earnings from petroleum revenues. The subsequent collapse of the petroleum market inflamed the latest crisis. Mexico's economic depression legitimated expansion of state authority through rationalization in the world system.

Crises such as economic depressions provide new insights into the study of land ownership and use. However, we suggest that changes in land reform that have been viewed as responses to crises at one degree of abstraction are an ongoing part of the more encompassing role of rationalization at another.

Land Tenure and Reform

Land tenure and reform have been viewed as the redistribution of land in a particular nation or as the attempt to create more productivity from the land. One view revolves around the redistribution of the land for peasants and small farmers in order to promote greater equality and social justice. The other focuses upon the techniques of creating greater productivity, including better use of the land through technological advancements, scientific knowledge about crop or animal use, credit arrangements, and related business matters.

While our focus is upon the relevant literature in land tenure and reform, it is important to emphasize that one of the basic roles of the state and the world system rests on the shift from communal to private property. When, for example, communal land that served elites and nonelites became redefined as the private land of the elites, the foundations for state centralization were already being constructed.

In some instances, the change to state control was relatively direct. Japan's rationalization is marked by changes that emerged during the end of the sixteenth century, systemic changes that established its present agrarian structure (Dore 1959).[2] The state developed a clear set of legal principles concerning ownership and use of land, standardization of measurement, and the use of national surveys by the state. While this system was administered by a single military authority, the rationalization of law that ensued led to the expansion of other forms of state control.

In the shift from feudalism to capitalism in Europe, the process of state formation was more protracted as the land that was used in common by the lord and tenants came to be redefined, initially as the private land of the lords and then later as the property of the lords administered by the nascent state (Huberman 1952). The concept of property, in general, has been viewed more recently as promulgating the expansion of capitalism and the primitive individualistic conception of property (Zeledon Zeledon 1984a; Vargas 1989). These changes emerged along with the rationalization of law and the increasing development of state agency, and the resulting revolutions over these changes in countries such as France often were directly related to land tenure and reform. Land ownership and use alterations became tied intimately to state penetration and commercialization (see Tilly 1964).

The cycles of reform and crisis throughout the world system, while having particular characteristics at one degree of abstraction—for example, the specific substantive alterations within a nation—have striking similarities at another degree of abstraction, the increasing process of rationalization of land reform throughout the world. The seemingly disparate land reforms of Europe in the seventeenth and nineteenth centuries, the U.S.A. in the eighteenth and nineteenth centuries and the Soviet Union in this century become less divergent from a world system perspective and the increasing processes of rationalization. Moreover, reforms in Latin America, Asia, and Africa in this century have been perceived generally as being instituted from many different crises. Yet land reform programs often emerge organizationally from the state within the rhetoric of citizen rights, law, well-being, and progress (Thomas and Lauderdale 1987).

The Incorporation of Central America

In order to examine some of the general processes of state expansion and rationalization of land reform programs, we present a brief synopsis of the incorporation of Central America into the world system. In general, Latin America was incorporated into the world system when a form of mercantilism was prevalent, one that emphasized its attendant concern with strict government regulation of national economies and foreign trade monopolies. Feudal arrangements still permeated social relations in Western Europe, and rational capitalism was as yet undeveloped. The opportunity for exploitation of abundant resources lay at the roots of the motivation behind the colonization of Latin America. Foreign countries colonized lands rich in mineral deposits or tropical areas, where the agricultural products of sugar, cotton, and chocolate could be readily produced and shipped to European markets. In Central America, Spain was the primary instigator of colonial rule and the production of these agricultural products engendered fewer obstacles than in South America (see de Janvry 1981).

Spain's Latin American colonies initiated various wars of independence early in the nineteenth century, and the United Provinces of Central America were among those colonies. These five states were factionalized and centered around major cities within the region and, in general, controlled by the portion of the population that claimed Spanish heritage. Much of the history of the United Provinces was dominated by civil war. The leadership that emerged from the civil war, led by individuals such as Francisco Morazan, attempted to weaken the church, encourage religious toleration, establish a progressive legal system, and confront the fear of control by Mexico. After numerous revolutions, Central America became the five nations shaped into the political units we recognize today. The five nations became independent entities, and the early part of the nineteenth century was marked by U.S.-British competition for these markets.

The United States was concerned primarily with excluding foreign influence and protecting U.S. interests. From the expansionist ideas of Thomas Jefferson to the commercial interests of Woodrow Wilson, the U.S.A. maintained its involvement in the affairs of the five nations. Although the idea of "Manifest Destiny" became increasingly less legitimate, the U.S.A. continued to have the single greatest influence over the region. Much of this influence stemmed from the Monroe Doctrine and the attempt to demonstrate the ostensible vitality and power of the U.S. form of democracy:

Rather than joining in the rush for colonies in Africa and Asia as the European powers did at that time, the United States called for an "Open Door" policy vis-à-vis the underdeveloped regions of the world and used its growing economic might to penetrate the markets and societies in these regions. Subsequently adopted by other imperial powers, this system of domination has been characterized as a "neocolonial system," one in which a metropolitan country holds sway over a formally independent country and extracts economic and political benefits from this arrangement. [Burbach 1982:12]

Nonetheless, the bottom line of the Monroe Doctrine was that European powers should not interfere in the political affairs of areas such as Central America. The composers of the doctrine were quite aware that France was resigned to intervention in Spain, Russia had neither the fleet nor the economic resources for action, Austria was expending its energies on suppressing republicanism in Europe, and, with the exception of Britain, the U.S. influence was dominant.

In the 1840s British interests in the region became more apparent as they created a state, Mosquitia, on Nicaragua's Atlantic coast. While most British activities in this period appeared to be aimed primarily at the expansion of trade, the U.S.A., with the impact of the War of 1812 still present in its foreign policies, became alarmed over the perceived expansion of British influence. Nonetheless, the imperialistic actions of William Walker, a U.S. citizen, noted the inability or unwillingness of Great Britain to exert great influence. Walker took political control of Nicaragua as he made himself ruler of that country, with U.S. recognition, for two years. Yet, rather than confronting Walker and the U.S.A. directly, the British tried to convince the Central American states to purge Walker from their region. Walker was overthrown. Within a few years the British surrendered the Miskito Coast and the Bay Islands.[3] While they continued to maintain control over Belize, British ambitions were curtailed throughout the remainder of the century (see Chace 1984, esp. pages 23–27).

In fact, Chace claims that:

As they would in generations to come, U.S. policymakers in the nineteenth and early twentieth centuries used the fear of another great power's possible intervention in the region to achieve their own goals in Central America. . . . From 1845 to

1860 there was only a remote chance that the British might engage in a conflict, however small, with the United States; after that, the possibility disappeared altogether. But in the United States the fear persisted, and whether because of political opportunism or genuine insecurity (just as in the case of the Holy Alliance earlier), the result was that [the U.S.A.] completely disregarded Central America's own political goals and realities. [1984: 32]

The Commodification of Land

A basic part of Central American reality is tied intimately to its land and crops. Coffee plants were brought typically to Central America from Jamaica at the turn of the nineteenth century. With European and U.S. investors' accumulation of agricultural lands and the ensuing expansion of coffee production, and subsequent increased dependence of the small economy on the external market, the relatively equitable distribution of land characteristic of the colonial period gave way to increased fragmentation of plots on the one hand, and concentration of plots through consolidation on the other. The majority of land came to be controlled by a few owners. Investments in Central America have been primarily in export agriculture, mining, construction, and transportation. The export agriculture, including bananas, played a primary role. Banana companies had a virtual monopoly over the sectors of production in which they invested; United Fruit, for example, had a major interest in the railroads, the telephone and telegraph systems, the electricity companies, and shipping lines that transported bananas outside Central America.[4] The demand for workers was seasonal and, since the workers were dependent on these wages, they were unable to accumulate sufficient capital with which to purchase their own land:

The traditional landowning aristocracy was overshadowed by a new elite, many of whom made their wealth in the nineteenth-century coffee boom. Coffee transformed Central America's agriculture in all but Honduras and in so doing created a new oligarchy. Modernizers in their time, the coffee oligarchy branched out into other areas of the economy, using their growing political influence to stimulate economic development. But it was development narrowly defined in their own interests. The road-building and export-financing programs that were the hallmark of their development scheme brought no benefits to the majority of Central Americans. Indeed, the coffee boom took place at the expense of the rural poor, as governments in Guatemala, Nicaragua, and El Salvador confiscated Indian and peasant lands to make way for expanded coffee production. [Flynn 1984: 32]

The introduction of the mechanized coffee processing mill in the mid-nineteenth century led to increased dependence on a handful of large producers who, with British credit, were able to purchase and maintain the expensive processing facilities. Prior to the mill, coffee processing was accomplished by the individual producer by labor-intensive methods: cultivating, harvesting, and processing the crop, often with family workers. The mill rapidly increased production levels and encouraged the demand for labor. By the 1860s importers had a near monopoly on the emerging coffee sector, purchasing the majority of the crop and providing capital in the form of credit to owners, who in turn advanced money on the coming year's harvest to small producers who used it to attract additional labor (Morris 1984). In addition, owners often provided property mortgages to small producers, yet subsequent foreclosures on advances and mortgages, common particularly during times of low international coffee prices, accelerated the process of land accumulation by large producers and owners.

Export products such as coffee, bananas, cotton, and sugar in Guatemala, Honduras, El Salvador, Nicaragua, and Costa Rica were defined as fundamental to Central American survival. As bananas became a common wage product throughout the Western hemisphere, a result of the invention of the modern refrigerated steamship, United States businesses began major investment programs in Central America, particularly Honduras, Guatemala, and Costa Rica (de Janvry 1981: 65). Technological development of these countries was implemented by U.S. corporations that required efficient railroad and communication systems to maximize the output of their banana plantations.

Concurrently, wages and land prices in coffee producing areas were high enough to induce many peasants to sell their small plots and either remain on the land as wage laborers or move to less expensive marginal land. Finally, deteriorating soil quality forced producers of all sizes to expand their holdings in order to maintain their production levels, and the large producers often expanded at the expense of their counterparts who could not afford to compete.

The small producers who kept their land had their profits increasingly absorbed by the new "coffee barons," individuals who had a tight monopoly on the processing and exporting of the crop, as well as on credit (Morris 1984; Paige 1975; 1987).

The 1883 Costa Rica census indicates that these trends were well underway by this time; 71 percent of the agricultural population listed wage labor as their primary means of support. Owners and exporters, who increasingly monopolized land, capital, and political power, were supported by a growing class of landless laborers and a declining group of small producers. Land was increasingly concentrated in the hands of a few owners since demand for workers was seasonal. Large landowners became more powerful and in effect constituted an oligarchy often dominating legal and extralegal policies, while the peasants were unable to save sufficient monies to purchase their own land.

Major redefinitions of land reform ensued through the encroachment of long-distance competitive markets into local ones (see Polanyi 1944).[5] The concentration of land in the hands of a small number of dependent elites continued to increase, with capitalists growing specialized crops for the world market (cf. Kaimowitz and Thome 1985). Peasant rebellions stemming from the capitalist oriented elites who eroded the traditional privilege of the peasantry were infrequent. Typically, the response of the small farmer displaced by the expanding coffee sector was either to become a wage laborer on coffee or banana plantations, or to migrate to unoccupied frontier land in the lowlands, where initially there were uncontrolled parcels of land.

Frontier land played a crucial role in setting the stage for potential land reforms. While frontier land often forestalled problems of land reform, protests from peasant groups often came from activities associated with part of the Catholic Church—activities that included literacy campaigns, cooperative business programs, radio schools, domestic support groups, and related social functions.[6] Land conflicts between elites and peasants resulted often in ad hoc land reforms guaranteeing the peasants access to land and limited title; however, in the absence of formal rational law, the titles were typically facades.

Many of these frontier lands are now under the management and control of the new land reform agencies of the state. This system is based on the continued expansion of cultivated lands and the maintenance of quasi-feudal labor organizations (Wallerstein 1974). Initially, the result has been local peasant movements that are directed largely toward the local elites and authorities. Increasingly, the movements shift their demands to larger target areas and organize politically to produce change in central state policies (Tilly et al. 1975; Skocpol 1979; Thomas and Lauderdale 1987).

In Central America, where some degree of political legitimacy exists, agrarian reform is touted as a workable alternative to peasant rebellion (Seligson 1980). In other parts of Central America, the state works in other ways. For example, when a form of land tenure prohibits access to the land, peasants are periodically forced out of subsistence production to supplement their incomes through labor in commercial or state agriculture (Winson 1978; Vargas 1989). The role of core countries in this matter continues along the same pattern as agrarian reform programs, often cloaking numerous types of counterinsurgency warfare (cf. Burbach 1982).[7]

Land reform has often been limited officially to concerns over the needs and patterns of agricultural growth, concern over the product per inhabitant, or an increase in the rates of investment in order to satisfy the cash demand of the market. Primary land reform emphases have been the agrarian enterprise and the activity of production—the agrarian contract. The factors of production—including lease contracts, partnerships, improvements, loan and restitution, agrarian merchandise, contracts of labor and credit—have narrowly defined the agrarian enterprise. Ostensible crises are adaptations to rationalization, not simply the internal problems (Lauderdale 1988b). Land reform is a structural process of rationalized markets and authority that often leads to conflict between dependent elites and the state (Paige 1987). While working initially for increased rationality in order to legitimate private property, the elites attempt also to create a system with relatively low levels of rationalization.

World System Impact

Land reform programs often devolve from a central bureaucracy that is rationalizing society and markets within the rhetoric of citizen rights, well-being, and progress (Thomas and Lauderdale 1987). The state's rationalization and legitimation of agrarian production is reinforced by intergovernmental organizations.

The United Nations Economic Commission for Latin America (ECLA) was organized in 1948 as a regional commission with members from the Latin American countries, the U.S.A., and three European countries with "possessions" in the Western hemisphere. ECLA promoted economic integration through the Latin American common market and directed attention to the asymmetry between the income elasticity of demand for imports from the center relative to the periphery. A primary goal for the state from the ECLA view was to increase rationalization at the local and regional levels (Hirschman 1961: 22). Ambitious ECLA programing techniques and premature responses to land reform programs have become the target of much criticism. The commission's overall emphasis on state and international rather than local control has also been viewed as problematic, although the critics have supported the ECLA objections to the lending policies of international organizations, such as the world bank and the unreliability of foreign capital inflow.

In addition, other international organizations affected the rationalization process. Initiated in 1960 by the U.S.A., the Alliance for Progress has been one of the main vehicles for promoting the Central American Common Market. As part of the reaction to the touted land reforms in Cuba, yet responding ostensibly to the post-World War II depression in Latin America, the alliance developed part of the Common Market to promote land reform and the industrialization of the region. The activities of international organizations as diverse as ECLA and the Alliance for Progress reflect the expansion of the state and the impact of the world system. They also emphasize the overarching view that land reform leads to industrialization.

Our perspective inverts the traditional functional approaches to land reform by examining the interactive dynamics of states' attempts to adjust to changes within the world system. Feudal arrangements no longer permeate social relations in Central America or the rest of Latin America; the logic of rational capitalism now dominates land tenure programs. As de Janvry (1981: 120) notes, "Today, Latin American agriculture is essentially capitalist throughout. Its social relations and the development of its forces of production must be analyzed in terms of the particular logic of peripheral capitalism that constitutes a historically specific phase in the development of capital in the periphery of the world system."

The structural dynamics create increased rationality that falls under the jurisdiction of the state's broad mandate for progress, as in the construction of new land programs. The land reform programs of Cuba initiated in 1959 and those of Nicaragua initiated in 1979 took land from the elites in those countries and redistributed it throughout society (cf. Deere 1985; Fagen 1987). Yet, the redistribution reflects the process of state control and expansion in a different form in that the land redistributed to the poor has typically been administered by a newly created state agency that moves the previously elite-owned land into communal organizations. Obviously, this redistribution is on the one hand a real change in property ownership and on the other is a reflection of the state's expansion under a different political order—one that is responding simultaneously to the needs of the nonelites and the rationalization of the world economy and polity.[8]

As with social welfare programs, the adoption and expansion of land reform by agrarian countries is related primarily to the structure of the state and to the world-polity environment (Thomas and Lauderdale 1987). The most striking aspect of land reform from 1960 to 1989 in countries such as Honduras, Guatemala, and El Salvador is the change in use of the land rather than alterations in distribution. There has not been any significant change in the distribution of land ownership in those countries, as most of the land continued to be controlled by a few owners (Fagen 1987). Nonetheless, the changes in the use of the land via state agencies and the proliferation of land tenure reform proposals by the state's legal system throughout Central America are part of the response to the dynamics of rationalization. Regardless of the outcomes of specific land reform programs, in terms of welfare and equality or class domination, they rationalize the countries agriculture: the agrarian enterprise is transferred from systems based on earlier modes of production to rational units that vary from small business ventures to agribusiness monopoly enterprises.

Conclusion

At one degree of abstraction, there is wide variation in the political forces, both elite and mass, that have shaped land reform programs and their implementation in Central America. Area specialists, for example, have made significant contributions by documenting the impact of different commodities and domestic political alliances among the Central American countries and the importance of such factors in any examination of land reform as a form of social welfare (Vargas 1989). Yet the work here points to the relevance of considering some of the striking similarities in land reform programs.

Land reform programs increasingly emerge and expand from a central bureaucracy that is rationalizing society and markets within the rhetoric of citizen rights, well-being, and progress. The political aspect of this process is tied to the rationalization of property rights and exchange and, in part, to elite support. However, it is more fundamentally a structural process of rationalized markets and authority that is not reducible to elite interest in rationalization (Giddens 1981). This is clearly demonstrated in the conflict between dependent elites and the state. The former, while initially pushing for increased rationality in order to legitimate private property, attempt to create a system with fairly low levels of rationalization. Yet the relationship between state and world system dynamics encourages increased rationality that is a primary part of the mandate of the state.

Land tenure and reform programs increasingly emanate from the state as a means of rationalizing agrarian organization and production. While the emergence of individualism as a legitimate order stemmed from the nineteenth-century evolution of a more formal, rational legal system in the core (Inverarity et al. 1992), another form of individualism surfaced later in Central America. There,

> the postwar expansion of capitalist agriculture, markets, and state power has tended to differentiate and "individualize" the interests that once gave peasant communities a strong internal cohesiveness. Nearly all contemporary Central American peasant organizations have had to struggle against peasant individualism in order to create cooperative or associational structures. [Kincaid 1985: 7]

The structural conditions for rationalization and the location of responsibility for progress in the state lead to changes in the definition and use of land.[9] The adoption and expansion of land reform by agrarian countries is related intimately to the structure of the state and to the world-polity environment. Our analysis of land reform programs points to their dialectic nature (cf. Basu 1987). They are part of a larger project of incorporating society into impersonal bureaucratic authority and capitalistic markets, yet they build this system of rationalization by touting the changes as fundamental to human progress and individual rights. *This dynamic suggests paradoxical consequences of centralizing authority and social rationalization.*

Appendix B:
The Rationalization
of Law in Costa Rica*

Rationalization

Rationalization is a phenomenon that expanded significantly in the late Middle Ages. Arising primarily from the unique dualism of Western civilization, national governments obtained authority over the means of attaining the goals of peace, justice, and security (see Deloria, 1973, for a useful critique). As the means to such collective goals, governments have been legitimated by a formal legal order and citizens who helped build, consent to, and are the purpose of the movement.

This conceptualization reflects Weber's perspective on the historical development of formal rationality (Lauderdale 1986b). Specifically, rationalization is the general process by which authority and exchange are brought within the purview of intellectual, calculable rules inherent in the world system (Thomas et al. 1987). This perspective focuses upon the increasing interdependence of nations in the world and the basic relationship between rationalization and predictability. The world system with a singular world economy has its roots in the sixteenth century. Since the appearance of the "world system," changes in individual national economies are attributable in large part to a society's position in the world division of labor and to the world economy's own pattern of rationalization. In addition, the world system increasingly exerts pressure on national governments, which shape decisions and processes that impact not only local economies but also political and environmental concerns (cf. Ashley 1986b; von Werlhof 1991). In essence, exchange under increasing rationalization becomes more predictable and includes processes such as monetarization, commercialization, and bureaucratic planning within the dynamics of the impersonal world market. Similarly, authority evolves into a more intellectually, calculable formal legal order with concomitant levels of centralization and incorporation.

Rationalization of the Law in Costa Rica

The evolution of the law in Costa Rica reflects the concern with the process of rationalization and its relationship with the concept of jurisprudence. The jurisprudence of interests found in the legal system in Costa Rica is concerned with the creation and application of the law and, importantly, with the concrete interests that attempt to influence that creation and application (Perez Vargas 1981). Legal decision-making in Costa Rica strives to fulfill the ideal form of formal, rational decision-making explicated by Weber. *Rational* refers to the use of explicit, abstract, intellectually calculable rules and procedures rather than sentiment, tradition, or particular interests. *Formal* refers to the existence of an autonomous system for deciding legal issues; disputes settled by distinctly legal procedures are characterized as "formal." This formal characteristic of the process separates it from decisions that are made on other grounds, such as those emerging from purely political, moral, or economic interests. Autonomy of the legal system may be institutionalized in several ways. For example, in the United States the constitution provides that judges will receive salaries that cannot be diminished during their continuance in office, thus reducing the influence of other interests. In Costa Rica the leading organ for the rationalization of law, the Supreme Court, maintains its autonomous position via financial independence.

The relevance of the rationalization of law and the evolution of a rational, legal system in Costa Rica becomes clear when we consider the problems created by earlier forms of law and the legal system. Part of the impetus for the United Provinces of Central America, a nation that incorporated the five Central American states and declared its independence on July 1, 1823, was a call for a new legal order. The civil war that ensued quickly after independence was fought partly over the injustice of irrational (substantive), informal law based upon narrow, particular interests. In fact, one of the primary priorities of the leader of the war, Francisco Morazan, was to establish a progressive legal system. Despite the failure of the United Provinces, those parts of the progressive legal system that contained formal, rational law influenced the independent entity that we now know as Costa Rica. For example, the law in Costa Rica has been increasingly characterized by the early emphasis on legal equality.

An emphasis on legal equality is markedly different from those legal systems that contain benefits for people of certain status. Medieval law, for example, contained a number of laws based upon status inequality such as the benefit of clergy and the doctrine of coverture (Inverarity et al. 1992). The reasons for the change in such laws based upon status inequality are complex; however, one fundamental factor emerges from an analysis of the role of changes in the economy. As many societies moved from feudal to capitalist modes of production, legal equality replaced those systems of law based upon conceptions of natural differences among people. Legal equality is viewed as a necessary part of the free movement of labor (also see Romero Perez 1984). While legal equality masks other forms of inequality, it promotes the process of rationalization, especially the role predictability (cf. Unger 1987). Also, as Weber noted in his general work on religion and economy, the affinity for long-run calculation had been influenced by numerous legal, political, and religious institutions in Western Europe.

The hallmark of the rationalization of the law and economy has been systematic planning with the advanced calculation of costs and benefits. Of course, certain periods in history are more conducive to this rationalization. In the United States at the beginning of the twentieth century, in a period commonly referred to as the Progressive Era, there were significant transformations. While there have been many changes in Costa Rica since the turn of this century, the last twenty years is notable for the phenomenal increase in the rationalization of law. The foundation for this increase was laid, for example, by the institutional achievements of the Judicial Inspection of 1921, the Unconstitutional Recourse of 1937, and, most notably, the Economic Autonomy of 1957. The Economic Autonomy achievement is notable because it established the independence of the judicial power via a guaranteed percentage of the budget in Costa Rica. This guaranteed budget helped accelerate the dynamic role of the Supreme Court of Justice in the transformation of the Costa Rican judicial system (Perez Vargas 1985).

The thirteen organizational changes in the judicial power of Costa Rica (Perez Vargas 1985) reveal the increase in the rationalization process. This change in the legal infrastructure reflects the emphasis upon the role of centralization and the coordination for long-term planning. Similarly, five recent projects initiated between 1983 and 1984 appear to have extended the rationalization process. The project for the creation of Alcaldías Civiles de Hacienda, for example, seeks among other things to bring prompt judicial procedure and relief to congested court proceedings. The project of the Civil Process Code provides, among other things, for an improved rationalized procedure to guarantee impartiality of decision-making.

These achievements and projects are especially striking when we compare Costa Rica with other countries such as the United States where the economy is clearly more rationalized. From many theoretic perspectives we would expect the country with the more rationalized economy to also have the more rationalized legal system (cf. Luhmann 1985). While there are aspects of the U.S. legal system that are more rationalized than the Costa Rican system, the *infrastructure of the Costa Rican system* is moving rapidly toward rationalization. Thus, while the economy has a major role in determining the *rate of rationalization*, it is clear from an analysis of the legal system in Costa Rica that we cannot neglect related political and cultural factors. Costa Ricans, for example, approved a constitution in 1949 that "prohibits an army as a permanent institution" (article 12) and in everyday life the citizens rarely mention the word "conflict," since they believe that conflicts are difficult to manage in a rational manner (see Brenes 1986).

Increased Rationalization

The future of the legal system in Costa Rica points to increased rationalization of law. Despite our cautions that rationalization of economy is not the sole factor impacting upon changes in the form and substance of the law, it is a major factor. And, as the world economic system continues to increase dramatically in levels of rationalization there are pressures on all countries involved in the world system to develop parallel forms of rationalization. Agreements with organizations such as the International Monetary Fund is necessary before foreign creditors will renegotiate Costa Rica's debt. Costa Rica's involvement with the World Bank's austerity requirements and those of the International Monetary Fund point to the problems associated with new forms of monetarization and bureaucratic planning. As the government in Costa Rica attempts to resolve the problems arising from the response from such groups as the major union organizations and the two principal teacher organizations, it will not only find itself increasing the level of rationalization of the economy but will turn increasingly to the legal system for assistance. Governmental response to such problems will undoubtedly need to be couched in a reliance on the predictability of legal and economic solutions.

Costa Rica has recently encountered new ominous austerity measures as well as an increase in the reaction of groups within Costa Rica who suffer from restrictions on consumption and wages. The attorney general of Costa Rica, Luis Solano Carrera, pointed out that "numerous new disputes and an acceleration of old ones" have ensued from the measures used to meet recent austerity demands. Prior to these demands, his office was already overburdened with attempts to create new organizations for dispute resolution, and the resulting increase in disputes by social movements and groups directly affected by the austerity measures has been significant. Thus, while the attorney general's office was attempting, for example, to provide more assistance for Costa Ricans needing public defenders, increased attention was necessary to attend to emerging disputes such as those arising from union reactions to the austerity demands and the efforts by social movements and protest groups to mitigate the already inadequate public housing situation (personal interview, August 13, 1986).

These problems, which include attenuated controversies over the number of Contras and Contra relatives residing in the camps, are exacerbated by the increasing number of people fleeing Nicaragua into refugee camps in Costa Rica. While most evidence suggests that Contra fighters typically use the camps only as rest stops, donations such as the half-million dollars in aid from the Netherlands for the victims of the Central American conflicts have been rescinded. The overwhelming influx of refugees, primarily from Nicaragua, in the past three years, has led to increased instability. New types of dispute resolution structures have become necessary to handle the current situation in Costa Rica, where approximately 10 percent of the population can now be classified as refugees.

One area that is crucial to the resolution of related disputes is agrarian reform. Since a large segment of the Costa Rican economy and social well-being revolves around the definition and use of land, the current thrust by specific parts of the legal system to promote agrarian reform is crucial. Costa Rica, and the other nations in Central America, adopted an agrarian reform law in the early 1960s. The "Lands and Colonization Law" passed in 1961, however, was basically unsuccessful in promoting reform. For the most part a number of preconditions were absent that are necessary for the successful reform and rationalization of the land (see Appendix A). One of the projects of the Supreme Court, the agrarian jurisdiction of 1982, is an attempt to provide the foundation for a rationalized reform. In addition, essential work continues to examine the basic structure and relations among land organizations and institutes (Barahona Israel 1984). These projects and studies are clearly fundamental to a successful reform, since the experience of other countries note the necessity of creating a finely coordinated organizational structure. The Supreme Court's emphasis in this area is also reflected in its recent studies published on related parts of the study of agrarian rights and problems (Zeledon Zeledon 1984b; Lazarus 1985; Torrealba Navas 1991). The seminal work by Ricardo Zeledon Zeledon on the importance of the concept of property is essential to the study of agrarian reform, since one of the preconditions for successful land reform has been traditionally a reexamining of the fundamental assumptions underlying the idea of redistribution or increased production. The continued study by the Congress of Agrarian Law of Costa Rica is one of the major sources for providing the theoretical and empirical base for the rationalization of the agrarian enterprise.

Despite the obvious importance of the rationalization of the agrarian enterprise and its close relationship to the rationalization of law in Costa Rica, the process of change will be tedious (see Appendix A). At one of the most fundamental levels, land disputes throughout the world between large landowners and "landless" workers has resulted often in ad hoc land reforms ostensibly guaranteeing workers access to the land and limited title; however, in the absence of formal rational law, most of the reforms have been only temporary. The activities of international organizations as diverse as the Alliance for Progress and the United Nations Economic Commission for Latin America (ECLA) reflect many of the varied political and economic problems encountered on the road to agrarian reform. Yet land reform is a national project that is occurring in different forms and at various rates of change throughout the world system. In this century, for example, we have seen reforms instituted from many different political forms in Central America as well as India, Egypt, Japan, Bolivia, Cuba, Eastern Europe, and mainland China. In general, these reforms were not only a response to the need for greater equality of land tenure, but also attempts to rationalize agrarian economic growth that takes the form of commercialization, largely through the encroachment of long-distant export markets into local ones. Costa Rica's experience with this process in the area of the banana industry illustrates the need for greater rationalization. The Costa Rican government's response to the enforcement of antitrust acts on banana monopolies by taking over part of the formerly private enterprise in the past and the more recent acquisition of banana production in the southern zone has led to the need for both increased rationalization as well as diversification.

In general, the two important aspects of land reform and rationalization are the redistribution of land toward more equitable tenure and attempts to create greater productivity within the national and world economies. The demands for greater social justice as well as increased productivity receive legitimation throughout the world system. Also, one of the basic outcomes of most successful land reform programs is the rationalization of the country's agriculture. Through successful reform the agrarian enterprise is changed from a politically and economically decaying system to rational units varying from small-scale projects to agribusiness to government cooperatives.

In essence, the rationalization of the law and the movement toward increased formal rational legal procedures and decision-making are fundamental aspects of social change in Costa Rica. In general, authority is evolving into a more intellectually, calculable formal legal order with concomitant degrees of centralization and incorporation. Specifically, using land reform as only one example, the process of rationalization is also a logical extension of Costa Rican culture. That is, Costa Rica's interest in agrarian reform is partially an extension of its more general and long-standing concern with other social welfare programs (see the following section for a brief discussion of agrarian reform problems). National welfare and agrarian reform programs increasingly evolve from governments that support the rationalization of markets and the legal system (Thomas and Lauderdale 1988). The rationalization of law in Costa Rica is also intimately tied to national concerns over citizen rights, justice, and progress, as well as peace.

Section I:
Agrarian Reform in Costa Rica

The Costa Rican agrarian structure has three complex, interrelated problems. First, in some areas the land is underdeveloped while in other areas it is exploited, a process which leads to the unnecessary destruction of potentially renewable natural resources upon some lands. Second, Costa Ricans are unable at this time to increase the level of agricultural productivity or quality by means of farm land enhancement. Finally, social and economic tensions arise from the unequal distribution of land and cattle productions, substructure of credit, transportation, and marketing, and wealth derived from the land. Incipient since the colonial period, these problems have intensified in recent years due to rapid population increases and subsequent exhaustion of colonization borders.

Until 1961, the spontaneous colonization of uncultivated lands ("squatting") served as the primary escape route for landless peasants and small landed estate owners, or "minifundists." In that year, squatting was prohibited by legislation in the law of lands and colonization (Ley de Tierras y Colonización) bill. The Institution of Land and Colonization, ITCO, established in 1962, was the first official body charged with resolution of Costa Rica's agrarian problems. The legislation of agrarian reform was a response in part to internal pressures; the population explosion was intense, the colonization borders were exhausted, and the developing industrial and manufacturing fabric could not provide adequate employment for the increasing labor force. In addition, this legislation was in particular a reaction to external factors, such as the Cuban revolution of 1959 and the U.S. insistence upon Costa Rican initiation of agrarian reforms. The U.S. pressure was applied on behalf of the Latin American members of the Alianza para el Progreso, and Costa Rica yielded to U.S. demands in order to reduce tension between the countries (Seligson 1980). The agrarian legislation retained the concept of private property even though the legislative body recognized its potential social function—that is, the land could be distributed justly in an effort to eliminate small landed estates (minifundios) and squatting. The private lands could be replaced with small and medium-sized farms, thus providing additional jobs and creating the possibility for strengthened local economies through owner creation of cooperatives. The new law considered the colonization of virgin timber as well as the redistribution of land with previous owners being indemnified justly (with cash or government bonds).

During the first years under the new law, economic resources were scarce and development of lands was minimal. In fact, between 1962 and 1966, there were only eleven colonies established on previously undeveloped lands (forests or jungles). Within this period, the ITCO estimates that there were about sixteen thousand five hundred families squatting, but their program was able to assist only 1,222. Even though ITCO granted legal title to lands to only squatters in these four years, the program was unable to attack the roots of the problem. By 1969 there was little improvement; only seven hundred families were aided and the incidence of squatting had increased.

In the 1970s, ITCO policies changed and they began to grant land titles to laboring minifundists. These lands, which had established roads and were located near towns, were again purchased from private owners. However, ITCO did not have sufficient funds available initially to create an extensive program and squatting continued consequently. In 1975, though, indirect taxes were deposited into ITCO funds, which allowed a rapid increase in the number of peasant settlements and the establishment of new development regions. These lands were expropriated primarily from the United Fruit Company. By the end of 1977, fourteen thousand people inhabited these regions with many more additional settlers from other distant regions on the way. In the Río Frio region, for example, the lands were expropriated even before the squatters arrived.

By the end of 1979, ITCO had established successfully over a hundred peasant settlements including the development regions. Of these, 29 were organized into cooperatives, 18 of which established collective holding of lands. Together, the settlements supported 5,428 families and encompassed 167,134 acres, which was equivalent to 5 percent of the total farm land registered in the 1973 census. These lands were scattered throughout Costa Rica excluding the West Central Valley, where there were no underexploited farms or unused available lands that could be expropriated by ITCO. Most settlements produced foodstuffs for exchange or sale on domestic markets upon lands that were either previously unused or designated cattle pastures. In Coto Sur, for example, a recently established cooperative harvests bananas which are then sold to the United Fruit Company. Finally, the average income of ITCO settlers surpasses that of peasants, and even though there have been many differences among the settlers, these are due to the differences in levels of initiative among them, and not to the nature of life within the settlement.

In addition to the peasants, ITCO has been granting land titles to those squatters occupying private or federal lands. This ensures squatters' access to land and agrarian credit which would

not be otherwise granted unless the farmer has an adequate mort-
gage to offer as collateral. There are specific ITCO land limits for
this category of squatters: 100 acres for agricultural lands and 300
acres for cattle pastures. These limits are imposed in order to avoid
the formation of large landed estates (latifundios) which might
cause problems for ITCO in the future. Toward the end of 1979,
ITCO had dispersed 28,079 land titles, which was equivalent to
more than one-third of the total number of farms and almost one-
fifth of the total farm acreage registered in the 1973 census.

The acceleration of ITCO programs since 1975 is transforming the landholding structure and the relative importance of different agrarian programs within Costa Rica. The next land and cattle
farm census is expected to reveal a decrease in the number of farm-
steads and small landed estates (minifundios) and an increase in
the number of peasant and medium-sized farms. Nevertheless,
ITCO reforms lag behind substantially in relation to the size of the
problem it is attempting to resolve. In the late 1970s, there were
over ten thousand families that needed to be established in peasant
settlements. To accomplish this task, ITCO required 165,351
acres, but had only 14,703 acres at their disposal. In the 1980s,
ITCO commissioned additional land but problems of landholding
and squatting persist (see Hall 1984 for a comprehensive analysis
of agrarian reform in Costa Rica; this section was constructed from
her findings and analyses).

Notes

Chapter 1

1. The concepts of politics and social control are central to the present study. For the purposes of this study, we propose that: (a) *social control is the process of defining and reacting to deviance* (cf. Sutherland 1924; Becker 1963); and (b) *politics is the process that influences the amount and type of social control* (cf. Matza 1969).

2. The role of power and the numerous sources of power are important in examining the form and substance of disputes, as well as the relationship between the types of dispute management and concomitant styles of domination. While the types of domination or power by the state or by persons of higher versus lower status is difficult to detect and measure in many informal modes of social control, it is nonetheless an important consideration for this study—Most thinking about deviance and disputes has separated the question of what leads people into nonconforming action from the question of what causes others to define those individuals or their actions as problematic (cf. Pfuhl, 1980; Liska, 1987). The first perspective relies on various interpretations which attempt to explain the dynamics that cause people to "break the rules." This approach is based on the view that law is a reflection of strong moral consensus within a society. This perspective has been challenged by work that can be traced as far back, for example, as the seventeenth-century work of Francis Bacon who argued that *the laws are like cobwebs, where the small flies are caught and the great break through* (Inverarity et al. 1983:9). On the other hand, the second perspective encompasses what largely is a reinvented concern with the factors that promote a social reaction, and suggests that the creation of stigma is linked intimately to more general studies on social conflict and power. More precisely, the social reaction perspective raises the question of who has the power to define people or actions as problematic or deviant.

Unfortunately, the social reaction that creates the label of deviant was considered by many scholars to be a straightforward response from a collective or the result of elite manipulation in the face of some dispute or conflict. Based upon oversimplifications, this representation of the social reaction perspective is untenable, since it ignores the dialectical sources of power and the often nefarious political processes employed by numerous forms of organization (Lauderdale 1980; Ben-Yehuda 1985).

3. The sanctioning process can include defining actors as nonconformists or deviants, and serve as a catalyst for a dispute or the initial settlement of a dispute. In this context, deviance is not inherent in actual behavior, but instead attention is focused upon the process by which action is defined as conformity under some conditions and deviance under others (Inverarity et al. 1983; Lauderdale 1984). Deviant status is socially negotiated—that is, people are not considered deviant until "discovered" as such by other disputants, agents, or representatives who have the resources to control such definitions. *These resources can be located, for example, within the interactions of informal control, including status hierarchies, or dynamics of formal control, including state power*—At most levels of analysis we are often able to identify leaders who create disputes or deviants for their own instrumental reasons, or we recognize the creation or reaction as a product of a more general collective action (cf. Meier, 1982). Many scholars have struggled over the question of whether dispute or deviance creation is a result of elite or collective action. Unfortunately, the historical forces that have laid the foundation for such dichotomous thinking plague even the more useful context of the social reaction perspective.

In essence, approaching the study of deviance from either a narrow consensus or conflict view is misguided, at best. Conflict, for example, at one level of social organization can lead to integration at another level (Simmel 1955). Role conflict can produce strain and disequilibrium for individuals, and the consequence in the area of voting is often integration since cross-pressured voters often become political moderates who react apolitically.

> Similarly, conflict at the intergroup levels (war between nation-states) may produce greater integration within the conflicting groups, so that the overall level of conflict might even decrease. Lest Simmel be cast into the fire as a functionalist, it is worth recalling that Marx made a very similar argument about the conditions under which classes would be formed. [Lauderdale and Inverarity 1980:23]

Moreover, criminologists and sociologists who have created, often in a rather Machiavellian fashion, the Durkheimian conservative strawperson are at a loss to explain Durkheim's work on the consolidation of power and repressive punishments or his treatise on professional ethics and civic morals. In the treatise he notes that "inheritance is therefore bound up with archaic concepts and practices that have no part in our present-day ethics" (Durkheim 1958:174; cf. Marx 1967). Chambliss (1979) presents a useful discussion of the pitfalls in imposing radical or conservative interpretations of Marx and Durkheim in his analysis of the creation of laws. Turner explicates recent confluences in his analysis of "the conflict functionalism" (1986:165–83).

4. Our initial theoretical perspective on social control conceptualizes social systems as containing a social space in which actions and actors are evaluated and defined. This social space includes moral boundaries that provide a sense of identity and a form of evaluation for actors. The boundaries give the actors information on members of the social system, the variety of their actions, and which actions will be defined as conformity or deviance. The social system or its agents negatively sanction those actors who ostensibly threaten the boundaries (Erikson 1966; Lauderdale et al. 1984; Ben-Yehuda 1985). We use the concept of social system because it encapsulates social collectives such as small groups, organizations, communities, societies, and the world system. While the degree of complexity differs dramatically at these different levels of aggregation, we suggest that many studies on each of these analytic categories reflect similar rule structures, dynamics, and social agents that define and react to diverse behavior. Specific cultural and historical conditions, under which these reactions and ensuing definitional struggles occur, lead to viewing, for example, particular disputants as deviants or, conversely, as normal, honorable people (see Grinde and Johansen, 1991).

5. In a study of the Zapotec village of Talea, Nader found that cross-linkage includes ties of locale, friendships, kinship, common work interests, as well as shared obligations and values (1964; 1990a). The study suggests that leveling and stratification—stratification in this case is based upon wealth, age, gender, and experience—are also useful in examining the type and amount of social control. Leveling is important to the dynamics of stratification because it offers an attempt to lessen hierarchical distinctions by mitigating the amount of inequality in a society. When a wealthy member of a community finances a large social gathering, for example, jealousies are to be reduced and differences in status are to be minimized. As Nader points out "Among these mountain Zapotec, it is both unappealing and dangerous to be too rich, too poor, too pretty, or too ugly" (1990a: 193). In some groups or societies this leveling process would be considered deviant, yet in others it is the norm.

6. In essence, we want to extend and modify recent research that examines a conception of social control as a dependent variable. One of our goals is to describe, examine, explain, and eventually predict the type and amount of social control in a particular context, in order to study social control at various levels of complexity (cf. Teubner 1983).

7. In a complex, heterogeneous society, for example, there may be a multitude of systems of informal social control existing alongside of, inside of, and sometimes in opposition to the formal social control network of the state.

8. Our emphasis on the structure and dynamics of conflict creation points to the role of institutional factors in the study of evaluation and

social control. Many norms or rules, for example, that have been institutionalized structure people's perception of and response to diverse behaviors (cf. Baer 1991). Whether these norms and rules are embedded in the infrastructure of a small collective or the bureaucracy of a large organization, they are central to the analysis of conflict such as deviance and disputing. In general, our focus upon the concept of the social system reflects the importance of the ongoing (corporate) relationship among people in various collectives, their membership in overlapping and conflictual collectives as well as the structure and dynamics of evaluation and social control (see Swanson 1971). In specific, our perspective on deviance points to the potential of examining deviance creation as part of the analysis of status negotiation, social mobility, and stratification (Lauderdale 1980; 1984).

9. It has become readily apparent that a reliance upon such classifications fails to grasp adequately the breadth and dynamics of conflictual situations (see Kierkegaard, 1968). Technocratic approaches have not led and are not likely to lead to thorough explanation, much less prediction of social phenomena (see Deloria, 1973). Discourse analysis and a few of the deconstruction perspectives, on the other hand, appear capable of salvaging major insights of ethnomethodology and refocusing systematic attention upon the control of agendas and informal dynamics of power (Trubek 1980–81; Ashley 1986a). One potential advantage of Ashley's approach to discourse analysis is its nascent ability to systematically delineate the processes of rationalization (cf. George; 1989 Mascia-Lees et al. 1989). While traditional concepts such as simplex/multiplex relationships or status of the disputants are useful, they only begin to unravel the complexities inherent in dispute resolution or management (Van Velson 1967; Miyazawa, 1987; Munger 1988).

10. The majority of serious crimes committed in modern societies may be in response to some perceived wrong. The process of "self-help," which Donald Black refers to as "the expression of a grievance by unilateral aggression" is especially relevant here (1984:2). By committing an act of violence against another person or that person's property, the aggrieved person risks the cost of being arrested, prosecuted, and convicted by the formal legal system. Nevertheless, in the case of homicide, Black estimates that "at least three-fourths of the nonnegligent criminal homicides are committed as social control" (1984:7). In these cases, the potential costs of engaging in informal social control do not seem to be much of a deterrent (see Black 1984:14–15). Therefore, we expect that some disputes may lead to the informal social control technique of self-help, even though the cost of initiating or continuing the dispute is high (Marx, 1988).

11. An attack of ridicule or mockery against a person's honor or social skills, or the theft or damaging of that person's property may evoke a response of self-feeling. And, depending on the social circumstances and how severe the offense, the reaction is likely to be very emotionally

charged. In fact, many individuals become so overwhelmed by "mood" that they commit acts they would normally consider unreasonable. The recognition of this process has worked itself into the formal workings of the law, particularly involving "crimes of passion" or "temporary insanity."

12. The struggle by sociologists to develop clear and useful research strategies has been tied intimately to various theoretical approaches. By theoretical approaches we refer to the collection of assumptions, terms, concepts, and means of ordering perceptions of reality such as structuralism, interactionism, functionalism, exchange, conflict, critical, and discourse analysis. It has been suggested by some reviewers that we accept a characterization of our evolving theoretical orientation as largely a combination of structuralism and interactionism. However, that label may be misleading. It may be misleading because there is significant variation in research that claims to be structuralist or interactionist, and many scholars who work primarily in the area of "theory" suggest additional complications. Following Turner, for example, our approach would be viewed in part as an analytical scheme, specifically a descriptive/sensitizing scheme that intends to "sensitize and orient researchers to certain critical processes" (1986:11). Our approach would also fit part of his metatheoretical scheme, since it asks what is the appropriate means of developing theory and what type of theory is possible given the subject matter? Yet others who are involved intimately in the development of theory present quite different views (cf. Giddens 1981, 1987; Luhmann, 1985; Hagan, 1988; Elster 1989; McCloskey 1990).

Part of the problem also revolves around the varying uses of theory development and theory construction. Theory construction has been concerned usually with the collection of assumptions, terms, and concepts that lead to testable hypotheses, while development appears more focused upon substantive theoretical traditions such as structuralism and interactionism. Our approach focuses upon the development of theory and in this context we view structure as emerging from agents (including the range from individuals to states in the world polity) who produce, reproduce, and transform it through processes of interaction. We attempt to emphasize the comparative and longitudinal relevance of these processes. In this sense, then, our approach is, in part, a nascent synthesis of structuralism and interactionism, since we view the dichotomy as unproductive in the present research (see Turner 1986, and Lauderdale et al. 1990, for a more complete discussion of these issues).

Chapter 4

1. The shift from competitive to monopoly capitalism in the United States, for example, created new categories of deviance as well as abolishing old ones (Inverarity et al. 1983). The classical thrust of Weber, Marx,

and Durkheim, and recent elaborations are central to future research on the changing definitions of deviance.

2. Greenberg (1981) provides a thoughtful analysis of why structural changes in a Chatino village are necessary for managing outside domination and ensuing conflict.

3. Multiple levels of analysis and degrees of abstraction can be useful in the analysis of the concept of deviance and its many related aspects such as stigmatization of individuals in small groups, extralegal punishment by formal social control agents, as well as conditions which lead to the construction of definitions of deviant societies in the world system (Lauderdale et al. 1990).

Appendix A

1. George Thomas, Robin Chladny, and Francisco O. Ramirez provided crucial comments on these issues. Ramirez (1981) presents a theoretical analysis of related comparative work in his examination of social integration and resource mobilization approaches to social movements.

2. See Dore (1959) for a historical perspective on the varied land reform policies in Japan, especially those dictated by the imperial clan.

3. Unfortunately, the typical instrumentalist focus upon the personality and cult of William Walker has distracted researchers from the structural conduciveness that led to his rule and the dialectic character of his support (see Skocpol 1986–87).

4. Minor C. Keith, the founder and head of the United Fruit Company, was given 800,000 acres in state lands in any part of the country as part of the 1884 government contract to build the railroad (Seligson 1980: 119). By the turn of the century, the company had become a major political force in Central America. Commonly called the octopus by campesinos, it quickly responded to various types of land reform. In Guatemala in 1954, for example, United Fruit was a major factor in removing the government of Arbenz and his comprehensive agrarian reforms. In 1988 other businesses and wealthy landowners (National Farming Union) opposed the recent land reform programs proposed by Cerezo's administration, which would provide aid to subsistence groups, especially the approximately four million Indians in Guatemala.

5. Paige, 1975, and Skocpol, 1979, provide more detailed analyses of other examples. Paige examines agrarian revolutions with an emphasis upon economic factors while Skocpol focuses more upon political factors in a general analysis of revolutions.

6. Periodically, the Catholic Church has exerted pressure on the state for land reform, primarily for the growing of subsistence crops in Central America (Morris 1988). However, an analysis of its other interests in Latin America suggests other dialectic processes.

7. Increased military spending apart from mass mobilization has somewhat negative effects (Stinchcombe 1983), although Gouldner (1970) suggests that the two increase together within the welfare-warfare state (see King 1987). Mesa-Lago (1978) examines Latin American regimes that extended welfare during or after periods of internal crises.

8. Recent Nicaraguan policies include an emphasis on creating state agencies to preserve the rain forest as well as organizations to combat the Central American shift from using land for the "harvesting" of cattle rather than crops. The Nicaraguan Institute of Natural Resources and the Environment, with environmental aid from other countries and international organizations, has been a central part of the rationalization process from 1979 until 1988. Other agencies have been erected to respond to the impact of the war with the Contras, which includes the displacement of fifteen thousand campesinos and the loss of millions of dollars in harvests annually.

9. Nonetheless, rhetoric persists as the world polity demands moderation, meaningful debate, and agreements to be stewards of the land. Yet core countries produce so much food from the land that it is destroyed and plowed back under ground (von Werlhof 1991).

Appendix B

*An earlier version of this chapter appears in *The Judicial Review of the Supreme Court of Costa Rica*, 1988, 44: 9–17.

References

Abel, Richard L., ed. 1982a. *The politics of informal justice. Vol. 1: The American experience.* New York: Academic Press.

————. 1982b. *The politics of informal justice. Vol. 2: Comparative studies.* New York: Academic Press.

————. 1986. The transformation of the American legal profession. *Law and Society Review* 20: 7–17

Ashley, Richard. 1980. *The political economy of war and peace: The Sino-Soviet-American triangle and the modern security problematique.* London: F. Pinter Press.

————. 1986a. Social will and international anarchy: Beyond the domestic analogy in the study of global collaboration. Paper presented at the Berkeley symposium on international studies, University of California.

————. 1986b. The geopolitics of geopolitical space: Toward a critical social theory of international politics. 1986 Annual Meetings of the International Studies Association, March 27, Anaheim, Calif.

Atleson, James B. 1989. The legal community and the transformation of disputes: The settlement of injunction actions. *Law and Society Review* 23:41–73.

Auerbach, Jerold S. 1983. *Justice without law.* New York: Oxford University Press.

Augelli, Enrico, and Craig Murphy. 1988. *America's quest for supremacy and the third world.* London: Pinter Publishers.

Bachrach, P., and M. Baratz. 1963. Two faces of power. *American Political Science Review* 56:947–52.

Baer, Judith A. 1991. Nasty law or nice ladies? Jurisprudence, feminism, and gender differences. *Women and Politics* 11:1–32.

Balbus, Isaac D. 1973. *The dialectics of legal repression: Black rebels before the American criminal courts.* New York: Russell Sage Foundation.

————. 1977. Commodity form and legal form: An essay on the relative autonomy of the law. *Law and Society* (Winter):528–69.

Barahona Israel, Rodrigo. 1984. Propiedad y contratos agrários. In *Constitución Política y Propiedad*. San José, Costa Rica: Editores Uruk.

Barkan, Steven E. 1985. *Protestors on trial.* New Brunswick: Rutgers University Press.

Basu, Amrita. 1987. Grass roots movements and the state. *Theory and Society* 16:647–74.

Bataille, Georges. 1985. *Visions of excess: Selected writing, 1927–1939*, trans. A. Stoekl. Minneapolis: University of Minnesota Press.

Bauman, Zygmunt. 1989. *Modernity and the holocaust.* Cambridge: Polity Press.

Baumgartner, M. P. 1984. Social control in suburbia. In *Toward a theory of social control. Vol. 1: Fundamentals*, ed. Donald Black, 79–104. New York: Academic Press.

Becker, Howard S. 1963. *Outsiders: Studies in the sociology of deviance.* New York: Free Press.

Benney, Mark. 1983. Gramsci on law, morality, and power. *International Journal of the Sociology of Law* 11:191–208.

Ben-Yehuda, Nachman. 1985. *Deviance and moral boundaries: Witchcraft, the occult, science fiction, deviant sciences and scientists.* Chicago: University of Chicago Press.

————. 1990. *The politics and morality of deviance.* Albany: State University of New York Press.

Berger, Joseph, David G. Wagner, and Morris Zelditch, Jr. 1992. Cumulative theory. Forthcoming in ed. J. Turner *Cumulative theorizing in sociology.* Beverly Hills, Calif.: Sage.

Biesanz, Richard, Karen Z. Biesanz, and Mavis H. Biesanz. 1982. *The Costa Ricans.* Englewood Cliffs, N.J.: Prentice-Hall.

Black, Donald. 1976. *The behavior of law.* New York: Academic Press.

————. 1984. Crime as social control. In *Toward a general theory of social control. Vol. 2: Selected problems*, ed. Donald Black, 1–27. New York: Academic Press.

————. 1987. The elementary forms of conflict management. Prepared for the Distinguished Scholar Lecture Series, School of Justice Studies, Arizona State University, Tempe, February.

———. 1989. *Sociological justice.* New York: Oxford University Press.

Black, Donald, and M. P. Baumgartner. 1983. Toward a theory of the third party. In *Empirical theories about courts,* ed. Keith O. Boyum and Lynn Mather, 84–114. New York: Longman.

Block, Alan A. 1988. The Khashoggi papers. *Contemporary Crises.* 12(1):25–63.

Blumer, Herbert. 1969. *Symbolic interactionism: Perspective and method.* Englewood Cliffs, N.J.: Prentice-Hall.

Bohannan, P. 1969. Ethnography and comparison in legal anthropology. In *Law in culture and society,* ed. L. Nader, 69–98. Chicago: Aldine.

Boli-Bennett, John. 1979. The ideology of expanding state authority in national constitutions, 1870–1970. In *National development and the world system,* ed. John Meyer and Michael Hannan, 222–37. Chicago: University of Chicago Press.

Bornschier, Volker, and Christopher Chase-Dunn. 1985. *Transnational corporations and underdevelopment.* New York: Praeger.

Braudel, Fernand. 1979. *The structures of everyday life.* New York: Harper and Row.

Brenes, Abelardo. 1986. Peace and war issues in Costa Rica. Paper presented at the European Psychologists for Peace Conference, August 8–10, Helsinki, Finland.

Burbach, Roger. 1982. Central America: The end of U.S. hegemony? *Monthly Review* 33:1–18.

Chace, James. 1984. *Endless war.* New York: Vintage Books.

Chambliss, William. 1979. Contradictions and conflicts in law creation. *Research in Law and Sociology* 2:3–27.

Christenson, Ron. 1986. *Political trials.* New Brunswick, N.J.: Transaction Press.

Cohen, Raymond. 1991. *Negotiating across cultures.* Washington, D.C.: United States Institute of Peace Press.

Collier, Jane. 1973. *Law and social change in Zinacantan.* Stanford: Stanford University Press.

Comaroff, John L., and Simon Roberts. 1981. *Rules and processes.* Chicago: University of Chicago Press.

Cooley , Charles H. 1902. *Human nature and the social order.* New York: Scribner's.

Coser, Lewis A. 1982. The notion of social control. In *Social control,* ed. Jack P. Gibbs, 9–22. New York: Academic Press.

Darenblum, J., and E. Ulibarri. 1985. *Centro América: Conflictor y democracia.* San José: Libro Libre.

Davis, Nanette J., and Bo Anderson. 1983. *Social control: The production of deviance in the modern state.* New York: Irvington Publishers.

de Janvry, Alain. 1981. *The agrarian question and reformism in Latin America.* Baltimore: Johns Hopkins University Press.

de la Cruz, Vladimar. 1980. *Las lunchas sociales en Costa Rica 1870–1930.* San José: Coedición Editorial Costa Rica and Editorial Universidad de Costa Rica.

————. 1985. *Los mártires de Chicago y el lo de mayo de 1913.* San José: Editorial Costa Rica.

Deere, Carmen Diana. 1985. Rural women and state policy: The Latin American agrarian experience. *World Development* 13:1037–53.

Deloria, Vine, Jr. 1973. *God is red.* New York: Gosset and Dunlap.

Dennis, Phillip A. 1976. *Conflictos por tierras en el Valle de Oaxaca.* Mexico: Instituto Nacional Indigenista.

Derrida, Jacques. 1982. *Margins of philosophy* (especially form and meaning: A note on the phenomenology of language), trans. A. Bass, 155–73. Chicago: University of Chicago Press.

DiMaggio, Paul J. 1988. Interest and agency in institutional theory. In *Institutional patterns and organizations,* ed. Lynn Zucker. Cambridge: Ballinger.

Dore, R. P. 1959. *Land reform in Japan.* London: Oxford University Press.

Dorner, Peter. 1972. *Land reform and economic development.* Baltimore: Penguin Books.

Douglas, Mary. 1966. *Purity and danger: An analysis of concepts of pollution and taboo.* Middlesex: Penguin Books.

Downes, David, and Paul Rock. 1982. *Understanding deviance: A guide to the sociology of crime and rule breaking.* Oxford: Clarendon Press.

Durham, William. 1979. *Scarcity and survival in Central America: Ecological origins of the soccer war.* Stanford: Stanford University Press.

Durkheim, Emile. 1958. *Professional ethics and civic morals.* New York: Free Press.

————. 1964 (1893). *The division of labor in society.* New York: Free Press.

Edelman, Marc. 1988. The early history of Costa Rica's labor movement. *Latin American Perspectives* 15(57/2):81–87.

Ekland-Olson, Sheldon. 1984. Social control and relational disturbance: A microstructural paradigm. In *Toward a theory of social control. Vol. 2: Selected problems*, ed. Donald Black, 209–33. New York: Academic Press.

Elster, Jon. 1989. *The cement of society: A study of social order.* Cambridge: Cambridge University Press.

Erikson, Kai T. 1966. *Wayward puritans: A study in the sociology of deviance.* New York: John Wiley.

————. 1986. War and peace in Oceania. In *The social fabric*, ed. James F. Short, Jr., 123–34. Newbury Park, Calif.: Sage Publications.

Fagen, Richard. 1987. *Forging peace.* New York: Basil Blackwell.

Fagen, Richard, and O. Pellicer, eds. 1983. *The future of Central America: Policy choices for the U.S. and Mexico.* Stanford: Stanford University Press.

Farrell, Ronald A., and Victoria L. Swigert. 1982. *Deviance and social control.* Glenview, Ill: Scott, Foresman.

Felstiner, William L. F., Richard L. Abel, and Austin Sarat. 1980–81. The emergence and transformation of disputes: Naming, blaming, claiming. *Law and Society Review* 15:631–54.

Fitzpatrick, Peter. 1988. The rise and rise of informalism. In *Informal justice?*, ed. Roger Matthews, 178–211. Newbury Park, Calif.: Sage Publications.

Flynn, Patricia. 1984. The roots of revolt. In *The politics of intervention: The United States in Central America*, ed. Roger Burbach and Patricia Flynn, 29–64. New York: Monthly Review Press.

Foucault, Michel. 1977. *Discipline and punish: The birth of the prison*, trans. Alan Sheridan. New York: Pantheon Books.

Frank, André Gunder. 1972. *Lumpenbourgeoisie, lumpendevelopment: Dependence, class, and politics in Latin America.* New York: Monthly Review Press.

————. 1984. Political ironies in the world economy. *Studies in Political Economy* 15:119–49.

Friedman, Lawrence. 1985. *Total justice*. New York: Russell Sage Foundation.

Galanter, Marc. 1985. The legal malaise; or justice observed. *Law and Society Review* 19:537–56.

Gamson, William A. 1975. *The strategy of social protest*. Homewood, Ill.: Dorsey Press.

Gamson, William A., Bruce Fireman, and Steven Rytina. 1982. *Encounters with unjust authority*. Chicago: Dorsey.

Garfinkel, Harold. 1956. Conditions of successful degradation ceremonies. *American Journal of Sociology* 61:420–24.

Geertz, Clifford. 1973. *The interpretation of cultures*. New York: Basic Books.

George, Jim. 1989. International relations and the search for thinking space: Another view of the third debate. *International Studies Quarterly* 33:269–79.

Gibbs, Jack P. 1989. *Control: Sociology's central notion*. Urbana: University of Illinois Press.

Giddens, Anthony. 1976. Classical social theory and the origins of modern sociology. *American Journal of Sociology* 81:703–28.

———. 1981. *A contemporary critique of historical materialism*. Berkeley: University of California Press.

———. 1987. *Social theory and modern sociology*. Stanford: Stanford University Press.

Gluckman, Max. 1955. *Custom and conflict in Africa*. Oxford: Blackwell.

———. 1965. *The ideas in Barotse jurisprudence*. New Haven: Yale University Press.

Goldberg, David. 1990. Introduction. In *Anatomy of racism*, ed. David Goldberg, xi-xxii. Minneapolis: University of Minnesota Press.

Goode, Erich. 1984. *Deviant behavior*, 2nd ed. Englewood Cliffs, N.J.: Prentice-Hall.

Goode, William J. 1986. Individual choice and the social order. In *The social fabric*, ed. James F. Short, Jr., 39–62. Newbury Park, Calif.: Sage.

Goody, J., and S. J. Tambiah. 1973. *Bridewealth and dowry*. Cambridge: University Press.

Gouldner, Alvin. 1970. *The coming crisis of western sociology.* New York: Basic Books.

Greenberg, James B. 1981. *Santiago's sword. Chatino peasant religion and economics.* Berkeley: University of California Press.

———. 1989. *Blood ties—Life and violence in rural Mexico.* Tucson: University of Arizona Press.

Grinde, Donald A., Jr. and Bruce E. Johansen. 1991. *Exemplar of Liberty.* Los Angeles: American Indian Studies Center, University of California.

Grindle, Merilee S. Whatever happened to agrarian reform? The Latin American experience. Technical Papers Series, no. 23, Office for Public Sector Studies, Institute of Latin American Studies. Austin: University of Texas Press.

Gurevitch, Z. D. 1988. The other side of dialogue: On making the other strange and the experience of otherness. *American Journal of Sociology* 93: 1179–99.

Habermas, Jürgen. 1979. *Communication and the evolution of society.* Boston: Beacon Press.

Hagan, John. 1988. *Structural criminology.* Cambridge: Polity.

Hall, Carolyn. 1984. *Costa Rica: Una interpretación geográfica con perspectiva histórica.* San José: Editorial Costa Rica.

Harris, Richard. 1985. *Nicaragua: A revolution under siege.* London: Zed Press.

Henry, Stuart. 1983. *Private justice: Towards integrated theorising in the sociology of law.* London: Routledge and Kegan Paul.

Hirschman, Albert O. 1961. *Latin American issues; essays and comments.* New York: Twentieth Century Fund.

———. 1970. *Exit, voice and loyalty.* Cambridge: Harvard University Press.

Hoebel, E. A. 1954. *The law of primitive man.* Cambridge: Harvard University Press.

Horowitz, Allan. 1990. *The logic of social control.* New York: Plenum.

Huberman, Leo. 1952, (1936). *Man's worldly goods.* London: Monthly Review Press.

Inverarity, James M. 1980. Theories of the political creation of deviance: Legacies of conflict theory, Marx, and Durkheim. In *A political analysis of deviance*, ed. Pat Lauderdale, 175–217. Minneapolis: University of Minnesota Press.

Inverarity, James M., and Pat Lauderdale, and Barry Feld 1992. *Law, justice and society*. New York: General Hall.

Inverarity, James M., Pat Lauderdale, and Barry C. Feld. 1983. *Law and society*. Boston: Little, Brown.

Kafka, Franz. 1969 (1937). *The trial.* New York: Vintage.

Kaimowitz, David, and Joseph R. Thome. 1985. Nicaragua's agrarian reform: The first year (1979–80). In *Nicaragua in revolution,* ed. Thomas W. Walker, 223–40. New York: Praeger.

Kaplan, John. 1983. *The hardest drug.* Chicago: University of Chicago Press.

Kidder, Robert L. 1980–81. The end of the road? Problems in the analysis of disputes. *Law and Society Review* 15:717–25.

Kierkegaard, Sören. 1968. *The concept of irony,* trans. L. M. Capel. Bloomington: Indiana University Press.

———. 1983. *Fear and trembling,* trans. Howard and Edna Hong. Princeton: Princeton University Press.

Kincaid, A. Douglas. 1985. *Agrarian development, peasant mobilization and social change in Central America.* Ph.D. dissertation. Baltimore: Johns Hopkins University.

———. 1986. The politics of quiescence: Costa Rican peasants and non—mobilization. In *Central American social movements,* ed. M. Edelman. New York: Grove Press.

King, Desmond. 1987. The state and the social structures of welfare in advanced industrial democracies. *Theory and Society* 16:841–68.

Kirp, David, Mark Yudof, and Marlene Strong Franks. 1986. *Gender justice.* Chicago: University of Chicago Press.

Koch, Klaus-Friedrich. 1974. *War and peace in Jalemo.* Cambridge: Harvard University Press.

Kozolchyk, Boris. 1988. Commercial legal relations between Arizona and Northern Mexico. *Arizona Journal of International and Comparative Law* (annual):28–33.

Kozolchyk, Boris, and James B. Greenberg. 1988. Living law: An interdisciplinary look at migration, land use, and violence in Mexico. *Arizona Journal of International and Comparative Law* (annual):66–104.

Lauden, Larry. 1977. *Progress and its problems*. Berkeley: University of California Press.

Lauderdale, Michael. 1986. *Social expenditures, economic problems, and Mexico's social welfare*. Technical Report, Social Work Research Laboratory. Austin: University of Texas.

Lauderdale, Pat. 1984. Experiments in social control. In *Toward a general theory of social control. Vol. 2: Selected problems*, ed. Donald Black, 261–81. New York: Academic Press.

———. 1986a. Social and economic instability in Costa Rica: Pre-conditions for militarization? *Policy Studies Review* 6:236–45.

———. 1986b. Agrarian reforms and the rationalization of law in Central America. 1986 Annual Meeting of the Political Economy of the World system, March 7, San Francisco.

———. 1988a. Domination, social movements, and change. In *The subsistence perspective*, ed. C. von Werlhof and M. Mies, 59–79. Bad Boll, Germany: Evangelische Akademe.

———. 1988b. Rationalización del Derecho en Costa Rica. *Revista Judicial de Corte Suprema de Costa Rica* 44:9–17.

Lauderdale, Pat, ed. 1980. *A political analysis of deviance*. Minneapolis: University of Minnesota Press.

Lauderdale, Pat, Phil Smith-Cunnien, Jerry Parker, and James Inverarity. 1984. "External threat and the definition of deviance." *Journal of Personality and Social Psychology*. 46: 1058–70.

Lauderdale, Pat, Steve McLaughlin, and Annamarie Oliverio. 1990. Levels of analysis, theoretical orientations and degrees of abstraction. *The American Sociologist* 21:29-40.

Lazarus, Alvaro José Meza. 1985. Derecho agrário y posesión: Elementos distintivos para la configuración de un instituto típico. *Revista Judicial*, no. 32, Corte Suprema de Justicia, marzo.

Lempert, R. O. 1980–81. Grievances and legitimacy: The beginnings and end of dispute settlement. *Law and Society Review* 15:707–15.

Lévi-Strauss, Claude. 1955. *Tristes tropiques*, trans. John and Doreen Weightman. New York: Penguin.

Lieberman, Jethro K. 1981. *The litigious society*. New York: Basic Books.

Lincoln, Jennie, and Pat Lauderdale. 1985. A new defense policy for Costa Rica: Constructing reality and the policy agenda. *Policy Studies Review* 5:220-30.

Liska, Allen E. 1987. *Perspectives on deviance.* Englewood Cliffs, N.J.: Prentice-Hall.

Llewellyn, K., and E. A. Hoebel. *The Cheyenne way.* Norman: University of Oklahoma Press.

Locke, John. 1960. *Two treatises of government.* New York: Mentor Press. [first published 1689, Cambridge University Press].

Luhmann, Niklas. 1985. *A sociological theory of law.* London: Routledge and Kegan Paul.

Maine, H. S. 1861. (1912). *Ancient law.* London: John Murray.

Malinowski, B. 1926. *Crime and custom in savaged society.* London: Kegan Paul, Trench Trubner.

Marquez, Gabriel Garcia. 1983. *Chronicle of death foretold,* trans. Gregory Rabassa. New York: Knopf.

Marshall, Jonathan, Peter D. Scott, and Jane Hunter. 1987. *The Iran-Contra connection.* Boston: South End Press.

Marx, Gary. 1988. *Undercover: Police surveillance in America.* Berkeley: University of California Press.

Marx, Karl. 1963. *The poverty of philosophy.* New York: International [first published in 1847].

———. 1967. *A critique of political economy, Vol. 1: The process of capitalist production.* New York: International Publishers [first published in 1867].

Marx, K., and F. Engels. 1965. *The German ideology.* London: Lawrence and Wishart.

Mascia-Lees, Patricia Sharpe, and Colleen Ballerino Cohen. 1989. The postmodernist turn in anthropology: Cautions from a feminist perspective. *Signs* 15:7–33.

Mather, Lynn. 1979. *Plea bargaining or trial? The process of criminal-case disposition.* Lexington, Mass.: D.C. Heath.

Mather, Lynn and Barbara Yngvesson. 1980–1981. Language, audience, and the transformation of disputes. *Law and Society Review.* 15(3–4): 774–821.

Matza, David. 1969. *Becoming deviant.* Englewood Cliffs, N.J.: Prentice-Hall.

McAdam, Doug. 1989. The biographical consequences of activism. *American Sociological Review* 54:744–60.

McCloskey, Donald M. 1990. The rhetoric of formalism in the social sciences. *The American Sociologist* 21:3–19.

Mead, George H. 1934. *Mind, self and society.* Chicago: University of Chicago Press.

Meier, Robert F. 1982. Perspectives on the concept of social control. *Annual Review of Sociology* 8:34–55.

Merry, S. E. 1983. Concepts of law and justice among working-class Americans: Ideology vs. culture. *Legal Studies Forum* vol. 9.

———. 1987. Legal ideology and social class. Prepared for the Distinguished Scholar Lecture Series, School of Justice, Arizona State University, Tempe, February.

———. 1990. *Getting justice and getting even.* Chicago: University of Chicago Press.

Mesa-Lago, C. 1978. *Social security in Latin America.* Pittsburgh: Pittsburgh University Press.

Meyer, John W., John Boli, and George M. Thomas. 1987. Ontology and rationalization in the western cultural account. In *Institutional structure,* ed. George Thomas et al., 12–37. Beverly Hills, Calif.: Sage Publications.

Meyer, John W., and Brian Rowan. 1977. Institutionalized organizations: Formal structure as myth and ceremony. *American Journal of Sociology* 83:340–63.

Meyer, John W., and W. Richard Scott. 1983. *Organizational environments: Ritual and rationality.* Beverly Hills, Calif.: Sage Publications.

Miller, Richard E., and Austin Sarat. 1980–81. Grievances, claims and disputes: Assessing the adversary culture. *Law and Society Review* 15:525-566.

Miyazawa, Setsuo. 1987. "Taking Kawashima seriously: A review of Japanese legal consciousness and disputing behavior." *Law and Society Review* 21:219–42.

Moore, Barrington, Jr. 1966. *Social origins of dictatorship and democracy: Lord and peasant in the making of the modern world.* Boston: Beacon.

Morris, Fred. 1984. Land reform in Central America. *Mesoamerica* 4: 4–7.

———. 1987. Costa Rica. In *Mesoamerica,* vol. 6, no. 9, 11–12. San José, Costa Rica: Institute for Central American Studies.

————. 1988. The region. *Mesoamerica* 7: 1–2.

Munger, Frank. 1988. Law, change and litigation: A critical examination of an empirical research tradition. *Law and Society Review.* 22(1):57–101.

Nader, Laura. 1964. Talea and Juquila: A comparison of social organization. *American Archaeology and Ethnology* 48(3, vii):195–296.

————. 1980. Alternatives to the American judicial system. In *No access to law,* ed. Laura Nader, 3–55. New York: Academic Press.

————. 1984a. From disputing to complaining. In *Toward a general theory of social control,* ed. Donald Black, 71–94. New York: Academic Press.

————. 1984b. A user theory of law. *Southwestern Law Journal* 38(4):951–63.

————. 1990a. *Harmony ideology: Justice and control in a Zapotec mountain village.* Stanford: Stanford University Press.

————. 1990b. The origin of order and the dynamics of justice. In *New directions in the study of justice, law, and social control,* ed. School of Justice Studies, 189–206. New York: Plenum Press.

Nader, Laura, and D. Metzger. 1963. Conflict resolution in two Mexican communities. *American Anthropologist* 65(3):584–92.

Nader, Laura, and David Serber. 1976. Law and the distribution of power. In *The uses of controversy in sociology,* ed. Lewis A. Coser and Otto N. Larsen. New York: Free Press.

Nader, Laura, and Harry F. Todd, eds. 1978. *The disputing process—Law in ten societies.* New York: Columbia University Press.

O'Barr, William M. and John M. Conley. 1988. Lay expectations of the civil justice system. *Law and Society Review.* 22(1): 137–161.

Offe, Claus. 1972. Political authority and class structure: An analysis of late capitalist societies. *International Journal of Sociology* 2:73–105.

Olson, Richard S. 1989. *The politics of earthquake prediction.* Princeton: Princeton University Press.

Orcutt, James D. 1983. *Analyzing deviance.* Homewood, Ill.: Dorsey Press.

Orloff, A.S., and T. Skocpol. 1984. Why not equal protection? Explaining the politics of public social spending in Britain, 1900–1911, and the United States, 1880s–1920. *American Sociological Review* 49:726–50.

Paige, Jeffrey. 1975. *Agrarian revolution*. New York: Free Press.

———. 1987. "Coffee and politics in Central America." pp. 141–190 in *Crises in the Caribbean*, ed. Ricahrd Tardanico. Newbury Park, Calif.: Sage.

Pampel, Fred C., and John B. Williamson. 1985. Age structure, politics, and cross-national patterns of public pension expenditures. *American Sociological Review* 50: 782–99.

Pashukanis, E. B. 1929. *Law and Marxism: A general theory*. London: Ink Links. [English translation 1978.]

Perez Vargas, Victor. 1985. El poder judicial de Costa Rica. *Revista Judicial*, no. 29, Corte Suprema de Justicia, junio.

———. 1981. *La jurisprudencia de interestes*. San José, Costa Rica: Universidad Estatal al a Distancia.

———. 1988. *Derecho privado*. San José, Costa Rica: Publitex.

Pfohl, Stephen J. 1985. *Images of deviance and social control: A sociological history*. New York: McGraw-Hill.

Pfuhl, Erdwin. 1980. *The deviance process*. New York: Van Nostrand.

Polanyi, K. 1944. *The great transformation*. Boston: Little, Brown.

Quadagno, Jill S. 1984. Welfare capitalism and the Social Security Act of 1935. *American Sociological Review* 49: 632–47.

Radcliffe-Brown, A. R. 1952. *Structure and function in primitive society*. London: Cohen and West.

Ramirez, Franciso. 1981. Comparative social movements. *International Journal of Comparative Sociology* 49: 632–47.

———. 1987. Institutional analysis. In *Institutional analysis*, ed. George M. Thomas et al., 316–28. Beverly Hills, Calif.: Sage Publications.

Romero Perez, Jorge. 1984. Reflexiones sobre la política acerca de la transición del fuedalismo al capitalismo.' *Revista Judicial*, no. 29, Corte Suprema de Justicia, junio.

Rowles, James P. 1985. *Law in agrarian reform in Costa Rica*. Boulder, Colo.: Westview Press.

Ryan, Alan. 1987. *Property*. Minneapolis: University of Minnesota Press.

Sacco, Vincent, ed. 1992. *Political deviance in Canada*. Scarborough, Ont.: Prentice-Hall.

Santos, Boaventura de Sousa. 1974. *Law against law: Legal reasoning in Pasargada law*. CIDOC Cuaderno 87. Chernavaca, Mexico: Centro Intercultural de Documentación.

Schlesinger, Stephen, and Stephen Kinzer. 1982. *Bitter fruit: The untold story of the American coup in Guatemala*. Garden City, N.Y.: Doubleday.

Schmidt, Steffen W., James C. Scott, Carl Land, and Laura Guasti, eds. 1977. *Friends, followers and factions*. Berkeley: University of California Press.

Scott, James C. 1985. *Weapons of the weak: Everyday forms of peasant resistance*. New Haven: Yale University Press.

Scott, James C., and Benedict J. Kerkvliet. 1977. Clientelism theory and development. In *Friends, followers and fractions*, ed. Steffen W. Schmidt, James C. Scott, Carl Land, and Laura Guasti, 439–58. Berkeley: University of California Press.

Selby, H. 1974. *Zapotec deviance: The convergence of folk and modern sociology*. Austin: University of Texas Press.

Seligson, Mitchell A. 1980. *Peasants of Costa Rica and the development of agrarian capitalism*. Madison: University of Wisconsin Press.

Seligson, Mitchell A., and Edward N. Muller. 1987. Democratic stability and economic crisis: Costa Rica, 1978–1983. *International Studies Quarterly* 31:301–26.

Shapiro, Martin. 1981. *Courts: A comparative and political analysis*. Chicago: University of Chicago Press.

Sherif, Muzafer, and Carolyn Sherif. 1964. *Reference groups*. New York: Harper and Row.

———. 1969. *Social psychology*. New York: Harper and Row.

Short, James. 1986. The social fabric as metaphor and reality. In *The social fabric*, ed. James Short, 13–30. Beverly Hills, Calif.: Sage Publications.

Silliman, G. Sidney. 1985. A political analysis of the Philippines' Katarungang Pambarangay system of informal justice through mediation. *Law and Society Review*. 19:279–301.

Simmel, Georg. 1955. *Conflict and the web of group-affiliations*, trans. Kurt H. Wolff and Reinhard Bendix. New York: Free Press.

Skocpol, Theda. 1979. *State and social revolutions*. New York: Cambridge University Press.

————. 1986–87. A brief response. *Politics and Society* 15: 331–32.

Smith, Carol, ed. 1976. *Regional analysis.* New York: Academic Press.

Snyder, David, and Charles Tilly. 1972. Hardship and collective violence in France, 1830 to 1960. *American Sociological Review* 37: 520–32.

Starr, June O., and Barbara Yngvesson. 1975. Scarcity and disputing: Zeroing-in on compromise decisions. *American Ethnologist* 2:553–66.

Stinchcombe, Arthur L. 1983. *Economic sociology.* San Francisco: Academic Press.

Stone, Christopher. 1975. *Where the law ends.* New York: Harper and Row.

Sutherland, Edwin. 1924. *Criminology.* Philadelphia: Lippincott.

Swanson, Guy. 1971. An organizational analysis of collectives. *American Sociological Review* 36:607–23.

Taylor, Mark C., ed. 1986. *Deconstruction in context.* Chicago: University of Chicago Press.

Teubner, Gunther. 1983. Substantive and reflexive elements in modern law. *Law and Society Review* 17:239–85.

Thio, Alex. 1988. *Deviant behavior.* New York: Harper and Row.

Thomas, George M., and Pat Lauderdale. 1987. An institutional world-polity model of national welfare and land reform. In *Institutional analysis,* ed. George M. Thomas et al., 198–214. Beverly Hills, Calif.: Sage Publications.

————. 1988. State authority and social welfare in the world system context. *Sociological Forum* 3:383–99.

Thomas, George, John Meyer, Francisco O. Ramirez, and John Boli, eds. 1987. *Institutional analysis: Studies of the state, society and the individual.* Beverly Hills, Calif.: Sage Publications.

Tilly, Charles. 1964. *The vendee.* Chicago: University of Chicago Press.

————. 1975. *The formation of national states in Western Europe.* Princeton: Princeton University Press.

Tilly, Charles, Louis Tilly, and Richard Tilly. 1975. *The rebellious century, 1830–1930.* Cambridge: Harvard University Press.

Torrealba Navas, Adrian de Jesus. 1991. Las fuentes del Derecho Agrário. *Revista Judicial,* no. 53, Corte Suprema de Justicia, marzo.

Trubek, David M. 1977. Complexity and contradiction in the legal order: Balbus and the challenge of critical social thought about law. *Law and Society Review* 11:528–69.

———. 1980–81. The construction and deconstruction of a disputes-focused approach: An afterword. *Law and Society Review* 15:727–47.

Turk, Austin. 1976. "Law as a weapon in social conflict." *Social Problems* 23: 276-91

Turner, Bryan S. 1991. *Religion and Social Theory*. Newbury Park, Calif.: Sage.

Turner, Jonathan H. 1986. *The structure of sociological theory*. Chicago: Dorsey Press.

Unger, Roberto M. 1976. *Law in modern society*. New York: Free Press.

———. 1987. *False necessity— Anti-necessitarian social theory in the service of radical democracy*. New York: Cambridge University Press.

University of Wisconsin–Madison, Law School. 1983. Conference on reflexive law and the regulatory crisis. University of Wisconsin: Disputes Processing Research Program.

Van Velsen, J. 1967. The extended-case method and situational analysis. In *The craft of social anthropology*, ed. A. L. Epstein. London: Tavistock.

Vargas, Elisabeth. 1989. Costa Rica. In *Mesoamerica* vol. 8, no. 10, 9–11. San José, Costa Rica: Institute for Central American Studies.

Vidmar, N. 1984. The small claims court: A reconceptualization of disputes and an empirical investigation. *Law and Society Review* 18:515–50.

von Werlhof, Claudia. 1989. On the concept of nature and society in capitalism. In *Women: The last colony*, ed. Maria Mies, Veronika Bennholdt-Thomsen, and Claudia von Werlhof, 96–112. London: Zed Books.

———. 1991. *Was haben die Hühner mit dem Dollar zu tun?* Munich: Verlag Frauenoffensive.

Walker, Henry A., George M. Thomas, and Morris Zelditch, Jr. 1986. Legitimation, endorsement and stability. *Social Forces* 64:620–43.

Wallerstein, I. 1974. *The modern world-system I: Capitalist agriculture and the origins of the European world-economy in the 16th century*. New York: Academic Press.

Weber, Max. 1954. *On law in economy and society*, ed. Max Rheinstein. Cambridge: Harvard University Press.

———. 1978. *Economy and society: An outline of interpretative sociology*, ed. Guenther Roth and Claus Wittich. Berkeley: University of California Press.

Welton, Gary L., Dean Pruitt, and Neil McGillicuddy. 1988. The role of caucusing in community mediation. *The Journal of Conflict Resolution*. 32:181–202.

Williams, Nancy. 1986. *The Yonlngu and their land: A system of land tenure and the fight for its recognition*. Stanford: Stanford University Press.

Winson, Anthony. 1978. Class structure and agrarian transition in Central America. *Latin America Perspective* 19: 27–48.

Wolf, Eric R. 1969. *Peasant wars of the twentieth century*. New York: Harper and Row.

Yngvesson, Barbara. 1978. The Atlantic fishermen. In *The disputing process: Law in ten societies*, ed. Laura Nader and Harry F. Todd, Jr., 59–85. New York: Columbia University Press.

———. 1984. What is a dispute about? The political interpretation of social control. In *Toward a general theory of social control. Vol. 2: Selected problems*, ed. Donald Black, 235–59. New York: Academic Press.

Zablocki, B. 1980. *Alienation and charisma: A study of contemporary American communes*. New York: Free Press.

Zeledon Zeledon, Ricardo. 1985. La escuela moderna del Derecho agrario. *Revista Judicial*, No. 30, Corte Suprema de Justicia, septiembre.

Zeledon Zeledon, Ricardo, ed. 1984a. *Constitucion Politica y Propiedad*. San José: Virst Editores.

———. 1984b. Problemas practicos del titulo, la posesion y la buena fe en la usucapion. *Revista Judicial*, No. 29, Corte Suprema de Justicia, junio.

Zelditch, Morris, Jr. 1986. The problem of order. In *The social fabric*, ed. James F. Short, 107–14. Beverly Hills: Sage Publications.

Zelmon, Joseph. 1988. Abstraction and theory. Working paper, Center for Sociological Research, Department of Sociology. Stanford: Stanford University.

Zucker, Lynn G. 1983. The role of institutionalization in cultural persistence. *American Sociological Review* 42: 726–43.

Subject Index

A

B

C

Author Index

A

Abel, Richard, 7, 38, 126, 132, 139, 149, 154, 180, 192
Anderson, Bo, 10
Ashley, Richard., 9, 183, 186, 194, 211, 224
Auerbach, Jerold, 192
Augelli, Enrico, 28, 189, 191

B

Bachrach, P., 163, 193
Baer, Judith, 224
Balbus, Isaac, 9, 34, 179
Barahona Israel, Rodrigo, 216
Baratz, M., 163, 193
Barkan, Steven, 111, 170, 197–98
Basu, Amrita, 198, 210
Bataille, Georges, 183
Bauman, Zygmunt, 29, 191
Baumgartner, M. P., 31–32, 35, 37
Becker, Howard S., 221
Ben-Yehuda, Nachman, 10, 38, 69, 90, 158, 183, 222–23
Benney, Mark, 9, 189
Biesanz, Karen, 39, 41
Biesanz, Mavis, 39, 41
Biesanz, Richard, 39, 41
Black, Donald, 1, 7, 8, 26, 29, 31–32, 65, 150, 180–82, 188, 224
Block, Alan, 42
Blumer, Herbert, 140, 158
Boli-Bennett, John, 154, 197, 211
Bornschier, Volker, 44

Braudel, Fernand, 193, 195
Brenes, Abelardo, 214
Burbach, Roger, 203, 207

C

Chace, James, 203–204
Chambliss, William, 222
Chase-Dunn, Christopher, 44
Christenson, Ron, 179, 183
Cohen, Colleen Ballerino, 224
Cohen, Raymond, 38
Collier, Jane, 154
Conley, John, 29
Comaroff, John, 7, 8
Cooley, Charles, 37–38

D

Davis, Nanette, 10
de Janvry, Alain, 197, 202, 205, 208
Deere, Carmen Diana, 209
Deloria, Vine Jr., 45, 193, 211, 224
Dennis, Phillip, 147
Derrida, Jacques, 183
DiMaggio, Paul, 197
Dore, R. P., 201, 226
Douglas, Mary, 136, 158
Downes, Daivd, 90
Durkheim, Emile, 29, 125, 184, 222

E

Edelman, Marc, 45

253